BUILD

LIKE A WOMAN

BUILD
LIKE A WOMAN

THE BLUEPRINT FOR
CREATING A BUSINESS
AND LIFE YOU LOVE

KATHLEEN GRIFFITH

ST. MARTIN'S
ESSENTIALS
NEW YORK

First published in the United States by St. Martin's Essentials,
an imprint of St. Martin's Publishing Group

BUILD LIKE A WOMAN. Copyright © 2024 by Kathleen Griffith. All
rights reserved. Printed in the United States of America.
For information, address St. Martin's Publishing Group,
120 Broadway, New York, NY 10271.

www.stmartins.com

The Library of Congress Cataloging-in-Publication Data is available
upon request.

ISBN 978-1-250-28699-4 (hardcover)
ISBN 978-1-250-28700-7 (ebook)

Our books may be purchased in bulk for promotional, educational,
or business use. Please contact your local bookseller or
the Macmillan Corporate and Premium Sales Department at
1-800-221-7945, extension 5442, or by email
at MacmillanSpecialMarkets@macmillan.com.

First Edition: 2024

10 9 8 7 6 5 4 3 2 1

This book is for every woman who is done and ready.

You reach a point where you are just done.
Done screwing around.
Done playing small.
Done pretending.
With yourself. With others.
Just done.
Where the new you
Needs to lovingly take the hand of the old you.
And say . . .
Thank you, but your services here are no longer required. You may
rest now.
There is but one precious life. And time she is fleeting.
I have big, beautiful, brave things to build.

CONTENTS

SECTION II: SKILLSET

Unleashing Your Dream

WE'RE BUILT FOR THIS . . .

AT SOME POINT SOMEONE WILL LOOK AT YOU AND CALL YOU LUCKY. THEY WILL cozy up to you, arms crossed under their chin, and say, "Tell me everything!" As if it would take five minutes and as if you were talking about a new pair of slingbacks you scored on sale. But you know this is not luck. Far from it. This is what starting a business alone—investing in yourself, losing money, making money, finding your voice (too loud or too soft, depending on the day), restless nights, legal contracts gone sideways, crazy selfie crying shots, happy-deal dances in the kitchen, hiring, firing, trying, failing, floundering in the deep end—looks like.

This is the house that was built on every high and low emotion. Brick by brick, block by block. Laying each one as perfectly as possible, only to have whole sections of your work destroyed overnight by a storm or ripped out simply because the edges didn't match up. Needing to start over because even if they don't know or notice, you will.

What no one tells us is we make our business and then our business makes us. Through this process, you come to know yourself wholly and completely, as if for the first time. You meet both the best and worst in yourself. You find yourself and destroy the parts of yourself that no longer serve you. The parts that were unfairly thrust on you by society, culture, family—those deeply entrenched ways of thinking and patterns of behavior. And the people who use you or hold you back. You will learn every superpower you need to lean into, every BS game you play with yourself to dim your own light. The ways you self-sabotage, those anemic qualities that need to be ruthlessly exhumed, explored, and exorcised. AND those insecurities, fears, and traumas that become your greatest weapons for mass creation. It's as if you started a business just to search your soul.

Only you, and you alone, could build this house. There will never be another one like it, as your business is an extension of you, and there will never be another you. Never. My friend, you are one in eight billion.

And oh will it be painful, but it will be every bit worth it.

I promise when you are well on your way (because there really is no end, is there?), in a quiet, utterly insignificant moment, probably under unflattering fluorescent light, you will experience this flash in the mirror that finally, for the first time, you would not trade places with another person on this planet. Your life, so perfectly imperfect, perfectly yours.

* * *

Now if you'll indulge me, let's drop back into the practical here and now, and what brought you to this book. Pretend for a moment you're a potential new small business client and we're meeting for the first time. I'd invite you to my office (none of this remote mumbo jumbo), warmly greet you at the door, and make sure you've got libations (plural) in front of you (hydration, you know). Your speedy staccato speech might signal you're a bit nervous, a bit wobbly about what you're undertaking and your business-building abilities. But I'd assure you that you've come to the right place. We'd quickly get down to brass tacks. Covering everything from the Build Like A Woman Blueprint to why you're here and what you can expect to gain. Snippets of our conversation might go a little something like this:

. . . *The purpose of BUILD?* Simply, to bet on yourself.

. . . This is for you if you're an aspiring or an existing entrepreneur. Whether you have an idea you're ready to explore or an existing idea. It's for all types: recent college grads, side hustlers, "want-more-in-life" corporate dropouts, full-fledged founders, or anyone looking for help navigating this confusing thing called a business. You're either at the idea stage wanting to bring your product or service to market, or fully launched, ready to level up. All sizes of businesses are cared for: solopreneurs to small business owners to scalers. All types of businesses are, too: product or service, across all categories.

. . . *What will you learn and accomplish?* By the end of this work, you will be well equipped to either start a business, or take your business to the next level, AND you will have designed a well-rounded life in the process.

. . . *What makes this BUILD blueprint different from others you've considered?* Typically, business experts focus exclusively on business-building tools, leaving you to scramble around to figure out your life on top of that. Everything cobbled together. They forget the person. You! That doesn't work out too well. This how-to hybrid combines life mindset with business skillset. I mined and methodically organized everything under the sun so you don't have to. You'll find it's the first of its kind.

. . . To delve a little deeper, this is the ultimate do-it-yourself entrepreneurial blueprint. First, we focus on life mindset work to create a winning mentality for success and a sustainable foundation. Next comes the business skillset work, the nuts and bolts needed to construct your dream business. Along the way, you'll get a crash course in leadership, team, strategy, marketing, money, creative, sales, and so much more. And all is geared toward the unique experiences of women.

. . . *Why is this so important?* Because you need to have a strong foundation in place so your business can grow to great heights and go the distance. And frankly, otherwise you'll often be miserable. With this mindset–skillset combo, there is nothing you cannot do and accomplish.

Know that while this is a proven method—an off-the-shelf, worth-its-weight-in-gold one—it needs to have YOU written all over it.

. . . *What landed you here?* Lay it on me, from your rudimentary here-and-now needs to higher-order existential dread. You might answer: "I want to leave my current corporate job, but somehow can't make the leap," "I feel like I'm just going through the motions. Walking-dead style. And I don't feel fulfilled," "I want to pursue what I'm passionate about and have more creative freedom," "I want to earn more," "I want to feel less stretched with more flexible time for family, my own health, and other priorities," "I want to get in the driver's seat for life on my own terms."

. . . I'd put money on the fact that you feel frustrated by your current situation and blocked in some way. And you might be overwhelmed not knowing how to improve it. So many experts and options out there. Too little preparation from college, regular jobs, and life in general. You're stuck. Overwhelmed. You want to take control, control, control back. You are hungry to get to the next level, ready for change, eager to improve your quality of life and smart enough to know you just need a clear path forward. A few more skills, resources, and knowledge in your toolbelt. This blueprint is here to give you just that.

. . . *"How will I know when I'm ready?"* you might ask. "You'll never be," I'd say. Just start where you are with what you've got.

Before leaving our hypothetical meeting, to help you in your pursuit I would hand you a copy of this book—a guide for women who want to start and scale a business and life they love. I'd let you know that you now have my methodology in the palm of your hand. For many years and over many holidays, I poured myself into it, so you don't even need to meet me face-to-face. My brain has been transferred, my soul summoned. As you leaf through this book and the rest of the introduction that follows, you'll find the origin story for this work. Know I'm shoulder to shoulder as you break ground in BUSINESS and break through to YOU.

* * *

Business over Barbie

Growing up, I lived in a town about thirty-five miles north of NYC. Our town was Stepford-like. For the most part, women worked inside the home. Men worked outside the home. It was a place of Jazzercise, eating disorders, and academic pressure that had kids on a low simmer at all times. Where nothing, from periods to sex to the nature of work, was explained and everything was always "all good." Despite running with a popular crowd, I felt like a total outsider. Reptile-like with skin that got put on backward, inside out, always scratching at my intestines. Simultaneously anxiously activated and reliably repressed, which I guess is part of the collective high school experience.

My Canadian dad had a rule in our family that you had to spend at least an hour outside every day, rain or shine, sleet or snow. Like lock-the-doors-until-the-timer-dings-level rule. When I was young, my nanny (I had the rare combo of two parents who had full-time childcare as they actually both worked outside the home) was an older, lace-curtain Irish-woman with a cackle. She would arrive proudly every day right on time in a monochromatic pantsuit, fully coiffed with a bright red lip, only to then change into her "work" clothes, usually a velour tracksuit. Nan would watch her soap operas inside while I would be left to the elements outside like a billy goat, eating blackberries, pushing friends in wheel-barrows, climbing the massive chain-link fence behind our house. That saved me, I think. There in the wild I would dream and scheme under a giant tree that dropped pine needles in my hair. Wily. Usually about selling something. That was my play.

It was during one of those mandatory evacuations that I concocted something called the Snack Attack Pack, which was basically a glo-rified set of snacks sold at a premium, brown-bag style. I would rap on middle-school morning announcements, "Come and pick up your Snack Attack Pack, surprising enough you don't feel your hunger com-ing back." Years later Marc Randolph, the cofounder of Netflix, told me that candy arbitrage is an early indicator for entrepreneurship. If that's the case, I had IT.

We had a guest house on property for rental income, and in between tenants, I'd have my friends come over to play "business." They'd sit outside my "office," and I'd ask them to hold my calls until they grew restless enough waiting for an imaginary phone to ring, at which point I'd ask for the perforated pink and yellow slips logging who called.

A few years later I dreamed up a TV show called "It's Time to Talk." The theme song was Shanice's "I Love Your Smile," not so subtly reinforced by a Cindy Crawford–inspired logo that I hand-drew on a piece of cardboard. I was the host and interviewed guests about subjects like animal testing on beauty products. At the end of the home video, I thanked my ten imaginary nineties' brand sponsors, from American Airlines to Nine West. Fast-forward to graduating from college when I worked in advertising and had a T-shirt side hustle called Deux . . . always creating through business.

Some of us are probably hardwired to be entrepreneurs and I was one of those. A born entrepreneur. But I never saw anyone who was one. And certainly not a woman coming up with a hustle, calling the shots. Charting her own very unconventional, unique path. Wild. Outrageous. Carving her own weird way. Unapologetic in her ambition.

All to say, for a long time I had no idea what I was, what to call it, or what to do about it. And frankly, there are still days I don't, because there are so few of us who've stepped out of the expected.

"Oh Shoot, That's a Girl!"

On weekends my parents would pull me out of my warm bed before dawn, in my thermal underwear, and sleepily put me and my brother in the back of our Ford Taurus station wagon. We'd arrive at a ski resort in Vermont, shiny and gleaming, the first ones there. They would buy two lift tickets for four of us to share—one adult and one child—

and put the passes on these circular rings that could move from jacket to jacket (at the time, non-transferable was not explicitly stated; had it been, trust me, these two law-abiding citizens never would have done this). My parents would watch me watch other kids in fancy Spyder suits train with coaches, their full day to my half. They never got me a lesson. I'm not sure if it's because it was too expensive or because they didn't believe in learning like that, but something magical happened one year. I went from being average to quite good. Like "Oh shoot, that's a girl" from the chairlift above me as skiers watched me tear down the slope good.

We still joke about it. But now as an adult I trace that growth spurt to my instinctively watching people ski down the mountain. Skiing right behind the best skiers I could find on the hill. I'd follow them as close as I could without getting called out as creepy. I'd have my skis mirror their tracks in the powder. The curvature of their turns. How high on the hill they broke. What terrain they would avoid. Counterintuitively, I learned things like to accelerate over ice, to not stop sharply (how's that for a life lesson?), to stay out of the backcountry unless you have a partner (also good). I followed the fundamentals, repeated, and then put my own signature on it.

That is the sort of guide you will get here.

I'm not trained with fancy degrees. I didn't go to Harvard (even though I speak there now). I don't have anyone in my family who gave me insider access to the world of entrepreneurship. But here is what I do have: That magical number of more than ten thousand hours in the chair running a business. Lessons from interviewing and mentoring with CEOs of Fortune 100 companies, billionaires, and self-made mavericks, on the cover of *Forbes* (I even sat down with Oprah). At least one hundred conferences, industry events, and programs attended. Been in rooms with the most powerful women on Earth, from *TIME*'s Women of the Year to *Fortune*'s Most Powerful Women. A quarter million spent on performance, wealth, and business experts who have coached me one-on-one. This unorthodox approach has gotten me named one of the "Top 39 Disruptors in Media,

Advertising, and Tech" by *Adweek*, "Leading Woman in Business" by *Fast Company*, and "Creative Innovator" by Condé Nast.

My classroom has been this thing called life.

Higher Ground

So here are my actual credentials, because you deserve to know who's with you on this journey. What really grinds my gears (despite daily meditation) is someone promising a quick-fix solution. Like, you know, making a million dollars overnight. Anyone who alleges to give you results they have not achieved for themselves is a con artist, not a true practitioner. You should have someone who is battle tested and a bit banged up from doing it for real in the real world.

While this may sound like a narcissistic rant, the reason I'm obsessed with sharing who I am and what I've done here is because I want you to trust me to blaze this path with and for you. I have bone-level respect for you. That, and as Peloton's Robin Arzón says, humblebrags are part of what gets us into trouble. We need to start claiming what we've done. No apologies. Right, Robin? So here goes . . .

To build different things, I have worn different hard hats: entrepreneur, investor, and business strategist. My company, Grayce & Co, advises some of the most iconic brands—Nike, Verizon, NBC, Hugo Boss, Google—helping them reach women. I have a reputation in that space as being one of the best in the world to do it. I have directed $500 million in marketing and generated over a billion dollars on behalf of my clients. Built an integrated team of five hundred people across three agencies in seven different time zones. Doubled an athleisure business. Developed a leading sports strategy for millennial women. Led acquisitions for a major telecommunications company. Launched a drink startup's business. Set up a software startup for investment within one year. I have demonstrable and very real results helping businesses achieve and exceed goals. Time and time again. Which has been rewarding and satisfying, and yet . . . I wanted to do more.

The whole time I was building my own business and my clients' businesses, I had a separate goal in mind: to democratize my own hard-earned business expertise, and specifically to guide women entrepreneurs just like me. I'd found, at first, that my schooling and corporate training did not prepare me for the stark realities of startup life. And the women's business books that were out there were big on "go, girl" messages, but short on the gritty details of actually building a business. I had to teach myself *everything*, from how to develop a business plan to how to adopt the right mindset and attitude needed for entrepreneurial success. I took notes every step of the way to create a vision that inspires with a rigorous plan that actually works. Once I had a taste of that, I wanted it for anyone else who wants it.

With that in mind, I was inspired to start a multimedia platform known as Build Like A Woman. This global platform reaches 125 countries and provides inspiration, tools, and community for women. It includes a content series with top entrepreneurs, a digital course, live events bringing together women from all levels of business, and the most exciting, newest extension of this overall initiative . . . this book.

My intention behind BUILD is for women to kick back against the cultural conditioning of a ceiling. For every woman to discover and unleash the Builder that resides inside.

Looking Glass

I'm truly proud of all that on paper. But behind all the bright, shiny stuff is all that you don't see. The tough times, blunders, faking it, feeling like a fraud or imposter.

I didn't start out knowing my purpose but was hungry, restless to find it. Elizabeth Lesser, author of one of my favorite books ever, *Broken*

Open, talks about sledgehammers and hummingbirds. Sledgehammers know exactly what they want (god bless) and drive at it with a vengeance, with reckless abandon; hummingbirds take longer to find their passion, zigzagging, picking up this and that, cross-pollinating, always in motion. I'm definitely the latter and bet many of you are, too.

At my first job as an advertising assistant, I hung up a quote by Diane von Furstenberg in my gray felt cubicle that read, "I didn't know what I wanted to do, but I knew the sort of woman I wanted to become." As we all know, life has a plan for when that will hit you—and it is rarely on your terms. For me, it came ten years later.

But first I went from assistant to the assistant of the assistants, then rising to be the youngest managing director of a global agency. I got to a place with a nice title and a stable salary. You know, where you don't have to choose on a given day between whether you will pick up your dry cleaning or order takeout. But on the inside, I was falling apart. I didn't feel alive. I felt uncreative and depleted. I had no personal boundaries. The leadership of the agency would say, "Jump," and I would respond, "How high?" My thumbs' reply time on that cell was down to ten seconds flat; this fembot had no off switch. My personal life was relegated to being flat out on the couch with a take-out box of lo mein balanced on my winded chest as I dissolved into a reality TV show, or drowning myself in a few too many glasses of Sauv Blanc. It was work-related recovery, numbing, or escapism. My life was far from integrated, and I was light-years away from being amplified.

On good days I felt like a rat in an experiment being prodded to see how long I could stay underground. I saw only darkness for years, or so it seemed, arriving at the office in the dark and leaving in the dark. Once I was so bleary-eyed from a series of 3:00 A.M. finishes and 6:00 A.M. starts that I had to go sleep on a park bench around the corner from my office. A *park bench*! A designer on my team landed in the hospital for exhaustion, needing an IV drip. A *hospital*! And not only did it not faze me, I wondered how soon she could get back to finishing up the pitch deck. For a year straight I clocked four planes a week. Up in the air almost more than on solid ground. I was so absent from my life that Dash, my dog, virtually had an around-the-clock caretaker. On bad days I knew definitively I had sold out, given my only life over to an imposter who was so pathetically ambitious that she (me!) kept four-inch heels in a file cabinet drawer under her desk, ready to throw on if the big boss came for a visit. (He did *not* like flats.) My one precious life.

Something inside me whispered quietly at first, with more ferocity and urgency over time: *There. Has. To. Be. A. Better. Way.*

My business was not launched courageously after some eureka moment. It was launched quietly in the dark, out of sheer desperation. An attempt at relief from the unfair barriers and unkept promises of the corporate world. An attempt to escape the exhaustion. It didn't happen overnight. I couldn't summon the emotional courage, gather the financial security, or reach the physical breaking point to make the leap immediately, but finally I left. Everything.

That inciting incident came over a NYC shroomtown pizza (four types of mushrooms) where a friend looked at my overworked, puffy, gray, truffle-sauce-smeared face and said, "You look like a ghost." Instead of taking a cab, I walked thirty-some odd blocks home, the city lights reflecting off the wet pavement as words from author Tama Kieves (who I'd met at a workshop years earlier) cycled over and over in my head: "If you are this successful doing work you don't love, imagine how successful you'd be doing work you do love." Those words haunted me in the best possible way. They didn't leave until I did.

Eventually. I creeped into my boss's glass office, head held low in defeat (and to feign reverence), and resigned. That's really how Grayce & Co was born.

The actual idea for my business—starting a strategy agency—came from seeing the obvious market opportunity, a white space, in the same industry I was already working in. Heck, only 1 percent of agencies were owned by women. At the time, no one was really focused exclusively on the niche of women-oriented strategy, ensuring accurate, multidimensional representation. Instead, virtually every media campaign was about engineering insecurity. Lack. Want. Fear. If only you buy X product you (woman) will improve. I knew that being a woman trying to *serve* other women deliberately, relative to the men trying to *sell* them haphazardly, could become my differentiator.

After the exit, I'd like to say it went from bad (corporate) to great (entrepreneurship). But it was more like from bad to worse. You see, I just replicated the same bad patterns from corporate, but now no longer had the practical stability of benefits, a title, or a paycheck.

Grayce & Co was named after my tiny, mighty grandmother Grayce (also my middle name) who was one hundred pounds soaking wet; she'd lived in her family's attic for a year to survive the Spanish flu (sound familiar?), ran a one-room schoolhouse grades K-12 on the prairies near Regina, Saskatchewan, and had five kids. I figured if she could do that, I could do this. Also, true that I named it Grayce because I couldn't come up with anything else to call this so-called company.

My first client was really just me, myself, and I functioning as an independent contractor in the nonprofit space, having them pay my newly formed LLC, created via googled instructions. Frankly this was the only client I could get while fearing a noncompete clause. There really wasn't much strategy to it.

My second client was a Fortune 50 brand (hello, learning curve!) and that is when the noise really crept in. All of a sudden I wasn't on autopilot, and I had a team (albeit small) that was looking to me. But I was like a skittish, wide-eyed cat hunched and clawing externally for affirmation: *Did the client like my presentation or did it fall flat? Does my team think this culture is legit or are they scoffing behind my back? Was my turtleneck too tight? Why am I not one of those cool founders?* And the worst incessant, nagging question of all . . . *What if I'm found out?* Imposter syndrome would be an understatement.

In the background, my family was generally supportive while raising a collective right eyebrow. That polite melodic "we shall see!!" refrain. Others were harsher. Someone close to me told me I was "delusional" to be attempting to operate in such rarefied business settings. A boyfriend called me Bamm-Bamm from *The Flintstones*, and I don't think he meant it as a compliment. And, oh, my poor employees. They looked dumbfounded, as they had left Big 3 consulting jobs to work for a woman who turned out to be a confused coward. Desperate for success at any cost. Willing to compromise herself. To keep a startup happy, I stood by as a woman on my team was forced to guzzle hard liquor as clients chanted, "Shots, shots, shots." Her humiliated eyes caught mine pleading as I furtively glanced away. To get a project I wanted done for free I went along with an influential's icky advances only to become trapped in his indebtedness web. Rage toward him . . . fury at myself.

That bad, contortionist behavior was on me. It took a long time to release myself from that stomach-churning shame spiral. I knew it was wrong, I knew I was wrong, but I didn't have guts. Yet.

Reactive. Lonely. No mentors. No guidebooks. Those were the early years.

The Turn

One day as I relaxedly sipped my iced tea at a weekly check-in, an advisor triggered my body into a blood-bubbling boil. "You are wasting my time until you stop pretending," she said, "and really confront the fact you likely have deep-seated trauma."

Like a snapping turtle, I bit back. "I'm not avoiding anything. I would know if I was."

But later that night, her words tugged annoyingly at my sweatshirt like a little kid trying to get my attention. I was still pissed at her, which on its own said something. What if I don't know what I don't know? What if my issues are buried *that* deep? What if this is why I am so insecure and reactive, easily irritated with myself and, in turn, others?

Something in me clicked to go . . . inside. Do inner work. Get help. Maybe if I tapped into myself, I wouldn't be so tapped out. I began to poke at my core beliefs, prod at my insecurities, pull apart all the rejection from others (and myself).

I invested the money I was lucky to have made, even as a crappy business owner, into elite coaches to study mindset, limiting beliefs, and daily habits. Read self-help books. Did coursework. Tried meditation and MBSR (aka mindfulness-based stress reduction). Erected friendships with other like-minded women. Tried everything from flying across the country for a high-performance workshop to joining a gratitude group to researching vulnerability, shame, fear, and bravery. Therapists taught me about trauma, a wealth expert about money and mindset. I ingested a steady diet of inspiration from women I admired. From Oprah on the power of daily meditation to Sara Blakely's visualization exercises for mental clarity to call in what you want. From Serena's rituals for performance to Eva Longoria's importance of saying "no" and Barbara Corcoran's mad money stash to celebrate wins (we are hardwired to work for reward!).

It was the first time in my life I set my ego aside. Where I embraced that the operating system that had gotten me this far wasn't what I needed for the next phase. Willing to go anywhere, try anything. I was open and humble.

In the process, doubt turned confident. Feeling "not enough" turned into "good enough." External orientation turned inward. Mind turned body.

What I learned is nothing works unless you work. Nothing works unless you are your own home. Unless you stop looking outside and turn inward. Unless you really start to cultivate and only listen to that knowing voice inside you, the only voice that really matters. Where you learn to depend on yourself, develop a relationship that is reliable. Where you embrace sometimes unsettling things about yourself, like: You know what, I'm a great creative visionary, but I'm a horrible day-to-day manager. Or I hate being strapped to a desk supervising an office, so my team needs to consist of self-starters. Or my energy wanes unpredictably at times—so when I need to, I cancel my meetings. I get silent and still. Even imagine quitting my own business. And a million more revelations. My truths. The turning point came when I became committed to figuring out who I was, accepting and respecting it. Then dug reaaalllll deep.

You will have your own truths.

Shockingly, I found all this "self" personal development work paid the highest dividends of all in my business. These realizations went back into my business. Actually, now businesses, plural. If you can stand in the truth of who you are and what your business is about, you will become unshakable. All the nopes and nevers (which is 99.9 percent of what you get as an entrepreneur) ultimately become white noise. Because a reactive life is a painful life. At any minute you can be blown by the opinion or outside thought du jour, losing luminescent tendrils of yourself in the process.

When I came to know myself deeply for the first time as a grown woman, truly know myself in my bones—the breadth and depth of my vision, imperfections, dreams, mistakes, and resilience—I came to know not a shaky, superficial confidence but an entrenched, knowing confidence. This became a force multiplier. I'll now bet on myself all day long. I'll take that bet any day of the week.

That is when things started to take off. That is when I became an unpredictable, dangerous woman. Waiting for no one and nothing.

Many years after posting that quote in my cube, life winked as it often does and I was invited to have a business meeting with this woman whose words I had stared at for so long: Diane von Furstenberg.

Us alone in her NYC Meatpacking District office as the universe laughed. Looming behind a twenty-foot, raw-edged wooden desk (while I sat in front of her), surrounded by vibrant braided chairs, an Andy Warhol portrait, bracelets jangling this way and that, stood DVF, with her big, breezy hair that she adjusted ever so slightly to underscore a point. She showed me that sometimes the best advice of all isn't dispensed. It's demonstrated. She showed me a woman who was brutally direct, pointed in her questions, and tough, but at the same time, utterly graceful, gushingly complimentary (of me), and generous, wrapping me in a beautiful lavender leopard print scarf as she spun me out the door. I was both terrified and bedazzled being in the presence of authentic power.

As women, I learned, we can be profound contradictions and that is not only OK, it is fundamentally, absolutely necessary.

Becoming a Builder

Architects like the late, great Zaha Hadid teach us so much about the best practices of building. A strong foundation is what allows you to create structures that seemingly defy gravity. Radical, cylindrical, whimsical, soft-curving facades jutting out on a horizontal plane as if effortlessly resting on thin air alone. Seemingly in motion. All with tremendous scale. What is not exposed, though, is the base: beams and buttresses methodically planted deeply into the earth. It is a fundamental design principle that fashioning a foundation with the strongest materials is what is needed to create something that looks dreamlike, futuristic, and floating.

Nature mirrors this, leaning toward creating a strong foundation first. Take the majestic oak tree. It starts as a small acorn that demands space, pushing out to create an invisible vast, deep, wide root system, deploying nutrients and energy there first. Then up goes the tree canopy. This enables it to stay grounded and withstand great storms. It's why oaks endure, many for well over five hundred years.

That's what this book does here. It starts by giving you a foundation, so you can create whatever castle in the sky you can imagine. Keys to your kingdom (queendom?).

But being a Builder can be scary. As author and spiritual leader Marianne Williamson said, "Our deepest fear is not that we are inadequate. Our deepest fear is that we are powerful beyond measure. It is our light, not our darkness that most frightens us."

So how are you going to amplify your glorious light?

It starts by imagining yourself a Builder. This isn't a flippant title, but a choice. A daily act of choosing. One where you consciously decide your vision has value and intentionally step into realizing that vision.

To Be a Builder . . .

To be a Builder is to claim authority and agency for your own life. It means having a bold vision and taking big swings.

To be a Builder means you want a unique life. Dare to carve out. Dare to uniquely exist. Dare to defy cookie-cutter culture. No matter if you're eighteen or eighty.

To be a Builder is to develop a deep power base. Prioritizing foundation first. Where you power you to power yourself. Then power others.

To be a Builder is to move in the direction of bravery. Trying, building, if blocked or broken down, taking things back down to the studs to try again until the good stuff stacks.

Ultimately, it's a perspective shift to believe anything and everything is buildable. This is how we build a better world.

The day you have the courage to launch your dream business, you start to move like a Builder. The day you team up with people smarter than you, you start to lead like a Builder. The days when you want to give up but don't, you become a Builder.

You make you. You build you. This is your life. Win, lose, or draw, it comes down to you and you alone. I am not responsible. Your best friend isn't responsible. Your momma isn't responsible for whether you sink or soar. You are.

There's a secret no one tells us. We can be average and do extraordinary things. This method is for real women who build in the real world. Women who see a business as a means to a better life. This is about realizing no Prince Charming or family member or investor is coming to "save" us and so getting down to the often unglamorous task of laying bricks . . . the BLDG Blocks of our businesses.

With the Build Like A Woman Blueprint you become the architect of your life. From coloring inside the lines to outside the lines to drawing new lines altogether. And with that, virtually anything you want can be yours. Anything. You can build something out of nothing. We are here to share what lights us up most and what cracks open our hearts. Find it and breathe life into it, beautiful people. This is your birthright.

There is nothing you cannot dream, nothing you cannot do.

We're built for this. It's time to BUILD.

PUNCHLIST

THIS PUNCHLIST IS HERE SO YOU'LL KNOW WHAT YOU'RE GETTING IN THIS BOOK. Simply put, this is for all of you who are ready for more. More freedom. More passion. More independence. More money. More confidence. More impact. More you.

There are many, many, many different types of businesses and many, many, many paths to entrepreneurship. The Build Like A Woman™ Blueprint will be most useful to women (straight, LGBTQ+, GNC, NB, femme-identifying) who want to build things, as it focuses on the unique experiences, encounters, and roadblocks women face collectively. It was deliberately created by women, featuring women, for women. To state the obvious, this book is told from the (privileged) perspective of an educated straight white woman. I share my own personal story and provide overviews on the state of women and our commonalities. That said, I don't speak on the specific struggles of individual groups as it's not my place, but where possible have included demographic data and other experts to represent a broader spectrum of women. In this book she/her/hers is used as shorthand, but *everyone* (including men) is included. There is no intentional exclusion here.

Now on to the book contents that will help you create *your* dream business and life! Here's what you'll get as you go:

☐ **Definition:** A Builder bets on herself, consciously deciding her vision has value and intentionally steps into realizing that vision, daily.

☐ **Path:** Anyone (yes, anyone), at any time, with any qualifications and any amount of money, can have a business. You may have bought this book with anything from a vague to a specific idea for a business and need a solid plan. Or you might already have a business and just want to make it better. Whether you are an aspiring or existing entrepreneur, there are many paths to entrepreneurship and all are thoughtfully cared for throughout:

    ☐ College Grad: Hesitant to enter the corporate system that has so often failed women. As a recent grad or someone still in school, you're ready to crack open the book and take your first entrepreneurial steps.

    ☐ Corporate Dropout: Weary from rat-race running for others. You want more fulfillment in life on your own terms and/or a softer life without the stress, the anxiety, the malaise that comes from the nine-to-five hamster wheel. You are primed.

    ☐ Side Hustler: Super busy, no self-care, and stretched thin. You are conflicted between a full-time job and running a business on the side . . . think Dolly Parton's remake, "Five to Nine." What will give and when to make the leap? You are hopeful this book helps.

    ☐ Re-Enterer: Swamped with caretaking. Kid on your lap, needy parents, no privacy. You want to earn and be taken seriously. This will be an A-to-Z refresher on how to carve out time for business.

    ☐ Don't-Knower: You wonder what's best? Corporate, nonprofit, government, or entrepreneurship? Don't know what business idea to even start.

    ☐ Full-Fledged Founder: You know what's up and are excited about sharpening your skills.

☐ **Overview:** This book contains the very best tools from my relentless sourcing and seeking. Everything is rooted in leading-edge thinking from subject matter experts, research in behavioral science, and my original concepts (breakdowns to breakthroughs,

SECTION I

MINDSET: ARCHITECTING YOUR FOUNDATION

1

PLOT

Understanding the Lay of the Land

I love to see a young woman go out and grab the world by the lapels. Life's a bitch. You've got to go out and kick ass.

—MAYA ANGELOU

DO YOU WANT THE HONEST TRUTH ABOUT THE PLOT OF LAND YOU ARE STEPPING onto? You are going to get hit hard when you start to build anything that threatens others' land, resources, but most of all their power. POWER! Most people only pay lip service to liking a strong, independent woman. A woman of contradictions with opinions, who refuses to stay in her box or on her pedestal. A woman who knows her power. Initially, you will get lots of propitiative encouragement in starting a business, but once you build something formidable, you will find yourself defending it with more than you think you can muster. Your teeth will chatter, your voice will tremble, your face will flush. But shoulders back, chin up, my love. You will find a fire inside you that knows no bounds. You will find allies. You will be OK. Better than OK. But unlike me, you should go into this new territory eyes wide open, on alert, from the start. So you will not be blindsided when they come for you. Because they will.

Women are born Builders but have been limited in the ways we have been able to demonstrate this ability. My mom, Elinor, was an editor for thirty years at a very well-known magazine where she was told if she had kids she couldn't be an issue editor. Imagine saying that to someone today? She had us anyway, knowing her career would essentially reach a screeching halt. And that wasn't too long ago.

In my own case, I stopped building every time I thought I was navigating business wrong. Turns out my XX chromosome was the issue. Most of my favorite stop-start stories seem to involve men (of course, lots of good guys out there, too), but I found that most didn't respect or take me seriously, let alone fear me. As a very-late-working, recent college grad, I asked for a pay increase. My manager's response: "You don't have a family to support, so why do you need this 'extra' money?" Leaving after-work drinks with clients, having sipped only one, the chief marketing officer called me a "little c**t." Being taught by a plumber (mansplained) the proper way to flush a toilet (one finger on the handle) in a home I still managed to buy for myself. Corporate rooms where I was shot down for speaking up. Needing to stuff and repress all that was me back inside me. Or that one time a guy got REALLY ANGRY at my simply saying, "I no longer want to partner with you." The mental seek-and-destroy terrorism that followed. The list goes on and on: mild put-downs, annoying advances, wealth inequities. Or. Or. Or. Huh? Huh? Huh?

Backlash is a confusing thing. Going from being beloved to hated in a flash just by defying someone or something . . . torn down as a means of control. The anger and blowback can be terrifying. Deafening and disproportionate. No one explains it's not you. And you don't dare ask. So you just fumble around in the dark, trying to minimize a negative opinion of you over your doing what is in the best interest of your business. You stop building and get small in an attempt to manage the entitlement.

So instead of wondering what the hell is wrong with YOU and analyzing all your nonexistent missteps, you can play within this system with more authority. You are going to be underestimated, devalued, and dismissed at times. Let's not let you do that to yourself as well.

What an unprecedented time to be a woman. Archaic belief systems, structures, and formal education have socialized us into believing that

our ability to build is limited to certain circumstances. This is changing. Slowly. But if you wait for the world to change around you, you will
not have your biggest life. Change what you do and the world around
you will change. I am not here to get you to join a movement to break
down those structures, although many of you may do that directly or
indirectly. I am here to help you to take control of your own thinking
and story, rather than the one you've accepted from someone else, and
in doing so, build new structures.

Many days my eyes well up hearing stories about women's grit, fire,
pain, and how they gracefully keep on keepin' on. Women who, despite
fear, still manage to take that step, enter that room, make that leap, steady
that pulse, take that seat, channel that energy, raise that hand, wage that
ask, defend that "no" . . . and so grow. Becoming daily, breathing, living testaments of strength.

So let's get smart. Whip smart. Let's make this OUR time.

The three BLDG Blocks you will get in this chapter are:

1. State of Women
2. 12M + You
3. Fear Means GO!

BLDG BLOCK 1: State of Women

The system is rigged. Opportunity is not fair play. This we know.
Women want to move up and have more. Do great things. Feel encouraged to create and lead. And have a life outside of business. To
take this on, we need to build a solid foundation, do the work to build
strategically and sustainably, and know the right steps to do all of it.
Now that you've got the goods. The playbook. This is about stepping
into your authentic self to create an integrated life, inclusive of a business, that defies the odds.

At first glance, this chapter may seem dense and dry like a stale saltine, but the dire data actually describes the eye-opening lessons that no one ever taught us in work, college, and even high school. So that said, let's start by looking at the state of women broadly, so you can see the full landscape and how important your ideas are to it.

Put those readers on, and let's go back in time for a women-oriented history lesson. Shall we acknowledge the challenges first? Three major forces are at play, bearing against you and creating difficult headwinds:

- **Familial Forces:** For women, doubting our intelligence and ability starts early. By age six, girls are less likely than boys to view their gender as brilliant.[1] Parents google "Is my son a genius?" more than twice as often as "Is my daughter a genius?"[2] Insecurity around capability is often reinforced at home.
- **Cultural Forces:** Ethnic, racial, gender, economic, and intellectual diversity are still not reflected accurately by media outlets. Instead, they provide a disproportionate number of images of women as young, white, and thin. Because of this, few women see themselves represented. In addition, only 24 percent of news articles are about women, and many of those stories are about violence and victimhood.[3] Women generally have a lower sense of self-confidence as compared to men. Culture cements insecurities, self-criticism, and a persistent sense of "not enough." One of the contributing factors is social media, which has a stronger negative impact on girls.[4] And I would be remiss if I didn't mention sexual violence. It's hard to believe, but one in five women has been the victim of rape or attempted rape in her lifetime.[5] Tentative hand raise. I'm in this godforsaken club that no one ever asks to be in.
- **Professional Forces:** Women's representation in professional fields is also strongly lacking. In the United States, women make up 51 percent of the population, but only 27 percent of the Congress.[6] Only 7.4 percent of CEOs in the Fortune 500 are women; none are Black or Hispanic.[7] You'll find more CEOs named David than all

women chief executives.[8] And among the country's top earners (those in the 1 percent), seven out of ten men have stay-at-home spouses.[9] But what if you become the more successful one? Chew on this double whammy: even when women make more than their husbands, they are still doing more childcare and housework than their spouses are. Women owe two-thirds of student loan debt (about $929 billion) and struggle more to pay it off since they are paid less than men.[10] And that promotion? Women (despite being equally qualified) only apply when they meet 100 percent of the criteria for a job whereas men apply if they meet only 60 percent of the criteria.[11] The World Economic Forum projects that gender equality in the United States is still another mind-boggling two hundred years away.[12]

Women still lag in business building.[13] The rate of women's entrepreneurship is only 16.6 percent.[14] To put this in perspective, entrepreneurship has only a slightly higher share of women as these male-dominated fields: sports announcers (12.5 percent), police officers (12.8 percent), and cab drivers (15 percent).[15] Oh, and 50 percent of women report giving up on their dreams.[16] Too many women are still sitting on too many ideas that have the power to change lives and the world.

So what's holding women back from starting businesses?

- **Support:** Women lack financial, emotional, and practical support, as well as tools and resources: 50 percent of women have never had a woman mentor,[17] and women-led startups in the US received only 2.3 percent of available venture funding, according to *Forbes* magazine. And if you're a Black or Latina woman, it's even more daunting: only 0.34 percent.[18]
- **Leadership:** "Feminine" traits aren't celebrated in leadership, but women have business-building superpowers. The *Harvard Business Review*'s "Women Score Higher Than Men in Most

Leadership Skills" summed up the results of one of the largest studies on gender and leadership to date. Actually, in twelve of sixteen identified leadership competencies, women scored higher: they take more initiative, display more integrity, are more results oriented, are more likely to practice self-development and to develop others, are more likely to inspire others, are better at building relationships through collaborative work, and are champions of change who reach for higher targets.[19]

- **Confidence:** Women don't believe in their ability. Less than 50 percent of women are confident they can start a new business.[20]

So that is how the deck is stacked. But there is hope. Things are looking up. Tailwinds are accelerating.

Women are rising. Powerful events like the Women's March attracted five million people across six hundred marches *worldwide*—it still remains the largest single-day protest in US history—proof that women are tired and ready to speak up and fight for what they want.[21] Political activist Gloria Steinem calls this one of the most important times for women in history.[22]

Economically, women are a force to be reckoned with. According to the Boston Consulting Group, wealth held by women has grown to about a third of global wealth.[23] That trend is accelerating, reports McKinsey & Company. In an unprecedented transfer of wealth in the United States, for instance—thanks to money jointly held by baby boomers passing to the longer-living female spouse and women also earning more—by 2030 American women are expected to control $30 trillion in household financial assets. In effect, more than the 2022 US economy ($25.5 trillion).[24]

We have more leverage than we realize. Mini revolutions and evolutions are upon us . . . we just need to keep building.

Today's New-Fashioned Women

In light of all this information, here is a temperature check on how women are truly feeling about themselves, their community, and the world at large. The agency I founded in partnership with the market research firm BeaconInsight, polled two thousand women ages eighteen to thirty-four. While some of this may sound obvious, I believe it is worth covering, so you are reminded you are not alone. I've often felt like I'm unique in my habits, thoughts, or struggles, but there are certain shared experiences. Our research revealed five key paradoxes that define us:

1. **We are aware of the bleak reality of our country, but less worried about it.**

   Despite increased awareness of the dire circumstances in the United States in particular, we recognize the power we have to effect change. And in light of chaos and turmoil, we are intensely optimistic when it comes to our own futures and are motivated to take even more agency over our own lives.

2. **We want to be sexy but not sexualized.**

   We do not wish to be sexualized, although we are proud to have a healthy sex life (lots of sex and good sex at that). We seek to define sexuality on our own terms. We are open-minded, sexually liberated, and not ashamed about it.

3. **We are fiercely independent but also dependent.**

   We crave authentic connection but are also more reliant on technology than any other generation, spending 6.5 hours per week on social media alone. And while 100 percent of the women we spoke to said they could not live without family and friends, 80 percent feel misunderstood by others.

4. **We feel in charge but also see obstacles outside our control.**

   We are cognizant of barriers we face, such as sexism and job market challenges, but we remain optimistic. We put our career and/or personal development ahead of marriage. We are inspired by possibility and want to live outside our comfort zone. According to our research, half of the women polled mention that ongoing learning and growth are top priorities, while 100 percent of women polled value career or pursuing a degree and state that being non-conformist and finding their own path is important, but they still want to feel like they belong in society.

5. We value holistic well-being but struggle to stay healthy.

We prioritize exercise as a means of self-care, not as a form of body manipulation. Nine of ten women we interviewed pursue good health so they can be successful in other areas of life. However, while 60 percent state that health and holistic well-being are essential, they struggle to find time and energy to manage their health and well-being.

Overall, our research indicates that we are multidimensional and have a fluid definition of self. We want to be supported and nourished in our complexity. We reject labels, because we cannot be easily defined. We loathe being pigeonholed, judged, or stereotyped. Know you're not alone.

BLDG BLOCK 2: 12M + You

That is the general landscape. Now let's get into specifics around business: you joining the ranks of twelve million other women as an entrepreneur.[25] With only 40 percent of US businesses owned by women, there's plenty of room for you at the entrepreneurial table.

After decades of phantom progress, as of late women have found themselves fired, furloughed, and forced to downshift from corporate jobs. Women didn't want to lean in. They wanted to lie down. The silver lining? As women get up, there is a new urgency, a new hunger to take control and build what is hers and hers alone. New businesses started by women are up dramatically. And experts say a tidal wave is coming with nearly 40 percent of working women predicted to jump from traditional employment to self-employment in the next two years. For those who dare to dream of starting a business, it is their number one goal in life.[26] Necessity really is the mother of invention. Welcome to the *real* rise of female entrepreneurship.

While you have real headwinds, tailwinds are also in your favor. Brands born by women that embody those feminine traits like openness, relevance, empathy, fairness, inclusivity, persuasiveness, transparency, authenticity, commitment, and emotion have 4 to 10 percent higher revenue, and those that make an impact on our well-being and have functional benefits outperform the stock market by 206 percent.[27] Women-led companies also tend to be more financially secure. Female founders achieve higher returns, and at larger startups, the likelihood of success increases with each female executive on the team.[28] Women are also more likely to share what they have with their communities. Women really are uber equipped to start businesses.[29]

Also, customers are shifting from buying big to shopping small and supporting women-owned businesses. This is why cult indie brands that ooze these traits are rising up. According to a study by Catalina Marketing, ninety out of one hundred of the largest brands for consumer-packaged goods experienced a share decline as over $20 billion transferred from large brands to indie brands.[30] Women are gravitating toward brands that celebrate women, not objectify them.

If you intercepted one hundred people on the street and asked about the best US entrepreneurs, the top-of-mind answers would probably be five men: Bezos, Musk, Zuckerberg, Jobs, and Gates. Those questioned would likely stumble and fumble trying to rattle off any women's names. To add to your lexicon, here are five equally accomplished women—out of ONLY twenty-five (!!) female founders in fifty-five (!!) years—scaling to IPO stardom:

- First Wall Streeter: Muriel Siebert, Siebert Financial, 1967, IPO value: $253 million
- Largest IPO valuation: Diane Greene, VMware (software), 2007, $19.5 billion
- Youngest: Whitney Wolfe Herd (thirty-one at the time), Bumble (dating app), 2021, $2.2 billion

■ First Black woman: Cathy Hughes, Urban One (media company), 1999, $79 million
■ Most Famous: Jennifer Hyman, Rent the Runway (fashion service), 2021, $357 million[31]

The dearth of female-led entrepreneurial endeavors has to change, and it starts with you. Let's commit today to protract those innate business-building talons.

BLDG BLOCK 3: Fear Means GO!

So if that is the ground you stand on, now to the air you breathe. You will encounter a fog called fear. It rolls in and rolls out. Often capriciously and without warning. FEAR has two responses as you've heard. Face everything and run. Or face everything and rise.

I'm one of the most fearful people on Earth and one of the most fearless. Just this morning I cycled through a host of fears: how a building alarm indicating a ground fault might mean everyone electrocuted before lunchtime, pimples on my chin signaling hormone imbalance, payment not hitting my account because the clients have (maybe?) gone bankrupt, wondering if I used too many egotistical I's in that email. But I also know that I've been terribly brave: took myself out to dinner alone, lit my metaphorical cigarette as he shouted "no one will ever love you," stared into the void of eight TV cameras, survived what felt like one hundred years of solitude, and watched my once high and lifted, now low and pointed breasts jiggle as I ran into the ocean at sunrise on my birthday. Know the fear that you may have can be met with equal parts ferocity . . . you just might not have met that fearlessness in yourself. Yet.

So with both feet firmly planted, how to face fear and do "it" anyway?

A young girl in Mexico contracted polio at the age of six. At eighteen, while in medical school, she was involved in a near fatal streetcar accident. This was the second time she had to learn how to walk again. Despite constant pain, she began to paint while in recovery, embarking on arguably one of the most renowned creative journeys in history. That woman is Frida Kahlo, whose art influenced, inspired, and adorned fashion, design, digital media, furniture . . . even a US postage stamp. The world would be worse off had she not faced her fears and persevered.

Recognizing fear as a very real variable in the day-to-day success (or failure) of a business, my team and I decided to study risk-takers globally, to better understand what differentiates overachievers, innovators, leaders. What moves someone from ordinary to extraordinary? We learned that fear should be your compass, navigated best by three actions:

Analyze the Risk

For a nose-in-the-mud view on fear, Pulitzer Prize–winning war photojournalist Lynsey Addario and I sat down at length to discuss her going on assignment, leaving behind two young children and a husband. Lynsey is what I would call the right BUILD Inspector on fear, as she's been in conflict-ravaged countries like Iraq, Afghanistan, and Ukraine, and continues to run in when everyone else runs out, despite having been kidnapped twice and held hostage. For a front-row seat on handling fear from a war zone:

> I'm often very scared, but I think part of my job is knowing how to handle that fear and what to do with it. So when I feel that sort of paralyzing fear come on, I have to say, "Okay, why am I scared? Am I scared because I have PTSD and it's natural for me to be paranoid? Or am I scared because legitimately we are doing something very high risk?" Sometimes if I'm in the midst of a gun battle and I'm facedown in the dirt, I have to speak to myself out loud, you know, in a voice and literally say, "Okay, you have to get up, have to get cover," because sometimes I'm so scared I don't even run away.[32]

So if fear takes you out, shake it off for a second or two, analyze it (could this actually kill me or is it just a passing bodily reaction?) and talk to yourself sotto voce. Say things out loud like "You got this" or "You're going to be okay." And, remember, managing fear comes from close analysis.

Set a Goal

Take Phiona Mutesi, a four-time Women's Chess Olympian from Uganda. When Phiona was three, her father died from AIDS, and several years later her sister suddenly died. Her family became homeless. At nine, Phiona couldn't read or write and dropped out of school because her mother could no longer afford it. One day, hoping to find a meal, she stumbled across a missionary project teaching kids chess, a game testing survival through aggressive strategy. She was hooked. Every day she walked three miles to practice and play, knowing she wanted to be a grand master, and nothing could hold her back. The ultimate underdog, she couldn't have started from further behind: growing up in one of the poorest, most violent slums and within a decade became one of the world's best chess players. She wasn't distracted by her circumstances, didn't let anyone scare her, and remained singularly focused. "Chess is a lot like my life," she said. "If you make smart moves you can stay away from danger, but any bad decision could be your last."

Practice, Practice, Practice

New Zealand–born sailor Laura Dekker had been sailing every day since she was five. At sixteen, she succeeded in becoming the youngest person ever to sail solo around the world. In her own words, "You don't have to know that you can do something. You just have to try." Risk-taking is a daily practice of engagement. Small risks give rise to bigger risks, which give rise to even bigger risks, and finally you trust yourself enough to handle uncertainty. All because you've built the muscle and trust yourself to follow that uncertain path.

What we learned from everyone we spoke to is that their risks were made possible by changing their relationship to fear—instead of avoiding fear, they engage it. The most successful risk-takers are just as afraid, just as fearful, as you or I . . . initially. But instead of avoiding fear or running from it (which ironically means being ruled by it), they embrace it, stay with it, dialogue with it, make it a familiar friend. They look at fear with curiosity: there is something here to teach me, something to learn. A knock on the door from fear is seen as a positive sign. In changing their relationship to fear, they are able to take risks, again and again.

If risk-taking depends on engaging fear, we then need to understand our biological response to it. Fear first existed to keep us alive, but it can also hold us back from living. Our brain still interprets events as either life or death. While we are now living in a world where losing our jobs or not getting a promotion is the worst thing to happen, it can still biologically feel as drastic as death.

Our response to fear is controlled by a small region in the brain called the amygdala, which is the size of an almond. The next time your heart starts to thump, your stomach churns, take a minute to laugh at the fact you are being governed by a teeny, tiny bunch of neurons. Who's going to let an almond run the show? Or as author Elizabeth Gilbert jokingly says: "Fear, I recognize and respect that you are part of this family . . . You are absolutely forbidden to drive."

Given that fear is one of the biggest impediments to success, let's shovel deeper into understanding it and the strategies to deal with it. A Princeton neuroscientist I interviewed said that fear is essentially about threat detection and protection. The professor shared an experiment where subjects were exposed to an image of a tiger in a room. When they were reexposed to the same image of that room, this time with the tiger no longer there, the fear center in their brain automatically lit up again, making them feel fear. They kept recalling the tiger. This shows us that once you see a room with a fear-inducing stressor in it (like a tiger), you associate the room with that stressor. You can't easily avoid the biological response to fear, even if the stressor isn't there anymore.

"There's power," I was told, "in acknowledging the fact we're safe, or if we can't do that, to choose a different environment that isn't associated with that stressor." Go to places where you feel cared for and nourished while you are out there doing what scares you. Amelia Earhart, the first woman to fly solo across the Atlantic, in 1932, captures confronting fear as follows: "The most difficult thing is the decision to act, the rest is merely tenacity. The fears are paper tigers."

Fear remembers if you run. I so believe in not running that I had a calligrapher draw in exaggerated black ink, "What would you do if you weren't afraid?" It's the first thing I look at before I face the day.

No successful woman got to where she is without confronting fear and experiencing failure; however, it's the way she responded that made her the Builder she is today. Brands are built upon a bedrock of failure. Fear means GO!

Builder Spotlight: Eva Longoria

A multitalented, multidimensional, multihyphenate, Eva Longoria is an actress, designer, entrepreneur, producer, director, and founder of the Eva Longoria Foundation, which is dedicated to unlocking the potential of Latinas. I'm leading off with Eva in these Builder Spotlights, given how well she sets the table for female founders. After our sit-down in Los Angeles, Eva shared how grateful she was to have had the conversation and posted this quote on social media about our meeting: "Here's to strong women. May we know them. May we be them. May we raise them." Right back at you, Eva!

On Building

. . . I came out of the womb a born Builder into a family of very strong women: nine aunts, three sisters, and a very strong mother. Everybody's educated. Independent. Successful. You're gonna make your own money. You're gonna find your own way.

On Breakdown → Breakthrough

... I get scared! Like I go, "Oh god, why did I say yes?" But I don't really doubt my ability. And if I don't know something, I will learn it. I don't go like, "I can't do it." I actually think being scared and nervous is healthy. I *hate* singing, for instance. It gives me anxiety and I start sweating. I didn't think I had a good voice but I had to do it for something, and I went through it and was like, "Oh, I can sing!" Like I never knew I could, didn't want to, but I did it!

On the State of Women

... Early on I had a really great mentor, Dolores Huerta. "One day you're gonna have a voice," she said, "and you better have something to say." And I was like, "What do you mean?" I didn't understand what that meant at the time and so I was like, "Why would I have a voice?" She said, "Everybody has a voice. And you have to think, 'What do you want to use that voice for, what is worth hearing in the future?'" And that's what inspired me also to get my master's. I always use education as a tool, and that knowledge empowers me to be brave.

... As women, we tend to say yes to family and kids and husbands and jobs. Like, "Yes! Yes! Yes, I'll do it." And then we're resentful! And that's the opposite of grateful. Learning how to say no is freeing. The anxiety is immediately gone because when you then say yes, it's something very special and near and dear to your heart.

On Women Entrepreneurs

... A lot of young women in the foundation tell me, "When I'm pitching to investors or talking to a bank for a loan, they don't understand me because I'm a woman or a person of color." My advice? Be comfortable with being uncomfortable. You've gotta walk into that room, have your mojo, put on your white male privilege pants and go, "I'm meant to be here, and let me tell you something about this product." Women want permission sometimes. So I always tell them, "I'm giving you permission to be great."

On Risk-Taking

. . . Moving to Hollywood was my biggest risk. I was twenty-one, living in Texas. I had just graduated college and I never aspired to be an actress. Literally one day I said, "I think I'm gonna be an actor." I don't know why, but I felt this guiding power. I had twenty-two dollars in my bank account. I knew nobody in LA. I was just like, "Okay, uh, what do I do?" I said, "Oh I'll get a job. I will find an apartment. I'm gonna go take a class, a workshop, and read some books. I approached it as a business. What do I have to do?" And that's really how I learn. You have to touch every rung of the ladder as you're climbing to your goals. You can't skip a rung. Then you miss that lesson. As my mother taught me, "You'll just figure it out." It's not easy, but it's worth it.

Nuts & Bolts: What do you most value in others? *Humor.* In yourself? *Compassion.*

2

DEMOLITION

Breaking Down to Break Through

Destruction is essential to construction. If we want to build the new, we must be willing to let the old burn.

—GLENNON DOYLE

DUN DUN DUN . . . THE *BREAKDOWN*. A NASTY WORD, USED TO FEIGN CONCERN, OF-ten wielded deliberately to provoke. A word suggesting we've melted down into a puddle on the floor, a puddle that is to be avoided or cleaned up. A word so shameful it should only be whispered in hushed tones in cloistered circles. The sign that you are either a failure with horrible judgment or poor decision-making or ill-equipped to properly direct your own life. In any case, wholly unstable. Or is it?

What if I told you a breakdown is often one of the best moments of your life?* What if I told you a breakdown is the perfect starting place for our work because it's how you break through to YOU. What if I told you that a breakdown can purely be the realization that you're done with the status quo . . . and are ready to start a business and change your life? So

---

* If the breakdown you are experiencing is a true mental health challenge, please get help.

many businesses are born out of a breakdown, with its shift in perspective pointing you in the direction of exactly what you are supposed to
build. We start here because the strongest buildings are erected upon a
cleared out, rock bottom, demo'd foundation. But first . . .

Two weeks before two hundred guests were to step into my story-
book wedding, and hopefully not step onto my fifteen-foot Italian lace
veil, everything shattered. My fiancé revealed (more like caved, via in-
terrogation) a secret life. And, oh, was it one dark underworld. Images I
couldn't unsee. Prostitutes. Plural. I felt dropped into an *Alice in Won-
derland* rabbit hole. Spinning. Dissociated. I called my best friend and
through gasped breaths asked, "What year is it?" This couldn't possibly
be the present day. Terror set in as I came to terms with the only option:
out. My love, my home, my business, my future, wiped.

Running on cortisol fumes, after an HIV test pit stop, I crawled to
my parents' home and got into my childhood bed. There I lay in darkness just wishing the hours away. The part I couldn't untangle was how
to trust myself, my judgment, because I'd gotten myself into this horrible mess. A shame-and-desperation-piled floor prompted something
unexpected. I decided to go on my nonrefundable honeymoon to South
Africa . . . *with my mom* (basically an insurance policy so I didn't feed
myself to the lions).

The first scene when I arrived were the rose petals on the bed, spell-
ing out what would have been OUR last name. Inhale. Exhale. I thought,
If you can get through this trip, you can get through anything. People say
nature heals, and I found that actually to be true as I dropped into the
rituals of safari. One night in bed surrounded by dusty air and Isak Di-
nesen's *Out of Africa* netting, I heard lionesses calling back and forth to
each other. Their primal roars rattled my chest cavity. I sat up. Through
wonder and tears, I roared back. Something in me shifted, numbness
turned vibrational.

You want the truth? Leaving that relationship was inevitable. Sadly, I
had started to resemble the Stepford wife I had vowed as a little girl, pine
needles throughout my messy feral hair, that I would never become. Like

when my then fiancé had encouraged me to quit my job so I could pursue "entrepreneurship." Despite knowing his definition was just a passion project cloaked in the code name of a business, I did it. "You don't have to make money," he'd said. "You just can't lose it." Me, coloring my naturally dirty blonde hair darker and darker as he was "a brunette guy." Doing dishes one night on the thirty-fifth floor of what had become my glass cage, alone again—the individual lights of the city blurring into a single neon haze as I zoned out—my right pinkie accidentally caught the angry edge of a broken dish. Bleeding into the sink, I felt . . . nothing. I had allowed myself to go from Technicolor to a light, muted pastel.

Clearly this was one big breakdown. The beautiful breakthrough came in meeting a new me: a woman who wanted independence and means, and with that change came the decision to build a business of real substance. But many women are not as fortunate, remaining trapped in this cycle without the means to escape, let alone rebuild. One's personal and professional worlds, I'd learned, are TOTALLY, at times diabolically, interconnected.

As it turns out, that which breaks us open, that which isn't working, is life steering us in a new, different, often better direction, known as a breakthrough. And not only that, what is breaking or broken can actually become the most beautiful part of our story. Scars become beauty marks.

We build. We break down. We build. We break down. We build.

So put on your hard hat and step onto that site. Know that walls will crumble, plumbing will clog, your crew will not show up, the roof will leak, the neighbors will make a mockery of your "ambitious" plans. But here's the thing. You grow into who you are meant to become as you fix things and keep building. What we make ultimately makes us. Before you know it, you'll be standing in front of something very real, so real your eyes will water and your knees will buckle in delight.

Coming up, the three BLDG Blocks you will get in this chapter are:

1. "Big B" and "Little b" Breakdowns
2. From Victim to Victor
3. The Heart Test

BLDG BLOCK 1: "Big B" and "Little b" Breakdowns

Breaking open, broken. Let's start by breaking down the breakdown. A breakdown means something broke or is breaking down to create space for something new. It's the demolition that's necessary for your beautiful new home: the life and business remodel.

Breakdowns tend to fall into one of two categories: a "Big B" or a "Little b" breakdown. Big B's are those cataclysmic, traumatic events that blindside you out of nowhere. It's a divorce. It's someone cheating. It's losing your job. It's those big, horrific life events that you don't anticipate. Little b breakdowns are those small, gnawing feelings that something is off, or wrong, or not quite right. It's not finding your relationship fulfilling. It's not feeling like you can be yourself at work. It's guilt in slowing down. It's promoting only a fake facade on social media. It's when you go to speak, then lose your voice. It's jumping from company to company, but no matter where you go, feeling lost.

We've all been there. Whether you've faced a major life-changing crisis or minor moments of stress and dissatisfaction, you have experienced some form of breakdown at some point in your life. You can bet on it. But the marvel of a breakdown is that it will bring about something bigger—a breakthrough. And it is all happening FOR you, not TO you. The reason I say FOR, even if you can technically point to something bad that happened TO you in the real world, is because whatever happened is still in your best interest. We have the great Stoic philosophers to thank for this concept. A breakdown gives rise to a perspective shift. It is in the midst of a breakdown—discomfort, dissatisfaction, or disaster; letting things fall apart or letting go; giving yourself permission to even have a breakdown—that you get the gift of forced clarity. An aha happens. You gain a new awareness, a new outlook. That once you see, you can't unsee. From there you break through to YOU.

You will find that the size of your breakdown is *in direct proportion* to the size of your possible breakthrough. And the more you surrender, the *faster* that breakthrough will come.

In many ways, the essence of being a *Builder* means you start to have a different relationship to breakdowns; when you see something is not operating well, you are then moved to create a new solution. You move anything standing in your way, out of the way. I want us to redefine and reclaim this word. Breakdowns are here to help us destroy, burn to the ground, turn to ash, take down to the studs, what is no longer meant for us. The magic of a breakdown in any aspect of your life is that it will have an impact upon the entire rest of your life. And breakdowns walk us to our breakthroughs, so that we can break ground.

Breakdown

Big B:

- A major, intense experience, event, or roadblock that comes in forcibly and is seemingly insurmountable.
- It enters your life quickly, like it must be addressed immediately.
- It feels like getting blindsided or hitting a rock wall.

Little b:

- A naggingly persistent, consistent feeling that a certain thing in your life is no longer working.
- It enters your life slowly, like you have time to address it.
- It feels like a pebble in your sneaker (or stiletto).

Breakthrough

A shift of perspective inside you that makes you want to take action outside (and build or break ground).

Breakdown → Breakthrough Examples

Hate my job → See that life is short . . . and start a side hustle

No intimacy → Want a soul mate . . . and begin dating

Feel alone → Desire connection . . . and join a MeetUp group

Out of shape → Decide health matters . . . and commit to a workout

Lose a friend → Find purpose eases grief . . . and collect for a memorial

It bears repeating: breakdowns come in many forms, from a minor upset to an actual traumatic event. Some decisions to start a business are precipitated by something large, but very often it's simpler than that. You don't need to have a seismic breakdown or anything bigger than a realization, a small whisper, that something isn't working (that you want to change) . . . a business becomes a vehicle for transformation.

In many cases a breakdown starts as a Little b. But when we ignore it because we are too busy, too stressed, too distracted, it comes back in a more elaborate costume with hands waving, hoping to get our attention. Until eventually, it's a full-on group of overdressed, cranky, tired protesters blocking the street in the form of a Big B Breakdown. We have to confront it head-on. Those breakdowns help with the deconstruction of beliefs and thought patterns that no longer serve you, so you can break through to new perspectives that open up new possibilities where you can break new ground.

Our life, if we listen, if we become more present in the present, is *always* speaking to us.

Over time, almost every Builder can point to a seminal Big B Breakdown that nearly took out the knees of her business, as well as a list of smaller Little b breakdowns too many to name. So for anyone who asks, "How do I know what to build," or, "How do I find my purpose?" and doesn't know where to start, look at what is broken. Take media mogul Arianna Huffington smacking her head on her desk from fatigue, a broken cheekbone, stitches required, which led her to create the wellness company Thrive Global. For her, the wrong path led to the right one.

In Bobbi Brown's case, she saw a defective beauty industry needing natural products (hence Jones Road Beauty) and had the insight of "beauty from the inside out, done simply" (hence her wellness brand, Evolution_18). Bobbi told me, "I have broken down in front of my husband, family, and girlfriends. And then you just quickly realize, *I got this. I can do this.*" What's broken sparked new enterprise.

Fashion designer Misha Nonoo bounced back after a Big B: "I was deciding to completely change my business strategy, and I actually think this came from my personal life breaking down. I'd been in a relationship and married for thirteen years, but the whole foundation of my life was crumbling. As I was analyzing my personal life, I put the lens on the business part. From a creative standpoint, I felt burned out. I thought, *I don't want to live like this. I don't want to work like that.* It was very difficult to go through all at once, but when you come out the other side, you'll achieve things that you never thought possible, with a very solid foundation." Silver linings abound.

As for Jaclyn Johnson, a venture capitalist and entrepreneur on Little b's: "Breakdowns? This week? Today? No, I mean all the time. Early in my first company, any fire, any negative email from a sponsor or client, whatever it was, felt like the end of the world. You're like, *This is it. Let's close up shop.* But you learn to weather the storms. At this point, years later, I'm a professional fire-putter-outer, and the things that used to scare the shit out of me I can deal with in four seconds. I'm now calm and know it's gonna be fine."

Quick sidebar: It might seem like I'm name dropping here, throughout the book, and in Builder Spotlights, but because I'm now fortunate to have a strong network, I figured why not let that benefit you, too? Many of the long strides I've taken were to try to keep pace with inspirational women a few miles ahead. I hope that by seeing that some of the best-known women struggle with the same things you do, you'll find the courage to keep charging.

In this breakthrough process, a powerful accelerant comes from identifying and claiming something you want to build next. Once you are in action, you are already leaving a breakdown behind. Now for the first of several Golden Tools that you'll learn about throughout the book: The AID Golden Tool—three steps easily remembered using this acronym for Acknowledge, Identify, Declare:

1. Acknowledge your breakdown (awareness).
2. Identify where you want to break through (perspective shift).
3. Declare what you are going to build next (action).

If you take nothing else away from this book, absolutely nothing but this breakdown-to-breakthrough concept, you already will have won. You anoint them as GOOD, GLORIOUS, even if they hurt like hell. And make no mistake, it's not one and done. They keep coming. I've considered shuttering my business many times and find myself in the fetal position listening to Sade more often than I'd care to admit. This breakdown concept, along with amplification (which you will learn about soon) are the two most critical cornerstones to Building.

Welcome breakdowns. Celebrate them. Congratulate friends in the midst of them. Good things are coming.

BLDG BLOCK 2: From Victim to Victor

Ever wonder why you have such a hard time being and building what's true to you? A bit hard to pinpoint but actually pervasive, degrading, and consuming as hell. Consider the pressure to be physically perfect. Bobbleheading our way through yet another obvious lecture. Putting ourselves last and experiencing GUILT (!) if we so much as lock ourselves in the bathroom for a few extra minutes to escape little fingers under the door. Feeling zapped as we fawn, freeze, flee our way through the day. The culprit? Turns out those familial, cultural, and professional forces we uncovered in chapter 1 have sneakily snuck into our lives.

The neutralizing tonic (to banish them)? Awareness.

Make no mistake, you are carrying the added weight of outside "do more" programming. And what seems like an innate people-pleasing gene was, in fact, injected into you. We are Good Girl–bred. Carry-the-invisible-load bred. Handle-whatever-junk-gets-thrust-on-us bred. Don't-rock-the-boat bred. Make-the-best-of-any-situation bred. It's why so many of us battle depression, anxiety, or autoimmune issues.

The "not enough" feelings are why we exaggerate, embellish, deceive, conform, manipulate, and betray. We do strange things, compromise our-selves when we don't have power or can't take up space. We sometimes find ourselves in situations that lack integrity. It's no surprise our legs are tired from all this running, arms heavy from all the spinning plates, and insides sick as we turn our judgment inward. Our guts intuitively know this is not right. We are at war with ourselves.

Entrepreneur Emily McDowell hits the nail on the head. "Finding yourself is not really how it works," she says. "Your true self is right here, buried under cultural conditioning, other people's opinions, and inaccurate conclusions you drew as a kid that became your beliefs about who you are. Finding yourself is actually returning to yourself. An un-learning, an excavation, a remembering who you were before the world got its hands on you."

You hear that? UNLEARNING. DOING LESS. RETURNING TO SELF.

A radically simple panacea . . . Enough of the "not enough" and "do more" victim mindset. As we write a new narrative and allow ourselves to be a "good enough" victor, we not only heal ourselves, we will find an unbreakable bond with other women. Again, it is not about learn-ing and doing more. It is more about unlearning and doing less. Just because you can do more doesn't mean you should. You can become a better Builder just by leaning into your core nature, getting back to your true self.

Current Mindset

"Not enough" forces bear down on you (i.e., be prettier, skinnier, smarter, etc.)

"Do more" forces push up against you (i.e., work harder, longer, stronger, etc.)

Future Mindset

"Good enough" forces release you, acknowledging you don't need to change anything about yourself (i.e., good enough mother, businesswoman, etc.)

Release perfectionism. Remember: good, not perfect.

Let anything go that's not serving you. You can want what you want even if that doesn't serve anyone else. You can build whatever you damn well want. Free of restraints and constraints. Without justification. Without apology. You can shed, release, discard, throw off any opinion or belief or idea or responsibility or expectation that does not sit well with you. You can drop the ball or balls plural. Let that shit go.

With this magical mindset shift (clearly I'm being a bit hyperbolic), you become free. If I could wave a wand and do that for you, I would, but you don't need no fairy godmother.

BLDG BLOCK 3: The Heart Test

It's probably sacrilegious to say building a business is "heart over head," but whatever. I said it. For a bit of a cold start here, I want you to pretend to cut off your logical, strategic, overactive, hypervigilant, ruminating brain. Go ahead! Seriously. Imagine lopping off your head. You are now headless. A headless businesswoman.

Next, I want you to make contact with your heart. Touch the skin over it. Feel that beat (an amazing hundred thousand beats per day). That deep, dependable synchronized rhythm. As you might recall from high school science, the human heart is split into two halves, each with an atrium and ventricle.

For the Heart Test Golden Tool, you'll want to run the idea for your business, which may have come during your breakthrough, via your heart. Like an internal heartfelt talk. As you consider your business idea, it should either:

1. Break your heart
2. Set your heart on fire

The energetic genesis of the best brands comes from your heart. (Of course, some new ventures are purely hands-on-hips, no-nonsense money-makers. Understood. That's OK, too.) But it is a return to love, really, serving that which needs to be birthed, healed, and set free. Ultimately, a heart-brain connection then kicks in to guide all business decisions.

So what's the first thing we do when we give birth? We name our baby. That gives a sense of place in the world. I cannot tell you how many people get paralyzed by what to call their company. I never felt goose bumps about the names of my businesses and was self-conscious about them when I started out. But "good enough" is good enough. For some thought-starters, think about someone or something of significance in your life (like the street you grew up on, which Beyoncé picked for Parkwood Entertainment) or naming your business after your mom (as fashion designers Rebecca Matchett and Stacey Bendet did when they founded Alice + Olivia). Don't overthink it.

The simple Heart Test is a good check-in to confirm you have a construction-worthy idea. It's the heartbeat of your BUILD Statement, developed in this chapter's DIY section, and in chapter 3 will be expanded into your BUILD Vision Statement, for your total life. And, finally, in chapter 9, it will be fine-tuned into your short BUILD Mission Statement for your business. This litmus test helps ensure your business will endure and can go the distance.

For anyone who's left corporate or is considering leaving, I think you might be able to relate to this genesis story. My second business lit my heart on fire. But my first business was born from a broken heart about how disparagingly women were marketed to, as I walked from one room to the next filled with men dominating the conversation, reaping the rewards (in reputation and $$$) while I played chameleon. Burned out, having given every ounce to that job. Every night, weekend, aging ovary, drop of my life force. For what? I'd become Humpty Dumpty. On my back, broken into hundreds of pieces, looking up at the darn sky like, *How do I put this shell of myself back together again?*

That shot in the arm came at an Inc. 5000 conference. As I looked at a room filled with more entrepreneurs than I'd ever seen, I thought, *If all these people can do it, why can't I?* I ran up to the step and repeat and said, "I'm just here as a date, but would you be willing, if you don't mind, if it's not too much trouble, to um, to take my picture?" Smirking, the photographer put down his long-lens camera, picked up my rinky-dink phone and took a single blurry photo. But that was all I needed.

Consider me now taking your pic capturing this moment in time. As you follow your heart. Whatever side it stems from.

Builder Spotlight: Tamara Mellon

Kicking up change in the shoe industry is serial entrepreneur Tamara Mellon. I sat down with her at her sun-drenched, mission-statement-filled office space in LA, with shelves lined with shoes. Like being in the best kind of a candy store—every color, texture, and style of the rainbow imaginable! Always gracious, she offered me a sleek and sophisticated pick: cutout white pumps to go with my LBD. When in her twenties, Tamara cofounded the luxury footwear brand Jimmy Choo (150 stores in

30 countries; sold for nearly $1 billion), and she is now leading the way with her own self-named, game-changing, rule-breaking brand. If you feel like you're in the midst of a storm right now keeping your business afloat as you make tough decisions and experience conflict or negativity, Tamara's example is a powerful, relevant shot in the arm. Picture this: you can go from selling Jimmy Choo for close to a billion bucks to bankruptcy to close to $100 million in funding if you let things get demolished, allow things to fall apart, and then rebuild.

On Building

. . . I was born a Builder and always wanted to create a business. Even when I was a young editor working at British *Vogue*, I knew there was more I wanted to do but it was just finding the opportunity. So I printed T-shirts and sold them at a store in London's Portobello Road Market.

On Breakdown → Breakthrough

. . . I had to put the first version of Tamara Mellon through a Chapter 11 bankruptcy because I wasn't going down the right path, and I needed to reorganize. But that was really risky from a reputation standpoint because I'd come off a huge success building Jimmy Choo. Like a huge high, selling it for just under a billion dollars. And then I had to admit to a kind of . . . failure. Going through the humiliating headlines of bankruptcy. But I knew that my vision was right, so I had to get through that storm to be able to execute what I wanted to do with this brand. The best thing I did was to keep quiet. Not trying to fight the bad headlines or defending myself, but just proving it with my actions. My anxiety can run away with me like a train. The other day I was completely overwhelmed by everything, and I was crying. And I thought, *Wait, let's just hit the pause button.* I got out my meditation app and listened to a meditation for ten minutes and did breathing exercises, and immediately felt better.

. . . I often say to myself, *Just get a good night's sleep, that's critical, and you can start again.* It's perseverance. Waking up every day and going in and not giving up. Just persistence. And it's just taking that moment thinking, *Today is going to be different.* Besides, I have learned two great things that I love: meditation and breathing exercises. It's a game changer. A hidden superpower.

. . . Life is messy. Everything we do is messy. You're always messing something up. That's what we have to embrace and not be ashamed of it.

. . . Negative people or situations just drain your energy. You can feel it. Other people are really inspiring and they lift you up. In my career I have put up with bad CEOs for way too long. That's something I've learned also: to speak up more.

. . . I've always thought I've not spent enough time with my daughter. I'm not the mother picking her up from school. I have to travel for work and do all these things. I'm always feeling guilty. And a couple of years ago at dinner she just rolled out her future. She said, "I'm going to work for another company, not you because that's nepotism. And then I'm going to go back and get an MBA and then I'm going to be the CEO of a fashion company." I was like, *I guess I wasn't such a bad role model after all.*

On Becoming a Victor

. . . My doubt comes from—which a lot of women feel—imposter syndrome. That's like, *I'm a fraud and someone's gonna figure it out.* Right? My doubt comes from a lack of education. In America that would be the equivalent of leaving school without a high school diploma. I'm completely self-educated so it actually proves that's also possible. Self-doubt comes when I walk into a room with a VC or private equity firm and I don't have an MBA or know their language. That would give me self-confidence, though they're not usually the mavericks who create great companies.

. . . From the lessons learned building Jimmy Choo, I wanted to create a completely different culture for my new brand—really becoming an activist for women.

On Matters of the Heart

. . . Only doing business, for instance, with people who have more than one woman on the board. Look, I was twenty-seven years old when I started Jimmy Choo. I was like, *I want to make beautiful shoes. I want to . . .* You know, I really had no idea. So after sixteen years of building Jimmy Choo, I wanted to change the things that bothered me about being a woman in business. We want our customers to feel loved by us. So we offer a special service called Cobbler Concierge and will repair your shoes for two years after you purchase them. For free. Could you imagine walking into a department store and saying, "Oh, I bought these two years ago. Can you repair them for free?" We don't think of her as a transaction.

. . . Take the leap. There is no perfect time to start a company. But first, can you pay your rent? You don't put yourself in danger.

Nuts & Bolts: What do you value most in others? *Integrity and honesty.* In yourself? *Integrity and honesty.* One thing you'd change about yourself? *Speak up.*

3

VISION

Imagining Your Future

Create the highest, grandest vision possible for your life, because you be-come what you believe . . . I don't have any limitations on what I think I could do or be.

—Oprah Winfrey

REMEMBER AS A KID HOW YOU WOULD BLOW ON A DANDELION AND WATCH THE seeds twirl off in flight like spinning ballerinas? A tickle of giddy, mis-chievous satisfaction, knowing they floated, dispersing seeds for miles, even though you'd watched your dad dig his trowel for hours to uproot their fuzzy stems from the stone walkway.

That's kind of what it is to have a vision. You imagine something way in the distance, blow with all of your life force, and then hope, pray, that somewhere that vision is tenaciously taking root. Somewhere there lies your field of dreams tinged as yellow as the sun. And even though you can't see it now, one day you might stumble across it.

In her mid-fifties, my mom was furloughed from a place she had worked loyally as an editor for thirty years. She loved that job, but a venture capital firm that had acquired the company had other plans.

She turned to me, glassy-eyed. "What now? What next?"

"Well, maybe we just start with what you love and figure it out from there?"

We brainstormed a list. Food and France rose to the top.

It just so happened I had seen a show about a woman named Kathie Alex (my name and my brother's combined . . . ahem, good sign) who taught cooking classes at Julia Child's former vacation home in the South of France (this was before all the *Julie & Julia* fanfare).

"What if you started a cooking tour business and took your first group there?"

Fast forward, my mom leapt into that vision without even knowing how and has for fifteen years led hundreds of people on cooking trips to Paris, Nice, Amalfi, Istanbul, Marrakesh, and more. These trips are more than trips. For one woman it was the first time she ever got on a plane. For another it steadied her during a rocky divorce. Everyone has brought something different in their suitcase and somehow left lighter.

I've had fun playing assistant on many of the tours. And the best part is watching her light up like a little firefly. It's truly never too late to start.

Though, starting a new business without a vision is not good; it's like skydiving without a parachute. A vision is what gives direction. It represents the future dreams and goals you have for your business (and beyond). It signals where you are going and what you want to ultimately achieve and become. Before any real action steps are taken, an established vision helps you build toward something crystal clear, and it keeps you inspired and motivated. Otherwise, you start off all over the place: too practical, too realistic, too simple, too static, too small; and frankly, just end up with something pretty basic. So do you want a basic business (and life)? Or a supercharged one? I'm guessing the latter.

In my work as a strategist, I spend a ton of time thinking about vision (sometimes it looks like I'm doing nothing for days) because it has a huge payoff. Vision is at the crux of what it means to be a Builder. A Builder consciously decides her vision has value and intentionally steps into realizing that vision. You come to believe you can create what you see in your mind's eye (no matter how outlandish it might seem). Visions are like snowflakes, as unique as the person who has them. No two are alike. You just have to take a beat and be still enough to see it.

That starts with a GARGANTUAN vision. I'm talking so freakin' big you probably couldn't do it in five lifetimes.

Now that you know what to build next, it's time to enhance it. Envision it. Live into that future you. This vision becomes a touchstone to make contact with daily. You will quite literally speak it into existence. Talk about it as if it's already real. It will be how you filter decisions (does this align with my vision?) and it will be what you lean on when the world doesn't show you any results. There will be periods (sometimes verrrryyyyy long) when you will not see anything—and I mean anything—in the material realm. Fruits of your labor come last. But fear not, your vision is growing, gestating. This is a time when you strengthen your character, resolve, and foundation. Not throw in the trowel.

Because you are building a castle, not a cabin.

My life at one point looked outright comical juxtaposed with my best friend who I'd grown up with since the age of five. She had a dreamy husband, two precocious boys, a stunning home in a swanky neighborhood, and a job as a real estate broker that kicked off serious moolah and freedom. Next to her . . . me. Single with no dating prospects, no kids, living out of two suitcases for two years, the proud renter of a ten-by-ten storage locker all the while working on projects to get to my "dream," which I had not earned $1 from and was paying for out of pocket. Manifestations of my vision not even a blur on the horizon. I had enough awareness to know that by traditional standards I clocked in somewhere between an odd duck and an utter F-up.

"Do you think I'm nuts?" I asked her one day as we sat side by side in Adirondack chairs (her porch, of course, not mine). She kept her gaze lovingly forward and without missing a beat said, "One day you're going to have the life we all desired deep down but didn't have the courage to chase down."

Wildly specific things take time.

In order to build something you haven't built before, you must do something—probably many things—you've never done before. Once you leave your comfort zone, you get into a creative state that allows you to actualize your vision. Creation and certainty do not coexist. This chapter is about bringing to life that vision.

The three BLDG Blocks you will get in this chapter are:

1. Play It Forward
2. Dig It Deep
3. Feel It Real

BLDG BLOCK 1: Play It Forward

To create a vision, you must treat your current circumstances as old news.

We are told that we should work and live within the current world we are given. "It is what it is," we are told. Have a nice, simple life, some cash in the bank, kids, and a dog. But think about it: the building you live in, the chair you are sitting on, the book you're reading right now were all created by someone. From Snuggies to Slinkies to shampoo. Often, that someone creates something that has never been seen or done before. And that someone probably spent years thinking, conjuring, and designing those objects before they were created in physical form.

Life can be so expansive when you realize everything comes from someone and that someone can be YOU. You can create things others use. And the best part? Your thoughts are absolutely free. Free thoughts, which you can control, change your circumstances. You can shape the material world and quite literally build your own world. Be the Builder. That is a large, rewarding life.

Have you ever been to Disney World? If not, you've probably seen pictures. A swamp was Disney World before Walt Disney's imagination got a hold of it. A literal swamp.

While you can look at these creations coming from time, money, team, etc., the real difference is a big vision. A willingness to think big, feel the emotional pull of the dream, and then the discipline to follow through with it. Even. If. There. Is. Not. A. Single. Other. Person. Out. There. Who. Sees. What. You. See. Who understands your vision. Chances are, you've not allowed yourself to play with your imagination very much, so allow me to reintroduce you two.

A vision can take hold at any age and with unexpected zigs and zags and zings along the way:

"One day I'm gonna sing the national anthem at a Super Bowl. Onnnee dayyy," she wrote on Twitter.

"I'm going to be a comedian," said the spunky, nerdy middle schooler.

"Maybe it's just too late for me," she trepidatiously told her dad, when considering starting a wedding dress line at forty.

Meet in order: Demi Lovato, Tina Fey, and Vera Wang. After her Twitter post in 2010, it took another ten years before Demi Lovato belted out "The Star-Spangled Banner" at the 2020 Super Bowl in Miami. But she did it. As for Tina's dream, at twenty-three, commuting on Chicago's L before dawn with a "bunch of Polish cleaning ladies," as she says, "I got a day job at the YMCA working at the front desk [and folding towels]. I had the worst shift imaginable. Five thirty in the morning till two in the afternoon. But I had my nights free to take classes at Second City." And that launched her career as a comedian. Vera? At age forty, newly married, still disappointed that her dreams as a figure skater never landed her in the Olympics, and smarting from not being chosen as *Vogue*'s editor-in-chief (a position snagged by Anna Wintour), she launched her vision for a wedding dress line. And, damn, has she made more than a few brides blush.

Remember: it is never too early or too late to start.

You create by what you give attention to, as action stems from attention. But here's the rub: if your attention is on your past, you will likely re-create it over and over. And that's OK if it's what you want. But if you want anything new, *you must give your attention to something new, a new vision for what you want in your life.*

Think about one breakdown you've experienced over and over again where you kept getting the same exact lesson, the same exact problem—let's say difficult clients or an unfulfilling job or the same bad boyfriend—on repeat. Why?

Consider that it likely happened because you only have a vision for what you DON'T want. You had not replaced it with a new vision for what you DO want.

One law of the universe that's particularly wild: I believe that nothing comes into being when it is based on need or lack or desperation. Nada. For example, I *need* work. I *need* sales. I *need* support. The message you are feeding is lack, insecurity, disbelief (a negative vision), which in turn just yields more of the same. When you focus on what you don't want, you will likely just get more of that as the universe can't distinguish between positive and negative asks. And that isn't any fun, is it?

To create anew, try focusing instead on the abundance you do have (maybe not in material form, but in other ways), make contact with that deep knowing, the fullness within that you have everything you seek already, in this moment. For example, instead of saying, "I need money," which might be true based on your current circumstances, you would say positively, "I have total wealth and abundance" and look for evidence in the smallest of ways: like fresh food from the garden, a healthy mind, a solid work ethic, a warm shower, etc. In turn, you start to feel less like you *need* something, and that's when stuff starts appearing for you and is attracted to you. Your words have power and influence.

A vision is what you would create if all constraints, all fears, all limiting and negative beliefs were removed. Really, if you could think/feel/do/become/create anything.

BLDG BLOCK 2: Dig It Deep

When you have a "why," you can bear almost any "how" (to paraphrase a famous nineteenth-century philosopher).

It is important to understand, at the deepest level, the "why" behind your vision. It's your business's root reason for being, why it should exist. And when you unlock that honest, authentic, fulfilling, soulful reason (i.e., the "why"), it allows you to not buckle when you have to do hard things (the "how"). That motivating "why" is what yields your drive: pure, potent energy that can supercharge you. But to tap into that energy you have to dig deep to get to the purest form of your intention.

I have co-opted and adapted a well-evidenced exercise that was popularized at the Harvard Business School called "The 5 Whys." Radically simple in concept but outsized in returns. (This works for pretty much everything in life, too.) Each time you ask yourself "why," you have this vision for your business go one question deeper.[1] Keep drilling down until you hit bedrock.

Here's an example: I want to quit my corporate job to start an acupuncture business.

The 5 Whys:

1. **WHY?** Because I am not satisfied with the work I am doing.
2. **WHY?** Because while it gives me job security and pays the bills, I don't care about it.
3. **WHY?** Because it doesn't align with my core values.
4. **WHY?** Because my real passion is helping people get well.
5. **WHY?** Because no one should have to be in pain and the world would be a better place if everyone was healed.

And if this type of questioning works for Sara Blakely, it could work for you, too. "My obsession with the word 'why' did two things for me in my life. It caused Spanx to become invented, because I asked, 'Why are pantyhose the way they are? Why are shapers the way they are? Do they need to be that way? Is there a better way?' That created a product. Then it made me recognize and find my purpose, which was to help women. I'm very, very passionate about helping women, and that came as a result of continuing to ask myself, 'Why am I doing this? Why am I inspired to do this in this moment? What is this connected to?'"

Or in the case of one of my mentors, Countess Albina du Boisrouvray, whom I met while consulting for a social impact agency, her "why" was born out of tragedy. Propelled by the untimely death of her son, who was a helicopter rescue pilot, the countess started FXB International, a foundation with a massive vision: to lift the world's poor out of poverty. Through her unique methodology, coupled with a powerful why, she's been able to realize her vision and lift an almost incomprehensible eighteen million people worldwide.

All charged visions are rooted in an electric why.

BLDG BLOCK 3: Feel It Real

Visualization, while powerful, has been misunderstood in that it has led people to believe that you visualize what you want, wrap it in positive emotion, and voilà! The check comes in the mail and the car appears in your driveway. While I am not going to debate the metaphysical efficacy of this approach, I will say that you need to pair visualization with action.

When coupled with all-important action, visualization is increasingly a technique that entrepreneurs, leaders, and all-star athletes like Serena Williams use before a game to get results. Studies have shown that mental practices are almost as effective as true physical practice, and doing both is more effective than either alone. According to *Psychology Today*, "Brain studies now reveal that thoughts produce the same mental instructions as actions. Mental imagery impacts many cognitive processes in the brain: motor control, attention, perception, planning, and memory. So the brain is getting trained for actual performance during visualization."[2]

AND we've got an edge. As women, we are often described as being "emotional" as if this were a bad thing. But when creating something new, the ability to identify and feel your emotions is, quite literally, a superpower. You've got an advantage! Creating a new vision rooted in emotion is what begins to create a new life; the positive emotion you feel for your creation is precisely what pulls it toward you (more emotion = quicker, bigger vision). Simply hold your emotion-filled vision in front of you to stay in the creative flow of ideas that generate inspired action.

Let's get touchy-feely! Think about the vision for what you are building personally and professionally, and what it could look like in a perfect world. Now to give your futurescape dimension—to visualize it—consider the following:

BUILD Vision Statement

Get Clear on Your Why

This vision will be the collision of what you want more of, how you want to serve the world, and why you are uniquely primed to do it.

Make It Crisp and Juicy as Hell

Give dynamic dimension—form, color, meaning, and life—to what you want to build. This is where the power of language comes into play. A vision is chock-full of detail. Loaded. The more specific, the better. Engage all five senses to breathe color, life, and feeling into this vision. It should feel so real you could almost touch it or taste it. Notice your feelings as you create the scene. Stay in that feeling. Your emotions may vary, but always close the scene with the outcome you desire, along with the attendant feelings of excitement or, at least, satisfaction. The more intense the feeling, the grander and faster your vision will become a reality.

Think Long Term

It's true that we overestimate what we can do in a day, but we also underestimate what we can do in a lifetime. Make sure you take a long view and play the long game.

Have a First-Person Perspective

It is critical that you are in the scene that you are creating. You are a director AND an actor. Merely observing a scene will keep you as an observer and, obviously, you want to be a participant and experiencer of your dream.

Relive How You Rocked It in the Past

Think of a time when you successfully created something you wanted. This could be buying a car or having a successful relationship. Anything that you really wanted, focused on, and created. It sometimes helps to build momentum by recalling lots of small things you created and use that energy to raise your belief in yourself and ability to build bigger things.

All of these elements come together to form your BUILD Vision Statement—your North Star—guiding you in every step of your Builder journey. Know each micro action, every decision will lead you either closer to your vision or farther away. Your vision will be realized not by grand events, but the smallest of small choices.

To better navigate uncomfortable new aspects of your business and realize your vision—negotiating deals and the like—my life coach, BUILD Inspector Mimi Duvall, suggests an idea she calls the Prepave. It's another of my favorite Golden Tools. Think of it as visualization's practical half-sister. They should always go hand in hand in your toolbox. Like I said at the onset of our business-building journey, I want to give you all the best goods without your having to shell out big bucks or time. Here's Mimi's advice:

In advance of a big meeting or important activity of any sort, write out how you want it to go. What is the overall feeling, what might this potential other person say (write out a script!) and what is the desired outcome?[3]

To make it even more tangible, you can use graphics or art clippings, create a vision board of what you want to see made real in advance of it actually happening. Like a merchandise line, your book or podcast cover or face on a Times Square billboard.

A burst of impassioned ideation preplanning what's to come, Prepaving is one of the best Golden Tools to help you excel in business because you emerge with a crystal clear picture of how YOU want everything to go.

When all else is equal, usually the person with the clearest vision and the greatest will is who wins the day.

When you *think* it, you *feel* it.

When you *feel* it, you *speak* it.

When you *speak* it, you *believe* it.

When you *believe* it, you *become* it.

When you are IT. You are LIT.

Builder Spotlight: Jessica Alba

Jessica Alba was one of the first Builders to say yes to being interviewed for Build Like A Woman. *I wanted to speak to her after she pivoted from the big screen to cofounding The Honest Company, which offers more than one hundred safe, effective, and affordable products for babies, beauty, and household cleaning. This actress-turned-founder has landed on the cover of* Forbes' *"Self-Made Women" and been named in the top twenty of* Fast Company's *"Most Creative People in Business." No thumb-twiddling ever, she's also the* New York Times *bestselling author of* The Honest Life. *AND when Jessica took her company public, 25.8 million shares sold at $16 each with a total IPO value of $1.4 billion—and netted her an honest fortune, a reported $130 million.*

On Building

... I am a born Builder. I grew up pretty fearless with an understanding that if you want something in life, you have to be creative in going about achieving it. You're not always going to have an easy path to success. But if it's important, you'll figure out a way to make it work.

On Breakdown → Breakthrough

... A lot of my major breakdowns happened before I started the company. I hit many roadblocks and false starts, had to find the right business partners, and spent time and money on different iterations of the business that didn't come to fruition. It took about four years of struggling before I was able to find the right business partners to even start Honest and get it off the ground. In hindsight, I realize that each lesson that I learned during these years brought me one step closer to making Honest a reality. With every challenge comes an opportunity to grow and learn.

On Vision

... The idea for The Honest Company came from my experiences as a conscious customer and a new parent. Making a happy, healthy home for my loved ones became my priority. Like many entrepreneurs, I saw there was a need that wasn't being met, so I had to create the company I was looking for.

... Undoubtedly my mom and my grandmother are some of the toughest and most resilient women I know. But when it comes to building my business, surprisingly, I've learned from Eleanor Roosevelt. She didn't let any hurdles get in her way, really persevered in the face of insurmountable challenges, and was completely committed to the need for social justice—that's clarity of purpose. Seeing her impact gave me an incredible amount of hope and determination that I could be successful.

On Her "Why"

... Having the courage and tenacity to believe I could start a customer products company was the biggest risk I've ever taken, with the challenge of pitching Honest to potential investors. But even in the face of rejection, I was constantly motivated by my desire to create this company. No one had any expectations of me in business, and it made me more fearless.

On Feeling It Real

... I sometimes second-guess my gut when it comes to parting ways with a person or an idea. Even if I have a gut feeling or an inkling, I need to have a lot of evidence to point me in a new direction. It takes a long time for me to wrap my head around leaving, so there has to be many different ways that it sinks in—it's not something that happens immediately or linearly.

... I've had to get over my own insecurity about not having the typical business trajectory or schooling. My education has always come from learning as I go, and jumping into tasks headfirst, whether in entertainment or business. I've overcome that by being realistic about what I'm good at and not good at, and partnering with people who have expertise in fields that I don't.

Nuts & Bolts: One thing you're afraid of? *Not seeing the big picture.* What keeps you sane? *Exercise, meditation, sleep, and my kids.* What keeps you going and building? *The art of the possible ... There's so much opportunity to do things better. And of course, my kids.*

4

DESIGN

Amplifying Yourself for Authentic Power

People tell you the world looks a certain way . . . And then at a certain point, if you're lucky, you realize you can make up your own mind. Nobody sets the rules but you. You can design your own life.

—CARRIE-ANNE MOSS

YOU'VE GOT YOUR BUSINESS VISION, BUT LET'S NOT FORGET ABOUT THE REST OF your life! Picking up the pen to write ferociously, courageously, and un-apologetically about the life you want to design for yourself, by yourself, can be terrifying, but you've got to be brave. Here's my own earnest scribbling from when I started writing this book: *I believe I can be the leader of my own life. I want to make my own life decisions. Buy my own home. Feel strong in my skin. Edit my circle. Invest all liquidity into my business. Share my little black book. Taste my own power. My script, not theirs.*

This chapter expands the aperture, so you can design your TOTAL life. Which is the entire point of this book. None of this business vs. life crap either, as if only one of these two areas matter. A new paradigm. Holistic and integrated across all key life areas, stitched together by your core values. Once you feel this integration, you can become what I call amplified. Which means meeting your brightest, highest, fullest, truest self. In laywoman's terms, being amplified means you are just completely yourself and don't give a dang what anyone else thinks.

Amplification is the path to authentic power. It's a widely propulsive force. Unique, different for every woman. And the single greatest X factor to our success.

One "un-amplified" day, I walked into a contract negotiation with a client and accepted what was offered. Exited stage right and scurried back to the relative safety of my computer lamenting what I could or should have said. Inversely I remember oh-so-vividly when my foundational understanding of "amplification" took hold. Fool me once . . . fool me twice, shame on me! For my next client, I was determined to do things differently. I used the ol' Prepave Golden Tool to create a vision for how I wanted this negotiation to go. Thought about my full life across every area and what I value most. I then hopped on the exercise bike to prime my body, reached for a clean juice to stay clear, wrote out my target number and also my walk-away number. Mind, body, and soul stepped into that room as one. The clients tried to get me to come off my position. But because my energy did not waver, because not an ounce of me was pretending to be anything other than who I was, committed to what I do, because I was completely integrated, they stood no chance. I left with half a million more dollars than I'd walked in with an hour before. They met me in a state of amplification.

When this idea of amplification first took hold in my own life, it felt like an out-of-body experience. I remember thinking, *Holy crap. Who the hell is this? And how do I get to see more of her?*

The power of personal amplification, so you can truly step into your authentic power, is the second most important concept in this entire book. But for you to reach amplification, you must first design your life (including your business) deliberately with the needs of your true self and core values in mind, so you can have total integration. Don't be afraid to consider reengineering things a bit!

In this chapter, we will explore how to live life more intentionally. In the long run this will help your business, because when you feel like you are on solid ground across all life areas, you can start to go after and stand for what you really want. You and your business become unleashed. Not only does it feel flat-out satisfying to have an integrated life to where you can be unapologetically amplified, but it also sets your business up for pragmatic benefits like more money and maneuverability in the marketplace.

The three BLDG Blocks you will get in this chapter are:

1. Integrated Life Layout
2. Value Values
3. X Factor = Amplification

BLDG BLOCK 1: Integrated Life Layout

Have you ever come home in a Pepé Le Pew stinky mood after a rough day at work? I've made my fair share of spite meals, preoccupied, replaying what happened that day at work, pinching sugar instead of salt until someone shouted "stop." Our moods don't stay behind at the "office" when we walk out the door. As if our business and personal lives are separate. As if we have two different worlds with two different identities. At best, there will be an inevitable conflict between each, where the demands of business success create friction and tension in your personal life. And, at worst, that it's not even possible to have both, and something's gotta give. The idea of work and life being separate is hugely misdirected. That ends today. "Working for the Weekend" should not be your theme song. Enjoyment should not be relegated to the "life" part of your life; it should be available 24–7–365.

We are entering a new age with new kinds of Builders. By architecting a new possibility for yourself, you can deliberately design the life you want and take the steps to build something more meaningful than you have allowed yourself to date. Designing a holistic, integrated life means thinking about your total life (i.e., business and everything else). Here you use the BUILD Business Vision you already created and then craft "lite" visions for your other life areas to extend your focus and be sure your full life is considered. These don't need to be as built out as your business vision. The connective tissue that will unite everything comes from your values, how you want to live, be, and show up across the board.

For this BUILD Integrated Life Layout (you'll find similar names and categories in performance and leadership programs), I landed on seven life areas; but as with everything in the book, make it work for you and expand as needed. But first, let's really start to unpack what we mean by integration.

In the old paradigm, we had two divided worlds: personal vs. professional.

In this new all-encompassing, more fluid model, we focus on seven life areas:

BUILD Integrated Life Layout

1. **Business:** Ambition, mission, and contributions
2. **Money:** Overall wealth, business revenue, spending, and saving
3. **Relationships:** Partner, parents, siblings, children, friends, teammates (crew)
4. **Environment:** Home, geography, living and working conditions
5. **Spirituality:** Purpose, connection, religion
6. **Passions:** Travel, entertainment, social, community projects, learning, pets
7. **Health:** Physical and mental well-being, exercise, meditation, self-talk, self-expression, nutrition, sleep, energy, appearance, personal accountability

The truth is that everything affects and impacts everything else. If you're not careful, all the good you're doing in one area of your life can be eroded by another. For example, you can have a great friend circle (thriving relationships), but are on social media like . . . all the time just to keep up with perfect strangers (poor mental health). Or you can be a rock star in publicity (business ambition), but are always buying leather pants semicompulsively, an unnecessary indulgence that you really don't need (spending money).

And I have to call myself out here. At the time of writing this, my relationship life area is pretty pathetic. I've got no partner and no kids. It's like I blinked and everyone had nuclear families, plus soccer game and unicorn sprinkle cake weekends, except me. Becoming a mom seems like a pipe dream at forty, racing against time. I've honestly struggled for years with unrequited love, but my business life area is a ten out of ten (and I'm still actively working on the relationship bit). This model is here because I've seen it work well for many women I admire. The more you can see that all aspects of life are strongly interdependent and integrated, the more you can transform breakdowns in any life area and deliberately design what you want so everything works in harmony.

Through the Integrated Life Layout you can be thoughtful about designing a full life that is connected to, but goes way beyond, your business. Why does this matter?

Because you have but one precious life. You don't want to waste it living someone else's design. You deserve a life with agency. One where you play the complex lead character who finds her own way. One where you can leave the conflict of separate worlds for the fullness of an integrated life and the feeling of an amplified state of being. And before too many years go by, taste your own magic.

BLDG BLOCK 2: Value Values

With life areas laid out, the next stop is to find the values that matter most to you. Ever noticed that when you aren't true to yourself, you can feel out of whack in life? Out of integrity with the core values that make up who you are? Maybe you believe in fairness but find yourself in your home environment angrily doing all the emotional and physical labor, feeling most of the time like a kitchen towel that someone just rubbed a snotty nose on? Or in my own case, identify with strength, but then in relationships act like a weak wimp, avoiding dating, blaming those darn app algorithms. Depending on what realm you are operating in, essentially segmenting, siloing, or severing off what you value most. Parts of YOU. Managing different identities, pretending, morphing, or shape-shifting is not only exhausting, it is the quickest way to diminish your power.

What you have now stepped into is being out in the open about everything. Where you tell the truth about who you are in every room. Show up as your full self, no matter the audience. So think of values as the glue that binds, holding all the areas of your life together, creating real integration and, in time, equal parts peace and power.

To unite your life based on your core values you'll want to think about—surprise, surprise—the few qualities you value most! This value set should resonate deep, deep within. And start with YOU at the center, spanning across all seven areas of your life. A few values that come to mind are: integrity, connection, courage, fun, humor, honesty, hope, generosity, grace, and gratitude.

Also consider those "feminine" traits, if they resonate with you, which can make for strong leadership DNA—empathy, caring, fairness, inclusivity, persuasiveness, transparency, authenticity, and commitment. In my own upbringing, the V word (gotcha . . . that's *values*) was so deeply embedded, my mom even pioneered an entire values-based cooking method and wrote a cookbook about them—talk about niche values infusion!

With values comes endurance and durability. You can go the distance without as much burnout, exhaustion, or upset. Values demonstrate your intent and immediately help you identify any pain points. In doing so, you don't waste time or energy trying to be anything other than what you value. And in business, just by nature of you bringing who you are to your work, you will likely create a business that is good for others.

Flashback to my twenties when I had the good fortune of meeting with designer Diane von Furstenberg. As clearly as if she was ringing a bell, her three values reverberated through the air: *style, authenticity* (no mincing of words or ideas . . . incredibly direct in her opinions), and *love*. As she has said, "There is no way to envision life without love, and at this point in my life, I don't think there is anything more important—love of family, love of nature, love of travel, love of learning, love of life in every way—all of it. Love is being thankful, love is paying attention, love is being open and compassionate. Love is using all the privileges you possess to help those who are in need."

An integrated life is always an expression and extension of your personal values. Excavate them. Bolster them. And you will find your essence.

BLDG BLOCK 3: X Factor = Amplification

Adele, Beyoncé, Serena, Swift, Lizzo, JLo, Dolly, Lucille . . .

They have the spark, they have the swagger, they have the sauce, and they seem to have found THE source.

This can happen for mere mortals, too. You don't have to be mononymous (I had to look this one up: be famous enough to have just one name) or even a traditional "success" for that matter. You could be Beekeeper Barb, just living on a farm, drinking your own nectar every day.

The point is to design a life that is a total reflection of you. A near carbon copy of everything you think, feel, and desire. Not what another goddamn person on the planet wants or thinks. Just you. Then this happens . . . Amplification.

Like a light switch, from deep integration comes amplification. Your power button naturally turns on. This becomes your natural state of being. It's like you meet you, the you always wanted to become. Pure potential you. You radiate brighter and vibrate at what seems like a higher electrical frequency. While humming "This little light of mine, I'm gonna let it shine," and others think, *What good shit is she on?*

So long as you stay integrated across your life areas, you show up intensely bright. Dimming only happens when you have a breakdown in a life area or when core values slip. Depending on whether you feel amplified or not, you are pointed upward (toward new heights) or inward (to resolve what needs mending).

Amplification presents as charging into places and taking up space. Bringing your total self into a room. Doing things without permission. Allowing yourself to claim all you desire, as weird or improbable as it might seem. Letting go of the knotted fear that you will get it alllll the way wrong. It means taking decisive, deliberate action. Having a center that is so strong, you cannot be moved.

In the real world, amplification looks like jumping in without a formal MBA, intending to build as you go. From the first Google doc titled "new business" to that Hail Mary email putting out your newly inflated rate. To sexy times date night every Tuesday and dramatic reenactments of bedtime stories if you chose them to that homespun outfit you made for a pitch to wanting to touch the sky even if you can't touch your toes. Mining yourself for gems that get you closer to your highest and best. Amplifying yourself inside out, not abandoning yourself outside in, as we have all done in so many ways, on so many different days. Where you allow desire. Unapologetically claim and go after what you want. Meet the moment. Stopping for no one and nothing. Just doing the damn thing. This is when you become a bad bitch not in some superficial sort of way to impress others. In your bones sort of way to serve yourself. Untouchability. Un-overwhelmability. Unfuckability. Pardon my French.

For us to live big, we need to lead amplified lives. Step into the fullness of who we are:

By confronting our breakdowns.

By trusting our inner voice and ensuring it can be heard.

By dialing up our unique genius and expressing it fully in every aspect of our lives, including our businesses.

By designing new possibilities . . .

Amplification is the catalyst to transcend how we've been nurtured to get us back in touch with our very nature, our sacred truths as women. It's so true that a powerful life means you don't wait for things to happen to you. You go out and happen to things.

For once, a positive life-altering side effect: your light lights the way for others. You doing you—bringing all of yourself to bear, without reservation or apology, with all of your might—is what other Builders need more than anything else. Because it gives them permission to do the same.

Builder Spotlight: June Diane Raphael

Actress, comedian, screenwriter June Diane Raphael won our hearts (and laughs!) as an icy businesswoman in Grace and Frankie. *As an activist, she wrote* Represent: The Woman's Guide to Running for Office and Changing the World. *To help moms at work, she created the Jane Club, the first workspace specifically for mothers. While home is LA, she swung by to see me in NYC decked out in a beautiful maroon dress and camel coat draped over her shoulders like a real boss. While I thought I would meet a comedian, instead I met a woman of deep conviction, as serious as a wake-up call after a heart attack. Make no mistake: June Diane advocates for all women across all definitions and all dimensions.*

On Building

. . . I've always been engaged in my community. Not sure that's actual building. But I do lots of activist work.

On Breakdown → Breakthrough

. . . My most challenging personal breakdown in recent memory was as a new mother. Hearing a screaming baby and knowing I needed to take a shower and get ready for the day and not knowing what to do. I felt out of control and helpless. It was a crazy feeling. In the shower I felt like I was in a movie and thinking, I've never done this before in my life. I took to my knees in the water. On my knees. It was a total breakdown. Thank god for supportive husbands. And professionally, I've had many Little b breakdowns. The nice part of training yourself as an actor is you get very used to the no. I'm now quite comfortable getting rejected. I've built up the part of myself that assumes most answers will be no.

On Life Integration

... The reason why I built the Jane Club for working mothers was I desperately needed it. Truly. I had just had my second baby and was breastfeeding, working, and writing a book. And I found myself pretending I didn't have kids. Not telling people I worked with, not wanting to say, "I have to go home," and somehow feeling like kids were a detriment to my work ethic ... When actually what I found is that motherhood has inspired me in so many ways and made my work better across the board, so much better.

... My own mother worked outside the home. A New York public school teacher, she was passionate about education. Always juggling and balancing, she leaned on community and was constantly igniting the village around her to get things done. She'd drop me off at a neighbor's house at 7:00 A.M., and I'd wait there until I had to go to the school bus. And there were days when I was picked up after school by a random person in her prayer group. I'd have no idea who she was but knew my mom had vetted her. That's a lesson I got very early from her: Children are the village's responsibility. She was always engaging and igniting the village around her.

On Values

... One of the core values at Jane is taking care of women first, like the oxygen mask idea.

... Really value the relationships with women in my life. There's a group of us from sixth grade on and we roll deep and strong, and I ask them for help and support, saying, "I really need you, I need you here tonight."

On Amplification

... The goal is not to succeed. The goal is not to do it right. That really stuck with me creatively. So much joy in failure and in flopping, and in trying something that you've no idea if it will work or not. Acting training focused on fail, fail again, and fail harder. You've got to take risks and be okay with things not working out.

Nuts & Bolts: What keeps you sane? *My children.* What keeps you going? *The other women around me changing the world.*

5

FRAMING

Creating an Actionable Plan

There's no map for you to follow and take your journey. You are Lewis and Clark. You are the mapmaker.

—Phillipa Soo

THE MORE AMPLIFIED YOU BECOME, THE MORE YOU WANT TO DO AND TAKE ON. THE more you take on, the more critical your daily holistic habits become. These habits are like the positively charged protons in atoms. So you can stay at high vibration, high frequency. An ideal state.

If you don't prioritize these daily practices, not only are you no longer amplified, things can go sideways in a hurry. Dare I share a few from my Rolodex of sideways adventures?

. . . Panic attack. Gasping for air, my breath narrowed. Electric pain from my front kneecap snaked to the base of my spine, jolting my body like the live third rail of a train track. It was my first panic attack, triggered by heaving heavy boxes in a move, plus a potential lawsuit.

. . . Depletion. Days of pouring myself into intense work often rendered me flat out in bed. Texts would go unanswered. Takeout orders with food would pile high in my bedroom. After being a recluse for days (plural), I'd turn my grimy NYC apartment back into *Architectural*

Digest and pretend nothing had happened. It was my dirty lil secret (quite literally) for years.

. . . Anxiety. A brain on fire. Middle of the night, my sympathetic nervous system would kick my conscious mind in the shins. "Get up!" Apparently we had been busy for quite a while. Fight mode. A T-shirt damp with pit stains. Disparate thoughts raced blurrily by: *Will this contract fall apart? What if I die alone? Was that a ghost? After all, this bedroom was once a deer meat hanger in the old farmhouse.* Something screamed I was not safe. Too early to send emails with a 3:04 A.M. time stamp, too embarrassed to wake a friend. Ruminating. Trying to calm my body from running away with my mind.

. . . Disassociated. Feeling nuh-uh-thing. Like not being able to taste without hot sauce. Like knowing a vista of the ocean is objectively beautiful but only being able to perceive it as a painting. Like hearing muffled words, but not registering what the person is saying. At one point I even went to a fancy schmancy place in Arizona and was instructed to hit a tennis racket into a pillow with all my might, so I could come back into my body again and feel. Something.

. . . Hemorrhoids! Ringing in my left ear. Like I said, sideways . . . on steroids.

What remedied these Whac-A-Mole-like flare-ups? Daily mindful maintenance. Getting consistent habits in place to proactively manage my well-being.

You see our bodies don't betray us. We betray our bodies.

So many of us have buried trauma, PTSD, or issues that have left us easily triggered by our go-to emotional response (anger, pleasing, silence, sadness, fear). Often in fight, flight, freeze, or fawn mode. This, in turn, leaves us with unhealthy coping mechanisms. Think alcohol, drugs, compulsive shopping, overeating, reorganizing the already organized, etc. And my personal favorite: overwork. Escaping in hard work itself. Yes, work to feel a sense of control—without even knowing it. Pain cloaked in accomplishment. A constant state of frenzied motion to outrun or fix the world outside, instead of the wounds that lie within.

Every time we don't hold the line, every time we are flat-out running on fumes, and instead of tending to that little girl who lives inside all of us who is pleading that she's being pulled too fast, tripping over her shoelaces, instead pushing her further, asking her four-foot frame to balance on the top of a precarious ladder to reach the food at the top of the refrigerator because someone realllllllyyyy needs a snack . . . ignoring that she might precipitously fall. Every time we internalize the nitpicking, how we could be "better," we betray ourselves. I've heard and at times believed: I chew too loudly. Make too much noise when I sneeze. Don't wear enough makeup. Wear too much makeup. Smell. Need to lose a few pounds. Have verbal tics to "improve," too. (In a pitch, one guy even scrawled my signature catchphrase "you know" on a legal pad then dramatically crossed it out!)

If we don't say *F-off* and maintain healthy practices, our bodies remember. And eventually they scream bloody murder at us to pay attention. Bodies are both a GPS system telling us where to go and an alarm system warning us when we get dangerously close to the edge. This mind-body connection cannot be underestimated. And when you deal with pressure—which happens with increasing frequency and higher stakes as an entrepreneur—without a release valve and good habits, you won't have a choice. The more you do, the more your body pays attention. Mental and physical pain episodes will immobilize you. You will come undone, unless you learn to ferociously mother yourself.

This chapter is about taking back control. Putting on those big girl pants to confront what needs to be confronted. Executing a personal plan governed by self-awareness and radical personal accountability. Implementing new habits, using habit hacks to increase your success, and up, up, upping the momentum will mean that, before you know it, you will have moved closer to your business vision. Discipline and determination lead to strength and stability. The business results will be so palpable, so demonstrable that you won't want to stop. You can never start these habits too early, because once you're in the throes of building a business, it's best if taking care of yourself is already second nature. To step into this, you'll take on a sixty-day challenge (for habit formation), which then has a daily sixty-minute prime (for optimal priming), which is then broken into sixty-second pauses (for intentional, in-the-moment decision making). Seconds become minutes, minutes become days, days stack into who you become.

You choose your own habits. No matter how well-intended, someone else cannot give you a blueprint for a home they themselves have never built. Ultimately, you are the architect.

The three BLDG Blocks you will get in this chapter are:

1. 60-Day Challenge
2. 60-Minute Prime
3. 60-Second Pause

BLDG BLOCK 1: 60-Day Challenge

Ever heard you are the sum of your habits? Like the sucker fish that religiously cleans algae to make sure the tank doesn't get out of whack with a toxic bloom. Ironically, it is the smallest of consistent micro daily actions that enable you to do the biggest macro things in the world. Habits are the disciplined, concrete steps you take toward the integrated life and vision you established. Habits protect and give a business stability. Habits also keep you in an amplified state because they keep your nervous system calm and energy high. And it all starts with self.

Groundbreaking research from Phillippa Lally, a health psychologist at University College London, indicates that it takes about sixty-six days to form a new habit and achieve "peak levels of automaticity." The prevailing idea had been that it is just twenty-one days to change or build a habit, but that is not the case (for most people)! So hang in there and do new things for approximately sixty days (the real sweet spot is sixty-six days), and you will be that person, according to this BUILD Inspector.[1] And it's not a biggie if you forget a day . . . just hop back in the saddle the next.

To help cement the process, think of the power of linking your desired new practice to one that's already well established. Like drinking a glass of water after your daily morning floss. Or coupling writing your business to-do list for tomorrow with that last sip of bedtime chamomile tea. That behavioral practice is called habit stacking or tethering and it leads to a higher success rate.[2] Good habits build on each other.

To change anything in your life, it's important to understand how to manage your mind—in other words, all the things that tug at you, slow you down, drain you, and pull you off course. To learn more about limiting distractibility in the face of stressors, I interviewed University of Miami neuroscientist Dr. Amishi Jha, another BUILD Inspector:

WE ARE MISSING OUT ON 50 PERCENT OF OUR LIVES! In meetings we go to, or books we read, or conversations we are in, we're not there about half the moments. Our attention gets hijacked. Especially under high stress, we ruminate. We loop on a past experience that's going nowhere. We catastrophize and worry endlessly about future scenarios that may never occur. We're not troubleshooting or problem-solving, we're stuck.[3]

So as entrepreneurs, what can we do about the mind's distractibility and manage better?

If we understand the way our mind functions, we get a better user's guide. So when we're trying to write a report, but the group chat keeps buzzing, the phone keeps going off, the children are calling, and you feel like you have no control over your own mind, realize *your mind is totally fine.* Your attention system is behaving exactly as somebody whose flashlight of attention is being yanked around like crazy. So turn off your notifications to limit distractions. And when the mind wanders away, be aware. *Oh, you know what? I really wanna look into that one restaurant I want to go to. I'll just hop on a call real quick and do that. No, that's a thought I don't need to follow right now.* Another simple solution is something technically called cognitive offloading. It sounds way fancier than it is, but it's a handy tool. Keep paper and pencil near you. Don't open up another tab on your computer. Instead, write it down, and then get back to the task at hand.[4]

This approach was anathema to my previous multitasking-under-the-guise-of-productivity self. My computer used to look like a file cabinet gone mad—dozens of tabs, drafted emails and chats simultaneously open. From rescheduling my doctor's appointment for the fourth time, responding to a girlfriend's hypochondriac text about her rash, writing that clever email opening (Greetings, hope you've had your coffee already!) to looking up what ingredients are needed for that bomb chicken parm, to googling why my dog threw up, all while adding (and then subsequently removing) new clothes from my shopping cart. Now I do one thing at a time, linearly. Even use one of those twenty-minute Pomodoro timer thingies!

Believe me, using this updated user's guide works better for managing your brain. So offload thought interruptions onto a to-do list. Be aware of ruminating in the future, or reliving or regretting the past. Stop losing precious energy by narrativizing every event. Your new future will be created in the now, so keep your attention there.

Of course, there are going to be days (many days!) when it's just really hard to focus, hence this habit helper that will encourage you to actually enjoy the discomfort of navigating newness. When you don't feel inspired or in the flow, this is where the power of healthy habits and routines—and, in particular, careful attention—can catapult you back into inspiration so long as you dig in instead of check out. You do this through focus. It sounds easy, and it is, except for the resistance you create to stay in the perceived safety of your comfort zone. Doing things or even thinking about doing things you've never done before will induce both excitement and fear. Your discomfort is a clear indicator that you are building something new and important.

Know that habits get easier and you will find momentum over time. It's like when I stopped working out for a bit, those first few weeks back felt like I was weight training with cement blocks instead of milk jugs; then I became a glistening bodybuilder (well, not exactly, but I did grow stronger). It got harder before it got easier. Which reminds me of physics class: $p = mv$. Perhaps you remember how momentum (or p) equals mass (or m . . . or *you* in this case) multiplied by velocity (or v). Once you start succeeding over a period (like sixty days), you start to build momentum. Taking off, however, requires a disproportionate amount of energy. The velocity must be increased initially until you hit cruising altitude, at which point less energy is required due to the momentum generated. And at some point in this journey, you grab the plane's PA system: You start telling people about wins (not winds) and what's on the horizon. You want to strike with new initiatives (or habits) when the turbines are hot. Then it's a matter of keeping the momentum. High performers take over the captain's seat.

All that said, pacing is like momentum's responsible seatmate. I'll go for weeks consumed by a project, working full-out because I'm either energized by it or need to get it done, and then take weeks off for recovery. Likewise, I love to work on Sundays when the world is quiet and my phone isn't buzzing and then take off a day during the week. It's walk (or crawl), then a burst sprint. Contraction, expansion. Rest, cocoon, or wall up, then take up space. Whatever works for you to maintain energy, so you can go the distance.

BLDG BLOCK 2: 60-Minute Prime

Back in the day, self-care meant external ta-da appearance stuff—a blowout with complimentary champagne, wing-tip eyeliner application, or getting eyebrow (or you-know-what) waxes. It evolved to Swedish massages, aromatherapy-infused salt baths, and gratitude lists. The future of self-care is an internal-external combo of morning habits as a foundation to root you—meditation, exercise, nourishing foods, and more—plus mini check-ins throughout the day so you can hold your center (and push back at the external world).

To do this we need to uproot the deeply ingrained belief that self-care is indulgent; that it's better to focus on everyone else's needs first. Then once others' needs are fulfilled, if any time or energy remains, we can do something nice for ourselves, so long as we feel a spoonful of guilt and dole out a dollop of rationale to those whining about our "selfishness" . . .

. . . Ever freak out when given an hour of alone time? Should you read a magazine, scrub the oven? Take up guitar? Learn French? Eradicate climate change? HOT DANG! Sooooo many things . . . anddd time's up!

. . . Get called a horrible, hateful, heartless hobbit of a mother if you ask your kid to so much as set the table? Apparently the same goes for laundry-folding, bed-making, dog-walking, dishwashing, room cleaning . . .

. . . Find yourself the last to eat, starin' at grits that are no longer pipin' hot, but congealed cold?

We must give ourselves permission to put ourselves at the top of the list, for at least sixty minutes a day.

Sheila Lirio Marcelo, cofounder of Care.com (incidentally one of only a handful of US women ever to lead her company, then valued at $500 million, to IPO status), speaks on the "care" void: "As women, as caregivers, we prioritize everyone else and put ourselves at the bottom of the list," she says. "To grow in leadership, you have to be a narcissist; focus on yourself, understand yourself, take time for yourself. It will make you a better leader." Your oxygen mask first.[5]

By tending to yourself, managing daily Anchor Habits intentionally and proactively, you won't get as depleted. No question, reactive self-care (the massage to reduce tension in your back, or face mask to offer a moment of escape from sticky little fingers) is well and good and should continue, but it's a Band-Aid. It doesn't care for you at the source. You need consistent, Anchor Habits that keep you grounded with those daily check-ins for good decision-making (credit again to Dr. Amishi Jha, who shared this idea with me). This preserves your energy, your fuel.

Like gas in the tank, you never know how badly you will need reserves until you do. No one wants to be running on an empty tank when something bad happens on the road of life. These habits are important because they help you weather tough winters. If you didn't like my gas example, think of self-care like stockpiling grain that you can draw down in the future. When you are strong and physically able, you want to fill those coffers. That's the time to work on your habits proactively, so you are holistically healthy going into a health or financial crisis (god forbid) or just a super-intense, demanding work period. Fix the roof when the sun is shining, not when you are knee-deep in muck.

So it's time to do your day: sixty minutes in the morning for optimal priming, for the next sixty days. This is an appointment with yourself, as important as any business meeting. These three Anchor Habits, done daily, make for an unshakable foundation.

Anchor Habits

1. **Sweat:** Exercise. The undisputed heavyweight champion of healthy habits. There are a gazillion health benefits to regular physical activity, but the most immediate for your day is that exercise ups motivation and confidence. Sweat that crap out. Wring it out. Get those yummy, feel-good endorphins firing. Some days this might mean intense cardio, others a light walk (with only a single sweat bead). Just move that bod!

2. **Silence:** Meditation, mindfulness, transcendental meditation and/or mindfulness-based stress reduction (MBSR). The names vary, but fundamentally this is a time to get silent and still,

follow your breath, escape racing thoughts, make contact with your truth, and ultimately strengthen your mind. As you deepen your practice, you will be better able to manage stress, navigate difficult decisions, stay steady, and remain present, no matter what the day throws your way.

3. **Sustenance:** Nourishing foods. From the dictionary, *sustenance* means "food and drink regarded as a source of strength; nourishment." It's so true we are what we eat. Food can fight brain fog, poor mood, inflammation, pain, you name it, giving you more energy and vitality. So double down on whatever makes you feel better, like veggies, fruit, water, healthy fats, green juice, nutrients, and controlled portions. Avoid what makes you feel worse, like sugar, processed foods, and copious caffeine. This is not a diet, but a way of life. Check in with a nutritionist (there's some great reading out there) before making any real lifestyle changes.

In my own case, I used to live like a whirling dervish. The demands of the world would govern how I'd start the day and how fast I twirled (ping, ping, ping, inbox read in bed). It's like I started each day holding my breath. I now find that by starting each morning intentionally with what makes me feel grounded, I can set the day's tone and speed. I'm now glued to daily habits like exercise, meditation, and healthy foods. My formula might sound like dullsville, Groundhog Day-in-the-life stuff, but every morning I make my bed first thing (judo chop those pillows), walk the dog, and get sunlight to wake up the whole system. After that, I down celery juice (chug), coffee, water, and a banana with almond butter while flipping through a design or poetry book for inspiration. Do a quick transcendental meditation. Then I either exercise or move with a simple walk in nature—all before sitting down to work. The clincher: outside requests only get reviewed in the p.m. All these things keep me sane.

To supplement those three Anchor Habits, here are a few additional practices that I do from time to time: gratitude lists, badass breathwork, extra sleep, aromatherapy, therapy, life coaching, journaling, affirmations, mantras, reading, podcasts, massage, acupuncture, nature, calling a friend, tapping, grooming, blowing bubbles . . . Wait, bubbles? Yes, Oprah keeps a bottle of bubbles on her desk. "When the day gets too heavy and I'm feeling overwhelmed, I may actually blow a few," she says. "Blowing the perfect bubble requires bringing your attention to your breath and placing it in the space of the present moment . . . kind of like bubble meditation. Being fully present automatically lifts your spirits. Clears your mind of distractions. Brings clarity. Even some joy, if you're open to it. Blowing bubbles reminds me of happiness."

Some of these habits will require spending cold hard cash, if you are in a privileged enough position to use disposable income in this way. Even so, you will likely feel guilty getting a massage to, *sheesh*, even glam, especially when the money could go to your kid's soccer cleats, but restorative practices help you manage stress and time so you can focus on what's important. And if you can't plunk down any money, remember what's freely always at your disposal: running outdoors, sitting in silence, taking a book out from the library, drinking H_2O, or even snagging face cream samples at the beauty counter.

You'll figure out what works for you. Trial and error. And it will change over time, based on your Integrated Life Layout. For example, if a relationship is a key focus area, grooming might come to the forefront, or if expanding your passions is important, reading fiction for fun might be in the cards.

Just mind your Me Time.

BLDG BLOCK 3: 60-Second Pause

Now that you have developed grounding habits for your internal world, you are about to get an "A" in handling things that come your way externally. Learn an enforcement tool to protect your newfound state. No successful woman arrived at where she is today without being incredibly intentional in her choices, incredibly protective of her time and energy—both finite resources. As things fly at you, invade your space, you'll learn to judo chop them down. And ironically, it starts with slowing down.

It's the 60-Second Pause.

It works this way: when things come at you that require a decision, check in with your body for sixty seconds. Your intuition will tell you just about everything you need to know. Does the ask feel peaceful or agitating? Like scarcity or abundance? Like a small baby you or a LARGE CONFIDENT YOU? Does it make you want to say yes (emphatically, loudly, proudly) or no? You and you alone will know if it's right for you. BUILD Inspector, life coach, writer, and three-degree Harvard "black belt" Martha Beck (who I spent a weekend seminar with) playfully sums up the body-checking process this way: "See if you feel warmer (happier, more alive) or colder (more miserable and dead). If it feels warmer, do it. If it feels colder, do som'n else."[6]

Another litmus test for knowing how to respond is you'll either feel a HELL YES ("I'm gung-ho in") or you'll start finger-wagging, irritated, a feisty knowing will kick back ("oh, no no no . . ."). Senses heightened, fiercely protective of your newfound peace.

But you can also take the time you need before communicating to the outside world. You don't need to make a split-second decision in the moment, which many will try to force you to do. With the 60-Second Pause, you can note what comes up, and take that initial inventory. Then say, "I need to think about things and get back to you." Sleep on it, run on it, meditate on it. Our bodies are tapped into an infinite wisdom aligned with our true self that is more knowledgeable than any amount of intellectual thought.

At a macro thirty-thousand-foot level, this is about the ability to see a major situation and choose to act differently. On a micro level—that a million small choices—your no's preserve where you want to go.

My twenties were spent with a gnawing icky, agitated, walk-on-eggshells feeling. I would lose myself in others' chaos, unpredictability, impulsivity, and nit-picking. I'd allow others to give a word of advice in my alleged "best interest" on how I could do more, improve more, or "understand better." I'd shapeshift to meet their divergent demands and ideas of who I should be. A client, a coworker, or a partner could spin me into a frenzy. Anyone know that lovely feeling? The world is going to tug at you in a million ways on a million different days, so *no* has to become your default setting.

And that is one way to establish boundaries. Because there is no building . . . without boundaries. Think of this as a home protection system. The alarm needs vigilant maintenance, so you aren't robbed blind.

To dig in deeper, when we say yes to what comes our way (which may feel easiest in the moment) based on outside forces (obligation, pleasing) versus our own truths, we become drained. Resentment goes into the body. And what evaporates? That all-important time and energy to maintain your habits and do your real work. Space. When we mindfully manage the minutes, listen to our truth, and say no (which may feel hardest in the moment), it translates to us feeling free. That pretty much means saying no ten times for every yes. A caveat here: to the external world, these decisions may seem illogical. Who would turn down that six-figure contract or wouldn't want to go on a second date with that chiseled face or agree to a coffee to "pick your brain . . . it's just an hour." Exercising no's will mean saying things like "Unfortunately, I will not be able to do that" as a full and complete sentence. And by the way, if you haven't had much practice exercising your voice, you might sound more like a sledgehammer, emphatically repeating yourself at a level ten octane: "I do not have time for this. I do not have time for you. I do not have time for this. I do not have time for you."

It's also important to note you can change your mind. Even after you feel warm and fuzzy and say yes. There was a podcast I had worked on for seven months with a potential media partner. When I started to feel cold, I torpedoed the deal. I did not feel listened to, the equity split wasn't fair, and the language seemed predatory (i.e., they hoped to garner a percentage of any future, impossible-to-pin-down TV work). Hello, Taylor Swift, Tina Turner. Know when to walk away.

No matter how much time or money you have invested. It's the sign of a very healthy person.

As you start this process, you will likely lose people who will be frustrated by you. On some days you will find yourself with more conflict than harmony. You will find yourself in more uncomfortable positions as you push back. But you serve them, or you serve you. Who will you choose? Know those relationships or things you lose in the process were never meant to be permanent; they were surface and transactional at best. Dealing with the blowback that comes from saying no pales in comparison to the regret of ignoring your gut. Neglected guts become gut wrenching.

Over time, this 60-Second Pause will put you in your truth. Help you stay mindful. You will feel your body become lighter, less exhausted. Your business will have enforceable boundaries that keep it fortified. You will meet your people, those who could never find you when you were not being uniquely you. You will find peace. In what you do, what you say, and how you move through the world. Cellular-level inner peace. No matter the conditions or surroundings or temperature in that workroom or boardroom. Stillness will reside in you. Never trade your peace for someone else's.

No one got anywhere big by cutting herself up into a million little pieces.

Builder Spotlight: Arianna Huffington

Arianna Huffington is incredibly successful, yet extremely open about her shortcomings. A story she often tells is of fainting at her desk from exhaustion, hitting her face on the hard surface and breaking her cheekbone. This marked a personal failing in not taking care of herself and was a turning point for her to change priorities. In her book Thrive, *she explains: "To live*

the lives we truly want and deserve, we need a third measure of success that
goes beyond the two metrics of money and power." That new framework
focuses on thriving with these life-enhancing habits: well-being, wisdom,
wonder, and giving. She is the founder and CEO of Thrive Global, founder
of the Huffington Post *(now* HuffPost*) and author of fifteen books.* TIME
featured her on its 100 Most Influential People list and Forbes *ranked her*
among the Most Powerful Women. I first met her at a Galentine's Day soul-
ful meditation led by her sister in NYC and by proxy when my company,
Grayce & Co, helped Verizon merge with a newly acquired AOL, which owned
Huffington Post *(how's that for a mouthful!).*

On Building

. . . One of the through lines to my life has been my love of helping
people connect and engage! And both of the companies I've built have
been platforms for that.

On Breakdown → Breakthrough

. . . I had a wake-up call in 2007 when I collapsed from exhaustion and
lack of sleep, cutting my eye and breaking my cheekbone on the way down.
I was diagnosed with an acute case of burnout and made changes in my
life, including renewing my estranged relationship with sleep and rede-
fining my idea of success. That led to several breakthroughs, including
my books *Thrive* and *The Sleep Revolution* and, ultimately, my launch of
Thrive Global.

On Habit Formation

. . . The pervasive belief that burnout is the price we must pay for success
is a delusion, and I'm inspired to accelerate the culture shift that allows
people to reclaim their lives and move from merely surviving to thriving.
    . . . My mother's favorite piece of advice to me was, "Failure isn't the
opposite of success, but a stepping-stone to success." That gave my sister and me the encouragement and license to try anything, secure in the
knowledge that if we failed, she wouldn't love us any less.

On Habit Priming

... I had long assumed the *Huffington Post* would be my last chapter. But as I became more passionate about the connection between well-being and performance, I felt the need to turn this passion into something that would help people change their daily lives. It was a call to action I just couldn't ignore, hence Thrive Global.

... What's also been rewarding about Thrive Global is proving that you can build a business, even a technology company, without being fueled by stress and burnout. So, I love the process of putting our principles into action.

On Taking Pauses

... I've struggled with that voice of self-doubt, which I call "the obnoxious roommate living in our heads." It's the one that tells so many women we're not good enough. But as [the sixteenth-century French essayist] Michel de Montaigne said, "There were many terrible things in my life, and most of them never happened."

Nuts & Bolts: What do you value most in others? *Authenticity and being present.* One thing you're afraid of? *Emergency texts from my daughters.* One thing you'd change about yourself? *Lower-maintenance hair.* What keeps you sane? *Single-shot venti cappuccino. And then another.*

6

CREW

Leading the People Around You

Leadership is hard to define, and good leadership even harder. But if you can get people to follow you to the ends of the earth, you are a great leader.
—INDRA NOOYI

PULL UP A SEAT . . . I REMEMBER BEING BRIEFED BY MY DREAM CLIENT, A BIG brand with a lot of swagger. They also gave a deadline of two weeks for an initial presentation. My consultancy was known for being fast, but not that fast. Instead of saying, "I've got an immovable commitment in that I will be under light anesthesia the day of the presentation for a girl thing (egg freezing)," I instead DID THE CALL FROM THE RECOVERY ROOM. In my gown and pink socks! Even ignoring the handsome anesthesiologist (just making sure you were still paying attention). This is what wounded entrepreneurship looks like. No surprise, as we were spoon fed that grit-your-teeth-do-whatever-it-takes anemic diet growing up. But there's a lot to unpack . . .

For a closer peek behind the curtain of my early entrepreneurial journey (better described as a decoupage art performance . . . I'm expecting judgment), I co-opted different styles of "leadership" and random business practices to lead my crew, otherwise known as team, before I found my own way. These were mainly messy misses:

Ms. Big Payments . . . Coming out of working for Fortune 100 companies, I gave corporate packages to my first employees. A top person got six figures plus a 35 percent performance bonus and 20 percent of annual company revenue. My take-home? Zilch. To fund the team, I'd sit in front of my computer dipping further and further into the red of personal savings while overhearing carefree chatter about last night's twenty-course omakase and complaints about our agency's lack of resources.

Cool Girl Culture . . . Perks, like team-building field trips to museums, abstract floral arrangements, Monday morning coffee musings, branded hoodies, rosé on tap, and a manicured, minimalist communal desk.

Rescue-Me Freebies . . . The immature fantasy of being saved led to my accepting months of free volunteer work for my company that was then accompanied by all-too-often backend "you owe me" slips. These were not the good permission kind. Entertainment. Introductions. Equity asks. Nothing is free.

Ad Hoc Admin . . . Little rigor around organization, intellectual property, contracts, payment. Even asking people to sign nondisclosure agreements *after* the fact. The audacity! While I was figuring things out (sorta or not at all), my team was forced to operate in a vague vacuum. Oh, and if anyone asked clarifying questions? I'd often snap back like a snake with a stepped-on rattler. At one point, I didn't have the emotional desire to run my business, so I abruptly, awkwardly, clinically fired my team. From nurturing den mom to cold ice queen.

Interestingly, though, it is through our personal healing that we become ready to lead differently. As we become more thoughtful, heartfelt, creative, deliberate, caring of ourselves, so does our treatment of others. We learn to take the time we need to be intentional instead of rushing to emulate someone else's style or simply flying by the seat of our skirts.

I call this paradigm shift from wounded leadership to mindful leadership.

Long story short, my definition of mindful leadership is now first and foremost about staying true to myself, my vision and values. Every day. Which also means not keeping what I really stand for in the closet: performance, professionalism, and positivity.

Realization #1, performance: I do like to keep my foot on the gas. Pretending my business was about slushy, touchy-feely team building all the time was a lie, so I needed to clean that up. I pivoted and set the expectation upfront with my crew that you must be self-motivated and hard driving. This is not for the faint of heart.

Realization #2, professionalism: I suck at operations, so I enlisted practical Virgo, Type-A help. No more after-the-fact contracts or work for free! I now run a tight ship that is detail-oriented and deadline-obsessed.

Realization #3, positivity: My pet peeve is a person who comes to the party holding hands with problems. The Eeyores had to go. Despite the challenges of "building while flying," which includes limited resources, aggressive time lines, and constant change, my belief is to focus on "what can go right" and bring solutions forward. I was after a team that would drive me to be the best possible version of myself.

Generally speaking, business comes down to being truthful about who you are, what you do, and what you offer. No more pretending to be anything else. To be a mindful leader who people want to follow to the ends of the earth—or at least till the end of a project—you must first know yourself, your values, and what you need (and certainly no more presentations from the recovery room!). From there you can build a crew around you. Because the head of the crew is YOU.

The three BLDG Blocks you will get in this chapter are:

1. Boss Up
2. Nailed It
3. Dream Team

BLDG BLOCK 1: Boss Up

You're about to step into the gloriously challenging, high-wire act of being a leader as YOU embrace your one-of-a-kind, unique, leadership style!

Wounded leaders, as described, may create business "success," yes, money too, but in equal parts burnout, breakage, crushed crewmates. You pay the piper. Yes, some wounded leaders have certain textbook toxic traits—bullying, lying, gaslighting, arrogance, hierarchy obsession, discrimination, self-interest. There are leaders who try to run from or numb their insecurities through work. Who bleed people dry because they are bleeding. Who wound because they are wounded. Some are the living incarnation of ruthless, nasty IPO heat seekers (blast radius be damned), masquerading behind kumbaya circles, promising color-coordinated fame, gloss, and glory. Certainly very bad characters exist, no denying that. But in most cases, wounded leaders just don't know who they are, so steal this leadership style or that business process to git 'er done. They are half-baked, unsure, insecure folks, running too fast with super-sharp scissors.

In comparison, mindful leaders have taken the time to do THE hard work to know who they truly are. This leadership, by my definition, isn't about a new prescribed "right way" of leading. It's about figuring out YOUR WAY of leading. To do that, you must first know your truth. Your vision and values. What makes you tick. Your traits. What triggers you. Usually this means deep introspection or healing work. By embracing yourself fully, you then can step up and into your own leadership and mindfully maneuver.

Here's the twist: This isn't about trading out a set of "wounded" qualities for "mindful" ones. Mindful leadership isn't at odds with ambition or being decisive or hard-charging or making money. It also doesn't necessarily mean embracing a soft style or emphasizing those "feminine" traits. This isn't a value judgment. You can be whatever you want to be. Even stand for values society doesn't deem "good" (though hopefully you'll use your more thoughtful traits, your foundation, to direct you in how you lead . . . like reasonable hours, fair working conditions, honest discussions, etc.). So long as you are aware, honest, and let people know what you are really all about. So long as you own it. Are consistent. And take personal accountability internally vs. blaming others externally. As a leader, you lose the right to feel bad for yourself. If you make a mess, it's on you to own it. Mindful leadership just comes down to the fact that you embrace and govern yourself. Fully.

And given that so many female founders—mindful people like you and me—struggle to speak up and speak out (a refrain heard in the Builder Spotlight sections in this book), here's a "little secret" from a therapist that should be helpful to us all. Nedra Glover Tawwab, a *New York Times* best-selling author and BUILD Inspector, unpacks why our voices diminish, even disappear, when our desire to please collides with difficult conversations: "You can be a 'good' person and still do things others won't like," she says. "Even when stated kindly, some things are hard to receive. So repeat after me: I can control my delivery, but I cannot control someone else's response."[1] A freeing reminder, isn't it?

Pro Tip: To keep your body free from someone else's emotional response, imagine a smokescreen or being in a bubble or on an island. You can see, hear, and appreciate their upset, but don't absorb it.

You won't find what follows next in your Harvard Business School textbook either. Transforming leadership really begins with embracing *all* of you. What is *all* of you? Glad you asked:

Mindful Leadership

Your Intelligence

Have you ever considered yourself not naturally smart or fast on your feet? A frozen deer in the headlights when someone asks you to validate an argument or substantiate a data set? Always on your heels? Even an outright idiot? I have. Often. Our society pushes the logical left brain as the standard for intelligence. Valuing scientific, empirical, analytical logic as the basis for business. It's made many of us who don't have IT, wounded, insecure AF. I'm calling bullshit. My brain is different. Yours might be too. That left part of my brain has been on holiday for as long as I can remember. For years I made up for it with high enthusiasm, people-pleasing, and work, work, work. The tough part is when you become too exhausted to be enthusiastic and too nauseous to ego-stroke. You are forced to reclaim your right brain's rights (in my case, creativity, intuition, vision). The world needs all forms of intelligence in business . . . and beyond.

Your Traits

Often "X"? (Fill in the blank: irritated, resentful, scheming, victimy, exaggerating, overpromising, immature, you name it.) If you find your operating system hijacked, chances are you have some wounding to confront. We are icebergs; around 90 percent of how we operate is subconscious.[2] The most successful leaders know this. Becoming a mindful leader means bringing to the surface, unearthing all buried character traits, everything that makes you YOU. Identify what you like and what you loathe in yourself. Then turn what was initially at odds with each other into fierce friends. Like you can be loyal, kind, empathetic, AND ALSO at times calculating, sassy, and aggressive. (News flash: Traits like aggression can be seen as "negative" when it's just us trying to get ahead or make things happen. What culture deems inappropriate behavior for women is often applauded in men.) It's not black-and-white. Reconciling all traits not only means you will no longer be at war with yourself but also that you can keep an eye on all traits, especially any slippery penguins, so they don't toboggan out of control.

Your Needs

Did you ever learn to deal with something really tough? A loved one with addiction? Divorce? An unpredictable family member? You became tough. Independent. A superwoman of sorts who can do it alllll. This may have become your identity and at times made you feel powerful. This felt *gooood*. When others seemed able to do only a little, you took pride in being able to do a LOT. Solve, fix anything. And now you find yourself having a hard time admitting you can't do something. Don't know how to do something. Don't want to do something. Gone unchecked, this might leave you feeling lonely. Like you have the weight of the world on your shoulders, with no one to help you carry a load that only seems to get heavier. That's where CREW comes in.

Mindful leadership is not about following a leadership template. This approach is for a different sort of woman no one has seen until now. Until you. You are one of one, so de facto your style won't resemble anyone else's. It will seem wonky and weird at times, especially at first. You will feel like an outlier. I've come to terms with the fact that I'm not the Anna Wintour *Vogue* type or that cool founder. Most of the time I'm in mismatched sweatpants with four-day-old hair in a topknot, using unmanicured, overexcited hand gestures.

Just do you. Do the damn thing.

BLDG BLOCK 2: Nailed It

By now, you've landed on your own intended style of mindful leadership—by knowing your form of intelligence, your traits (good and bad) and your unmet support needs. But how do you become this mindful leader? How do you practice being her on a daily basis? Feel that deep-seated wisdom, strength of character? Approach business decisions thoughtfully, from a place of rock-solid stability? That truly starts with self. The most important relationship is the one you have managing yourself, as that is where all leadership stems. Stepping UP TO the role of mindful leader demands stepping INTO you.

This begins with (and I get this sounds trivial, but it's major; life-changing) *keeping your word*. Becoming a woman of her word. And *doing hard things*. Nailing this combo boosts self-talk and drowns out the noise.

Let's start bottoms up with drowning out the noise. I've been called "delusional, narcissistic, crazy, disingenuous, manipulative," and worse. Fortunately, not all at once.

I've also been called "inspirational, visionary, magical, extraordinary, resilient, special." Some of my team even have a benevolent pet name for me: Queen G.

To be a mindful leader requires you to give up caring about what others think, good or bad. The endless chatter, scrolling through those head-scratchy comments from your social feed, or that business meeting. You'll need to override years of nasty/dumb/ugly programming and, conversely, the craving of heart-lifting, ego-satisfying, sugar-fix flatteries.

"So how do I ACTUALLY do that?" is a question I've often asked myself and one that women seem to really get on line for. One thing I learned is that affirmation can't be found externally. Not in lapping up others' positive compliments or quieting the criticism. Not in the CEO title, wire transfer, *Forbes* feature, or any of the tangible things. Precarious and conditional, temporal and fleeting, these external validations leave you even more insecure. It's an endless hunt that always leads to a vacant rabbit hole.

What I know for sure now is . . . it's 100 percent an inside job. Found in plain sight. Affirmation comes from what you reallllyyy believe about yourself, deep down. My leadership has grown the most over the years from what I've dubbed the Nailed It Golden Tool.

1. Always keep your word to yourself. Make that ironclad. Just do what you say you are going to do.
2. Don't give up when it gets hard.

This concept is so life altering that I have a gold nail head for a bracelet wrapped around my wrist. A reminder that I have nailed it in the past and now just need to nail today.

Straightforward in theory, more complicated in practice. Pinkie-promise you'll do this . . . keep your word and don't stop when things get hard. A leader is defined by how she recovers each time she hits the mat, when everyone or no one is looking. Because it does get hard. You'll want to take the subway at mile twenty to the marathon finish line. Abandon the industry completely when you have to deal with a scary situation. Skip out on the deadline or forgo the 60-Minute Prime that no one is tracking. Who will know anyway? But you will. You will know if you nailed it. You have to model leadership for yourself before you can model it for others. You have to feel good in your own skin so you aren't reactive to others' prickles or tickles. Emotionally regulate. Stay rooted in your habits. True to what resides in you. Honor what you want rather than what the world tells you to want. This is where you watch yourself. You start to respect yourself in a different sort of way from somewhere deep within.

Your self-talk transforms in this process. What you say to YOURSELF. What you call yourself in the dead of night. When you look in the mirror for those few extra beats. No longer a vinyl record of critiques caught in a groove. Or being your own relentless, toughest critic: "I should have this figured out by now," "I'm out of shape," "I'm going to be alone forever." Or no longer hearing those competition critiques that stem from scarcity, like "God, why haven't I done THAT yet?" More like: it's possible for me, too.

The more you keep your word to yourself and do those hard things, the more those cutting words get exchanged for kinder, more patient, loving words. Confidence uproots criticism. It gets quieter inside. We tolerate less, because we've learned to expect more, having fought for ourselves. As our daily dialogue with ourselves shifts, both outside approval and disapproval become moot. We stop caring. An internal resolve and relationship builds in yourself that becomes unshakable in the outside world. In the words of Reese Witherspoon: "Other people's opinions of you are none of your business." And when negative self-talk does rear its head, you know it's a sign you are stressed, tired, or spun out and need to double down on being extra loving to yourself.

Nailed it! It's a beautiful gift to learn you can trust and rely on your own word. It's as simple and as difficult as that.

You are a QUEEN, no matter if anyone can see that crown but you. Act like it.

BLDG BLOCK 3: Dream Team

No experience. No family entrepreneurs. No network. No business partner. No dedicated team. No investors.

These are things that might be running through your mind as you consider starting or scaling a business. But I'm here to say: no problem.

The foundational secret to people who achieve their goals and those who don't? A crew. A circle. Valkyries, Amazonians, warriors, wing women, construction forewomen, coconspirators, cheerleaders, consiglieres. People ready to rock with you, no matter the name. Stepping into mindful leadership means no longer going it alone. Where you believe in yourself. Believe in other people. Believe in other people believing in you. Let that wash over you. Building a team who will fight, fight, fight for you. Who will be there for you. Who will carry you. Who will help plan, harness networks, provide accountability, and hell, even throw a life jacket as needed. The saying is so true: "If you want to go fast, go alone; if you want to go far, go together."

But going it together doesn't mean it's a big operation. If you peered behind many high-profile women's tinted glass windows, you'd say, "Wait, is this just YOU?! No massive team, just one woman on a mission with light support. Same is true for everyday Builders, from the woman who was inspired by her Latina heritage to fill candle orders out of her storage locker but still managed to garner megawatt national press, to another who rolled out premium-looking perimenopause kits on a dime. Even if you are just technically a one-woman band, encourage others to grab a tambourine (or cowbell) and follow along in the procession.

We can be small and do big things.

So now it's time to meet your crew. In terms of formation—whether product or service—know this is SO individual. There is no fast-and-easy answer, as everything depends on what type of business you have, how much money you have and where that money comes from (services, product sales, outside investment, etc.), what stage of building you are at, and what your unique skills are as a founder. You create a team around these distinct variables but, no matter what, this framework can be helpful for planning:

The Crew: Self→ Core Group → Day-to-Day Team → Subject Matter Experts → Advisors

Self: All teams start with you, knowing yourself (as we covered).

Core Group: This is your most personal, immediate, and intimate circle who support you personally as you build. Dream catchers who hold your heart, allow you to offload your deepest insecurities and are trusted most with confidential business information. Think Rock of Gibraltar. And don't underestimate the power of MOM (for those of us lucky enough to have that support).

Types: Friends and family plus maybe an emotional support animal (seriously!).

Compensation: Meals, trips, massages, anything that signals "thank you."

Day-to-Day Team: This is your closest professional circle who participate in practical, day-to-day building. They help your business have a consistent presence in the market.

Types: Assistant, community manager, operations manager, product manager (if product or tech business), social media manager, website manager.

Compensation: They could be full-or part-time employees or contractors. Often a flat monthly retainer for ongoing, baseline support or an hourly fee.

Subject Matter Experts (SMEs): This is one of the best ways to supercharge and supplement your team's capabilities—subject matter experts. Assassins. The best in the business. These tend to be senior or highly skilled people for a specific project who you generally could not afford day-to-day. But they are supremely effective at performing specialized tasks (and can keep you from making costly mistakes!).

Types: Publicist, marketer, salesperson, designer, copywriter, content creator, lawyer, accountant, financial advisor, business coach, personal growth coach, and other skilled workers.

Compensation: They tend to be contractors. Typically, you invest in SMEs in a targeted way and pay them a project fee for specific deliverables or an hourly fee.

Advisors: This is how you get smart—learning from advisors or mentors who have reached the summit you seek. You know, been there, done that. With a name that carries clout, they embody success, power, influence. You can tap them informally for practical advice on strategy, business questions, introductions, etc. Or in a more formal capacity on business philosophy. (For this, you might profile or interview known figures in your industry, which can also help elevate your knowledge and credibility.)

Types: Advisors could be executives, entrepreneurs, or even celebrities.

Compensation: Think about a mutual win-win. Sometimes that just comes in the form of delivering an obnoxiously large bundle of white lilies!

If you're like me, you started a business in part because you don't like being told what to do. That's kinda the fun of building a crew. You can do whatever works best for you. That said, here are the questions I get asked most about crew.

Top 10 Crew Q&A

1. *Is there a formula to flex big while staying lean?* Many make the mistake of hiring too soon. Bigger is not necessarily better. Keep your initial team tight. When business lands, you can just use funds to surgically bring in extra help and subject matter experts instead of having full-time employees (where you must have additional business just to feed the beast). Think about a setup that allows for low overhead and limited expenses, so you don't burn through too much cash and you have a longer runway. Runway = survival.

2. *What's the best org structure?* Nix the traditional pyramid scheme with a top-down hierarchy and think more of a circular structure. Drawn with you at the center, radiating out to include other groups as needed. This allows you to be as small as a one-woman show, but also get as big as you want . . . or anything in between. You can expand and contract fluidly. Assemble and disassemble. All based on what the business requires at that time.

3. *Who should I bring on first? MVP?* Let's call her a forewoman, someone generally responsible for overseeing daily operations at a worksite and in charge of the construction crew. If you get only one person, it should be this operations person who can give you practical support and peace of mind. Think of her as your Jacqueline of all trades, boots-on-the-ground backup, and security blanket! If this person represents the traits that you just ID'd as important to you, she will have a demonstrable impact on your business.

4. *Should I duplicate or complement my skills?* Your first inclination might be to bring on a Mini-Me. But really think about complementary skillsets to you, as replication is not what you want starting out. Instead, focus on what you are *uniquely* good at (according to popular theory, if people spend 70 percent of their time doing what they prefer doing, they'll have a dramatic increase in success) and then build a team around that approach—augmenting your super skills.

This strategy helps the business do more in less time (efficiency) and increases your chances of positive return on investment (ROI), not to mention more enjoyment. For instance, if you are more creatively driven, you'll want a complementary numbers person. If you are a technical behind-the-scenes product gal, pull in a counterpoint who can make noise in the market. Or if you're not ultra-organized, get that pragmatic assistant, for starters.

5. *What are ways to save if I have a tight budget?* If you don't have many spare dollars, think about: interns, barter services, talent that is a bit green (helps your pocketbook) and, with your mentorship, has high potential. Some specific examples: bring in people on a commission basis (they eat what they kill, so to speak). To get legal counsel, you might position your company as a future big client that falls into an incubation track for now and settle on a small minimum retainer. Or to get a financial advisor, you might give a flat yearly percentage of the money managed on your behalf; in return, you get someone seasoned to advise you. Another trick? Use remote contractors from places that are less expensive (in major cities you pay a premium). Also, a compelling vision provides a financial benefit to you the founder, as it will bring people onboard motivated by things outside of money alone. And if all else fails, heck, see if your local church group or Nellie the neighbor might push up their sleeves for you.

6. *How should a crew evolve over time?* I've had different crews at different stages of growth and for different ventures. To start out, I needed to create a basic footprint or "shingle" in the market, so all my budget went toward SMEs. I found a developer (to create a website) and a designer (to help me with a logo, branding, and deck so I could pitch my business). Midway through, I found a day-to-day group consisting of a social media manager and business manager who focused on supporting me as I concentrated on getting publicity—to make my business presence known. To scale up later in my entrepreneurial journey, I found the most

valuable teammates to be highly vetted SMEs who could represent my brand with clients and potential partners.

7. *How do I locate a crew?* Freelancing websites and social media (your network really is your net worth, so ask for referrals and don't forget to check references).

8. *What sort of paperwork will I need?* Before beginning work with anyone, it's good to get foundational company contracts drawn up. Usually starting with employee or independent contractor agreements for any full-or part-time employees. Any external partnerships will need paperwork in place too: letters of intent (LOIs), client service contracts, separation agreements, employee offer letters, terms of service and partnership agreements (industry specific in sales, consulting, media, etc., all different in scope, but all attempt to define the work formally). Most tend to include a high-level understanding, SOW (scope of work), IP (intellectual property) rights, NDA (confidentiality or nondisclosure agreement), competitive limitations, insurance and benefits, liability, time line, and compensation. When starting a business, a standard contractor work-for-hire agreement tends to be the first legal document to draft. Typically, when serving as a vendor to others, they will make you default to their paperwork, so getting your own scope of work drawn up can be secondary. Bottom line: Figure this out with a legal expert.

9. *How should I protect my business?* If you don't have contracts in place BEFORE work starts with others, you can be left in a pig wrestling pit where everyone has shit on them—to the point where you can't figure out who owns what mud. Trust me, I've had to pay out six figures on lawyers. It's much better in the long run to have hard, awkward, contentious (at times), spiritual, and practical conversations upfront. In conversations, you will ferret out those who say things like, "If I help you, I'd want a cut, a piece of the action." When it comes to IP, usually you can't promise crap. You need to own it all 100 percent outright. Yourself. And if you

do decide not to, scrutinize that contract backward and forward before signing on the bottom line. Spending more time upfront with protracted contract negotiations and tough conversations ironically makes things more efficient in the long run, as you don't spend months on the back end trying to unwind and untangle or end up turtled. Try channeling Aesop's Tortoise and Hare fable from more than 2,500 years ago . . . slow and steady wins the race!

10. *Is there a leadership hack here?* The key to getting ahead is the opposite of the heads down (as in, do the work), thumbs up game we used to play as kids. The key to success counterintuitively lies not in doing more work, but in passing as much as possible onto others. And studies show that men are better at this learned behavior. While men are supreme directors and delegators, we, as women, can be uncomfortable offloading tasks and directly communicating. Generally speaking, men lead business like a general, exclusively focused on the public-facing big picture, farming out the rest. Women, on the other hand, lead like Gumby (or Elastigirl), pulled this way and that trying to do it *alllllll* themselves . . . until SNAP. Better to do a few things well and delegate the rest (if you can) by, again, focusing on your super strengths. The name of the game is delegate, delegate, delegate.

Codifying your leadership style and team structure allows you to convey your point of view (i.e., what you stand for, what you expect, and how you operate) clearly and cleanly to others. Even before you work together. Transparent enrollment from the outset creates an energy where everyone feels safe, because they know where you stand. Authentic relationships are created and trust is built over time, not immediately given.

And if you've still got a hangnail hang-up that it's reckless to have others join your parade, after all, what if it doesn't work out? Think about the journey. Will y'all have still learned and experienced something interesting? Will y'all have had a good life and a business run for many years? And what if it DOES work out?

While you want a crew, this is ultimately true: everything does come back to you, and you need to depend on you. People come and go. Money to afford a crew comes and goes. Sometimes that crew will be robust, sometimes it'll pretty much be a free solo climb. So it's important to always remember you can do a lot virtually alone. Over to leadership coach Tara Mohr to bring us home: "No one else is going to build the life you want for you. No one else will even be able to completely understand it. The most amazing souls will show up to cheer you along the way, but this is your game. Make a pact to be in it with yourself for the long haul, as your own supportive friend at every step along the way."

Builder Spotlight: Jennifer Fisher

The interviews that stress me out most are those with stylists. The day I was supposed to meet with Jennifer Fisher, I procrastinated so much when picking out what to wear (an awkward combination of cowboy boots, long floral dress, and black leather pants) that luckily I had only a few blocks to run from my NYC apartment to her Flatiron jewelry showroom, or I would have been tragically late. Once a hotshot movie wardrobe stylist, she'd made herself a fourteen-carat gold commemorative necklace following the difficult birth of her son—a personalized charm, a talisman to keep her close to him. Soon everyone on set wanted one. And when Uma Thurman wore her own customized JF necklace on the cover of Glamour, *demand took off. Jennifer's second career was born, an accessible luxury jewelry brand: hoops, ear cuffs, charms, and necklaces. And most recently, Jennifer Fisher Kitchen, focusing on food and lifestyle. She has a tight crew, including her husband as a business partner, while keeping herself (and her gut) at the center.*

On Building

. . . Does bossy mean leadership? I think I always was a leader, always had an opinion. It became a matter of learning how to use my voice.

On Breakdown → Breakthrough

. . . There are days I'm having the worst day and just want to cry and that happens; and if you say that doesn't happen, you're lying. There are days when you are afraid of something or don't want to do something or as a parent you didn't handle something well. You know, things that I could have done better, but I still learned a very valuable lesson.

On Bossing Up

. . . I'm in foreign territory. I've never built a business of this size before.
    . . . Every day something goes wrong or isn't perfect. Building a business is difficult.

On Nailing It

. . . It's weird. As a female you want to please people, but the best thing is to please yourself. And once you take that leap of faith in yourself, you own that.
    . . . And once you learn how to use your voice, there's no coming back. You become a leader. And trust your gut. If something doesn't feel right, it probably is not.
    . . . Every day we make decisions. As a female entrepreneur, you may think you are given an opportunity only once. Maybe so, but in passing on whatever it is that's not really right, something larger can come, something that feels right. It's very powerful, saying no.

On Dream Team

. . . A few years ago I had to turn over my team, which was really hard. I now know that I couldn't have gotten to the level that I am now if I'd stuck to my old ways. It's all about evolution. It's not right or wrong, not good or bad. It's learning that in order to evolve you have to change.
    . . . My good girlfriends who have nothing to do with fashion are my huge support group. It's nice to talk and learn from people outside of what we do. And those people who are mentors and building a board for the company help me learn about how other businesses are built, which is also really so beneficial.

Nuts & Bolts: What do you value in others? *Honesty.* In yourself? *Honesty.* What helps you stay sane? *My family.*

SECTION II

SKILLSET: UNLEASHING YOUR DREAM

7

CONSTRUCTION$$

Cashing In on Your Business

We all know money is power. We women won't be equal with men until we are financially equal with men.

—SALLIE KRAWCHECK

YOU MAY HAVE BOUGHT THIS BOOK WITH ANYTHING FROM A VAGUE TO A VERY specific idea for a business. Or you may already have a business and want to make it better. Regardless, rest knowing you now have a rock-solid foundation. You've leapt through the macro, foundational mindset work of Section I. You went on a self-discovery process, everything from understanding *fear* and determining exactly how you can engage it, to identifying your *breakdowns* and what you want to build; elevating that to a bigger *vision*; then designing your *Integrated Life Layout* complete with the game-changing X factor (*amplification*) to figuring out your *framing* with all those day-to-day well-being practices; finally stepping mindfully into your leadership style and deciding who you want in your *crew*.

All in all, now grounded, well-rounded . . . a breakthrough you.

You've been on the jobsite long enough for me to now bring out more micro technical tools (think buzz saw or pneumatic staple gun) and tighten the screws. What I'm about to share in Section II are business skillsets: this is what F100 brands (Nike, Verizon, NBC, etc.) and startups pay my company up to a million dollars a pop to develop, because that is what it takes to build a standout business. Of course, in their case, my team and I do the work for them, but now through the end of the book, you'll get some of the same tools and templates we use. A proven step-by-step road map. Simplified, mind you. While distilled into a book, these are the most necessary steps. This caliber of formal training—used at the highest levels of business and adapted from the big leagues—is what I uniquely have to give you.

Even if you are not initially comfortable operating this equipment (yet), don't sweat it. I just want you to get familiar with the general idea. You can always come back to these tools later (although you can muster this lift now with some elbow grease). And if you are a business newbie interested in product development (product design, prototype or proof of concept, and commercialization, i.e., manufacturing, distribution, and fulfillment), a heads-up: since developing your MVP (minimally viable product) or optimizing the one you've got is as unique to each business as a fingerprint, you'll likely want to bring in specialized experts for that part of the process. Same goes with your tech stack (i.e., the tools you pick to sell your physical and/or digital offerings). Nevertheless, for just about everything else, you'll have a strong base in place.

Now it's time to unleash your dream using micro skillset work. The actual nuts and bolts of business building. The nitty gritty. We start wide and go slow, so we can get deep and move smart. In this section, we look at finances, ideal customers, brand building, marketing and sales, powerful planning and pitching. And for the pièce de résistance, you'll ladder up to launching or relaunching your company in 2.0 form! By the end, you'll have an actionable plan and be ready to move into execution mode.

Lying around for you to pick up and put in your toolbox are more Golden Tools—my favorite, tried-and-true techniques to grow a business. While you may unknowingly do some of these things already, once you formally codify and consistently put them to use, they become transformative. Surprisingly effective in the business realm, since they are so unusual and unexpected. These proven shortcuts will give YOU an edge.

Now let's dive into an over-the-tippy-top, financial motivational tool. It involves—insert Will Ferrell's *Elf* voice—*presents*! We are hardwired psychologically (won't bore you with the research, but it's there) to seek rewards. Tangible, physical, pleasurable rewards that we can see, feel, taste, touch—that cause the brain to release a feel-good hit of the neurotransmitter dopamine. Something beyond money, which, as an inanimate object, often goes straight into our bank account, sight unseen. To achieve success, coupling a goal with a positive reinforcement (aka, the REWARD) when you accomplish it has a powerful compounding effect. That's the Risk & Reward Golden Tool.[1]

Anytime I am about to pursue a major goal, I put something on the line that I reallllllyyyyy want. It's the rabbit on the greyhound track. When the goal comes true, I get a treat. When I crazily pursued and landed a seven-figure client (risk), I got to treat myself (reward). Like a baller, I took my mom to a resort in Napa Valley, where we drove around vineyards in an obnoxious Mercedes SL550 convertible pretty much in our bathrobes. Like schoolgirls, we then went to purchase a gold bracelet (aka the reward). When I told all the women in the store the backstory (my first BIG client), they all celebrated as if it had happened to them. They told me about the businesses they wanted to start. Forget breakfast at Tiffany's. We raised the roof at Cartier. That is the joy this process brings. When someone sees you realize a dream and defy the odds, you breathe magical crystals of possibility into their lungs.

Over time, as I lassoed around more bullish thinking, I stuck with the bracelet theme and started proactively designing rewards in advance of closing a deal to motivate me even more in the material realm. In one case, a custom diamond blingfest with a woman jeweler. I promised myself I would not wear this glimmering light show unless the deal closed. Alas, the bracelet arrived and was too big, so I had to send it back to get resized. Meanwhile, I was still negotiating terms with lawyers. But with God as my witness, the final bracelet arrived on my birthday, nearly eight months after I'd started the design process, on THE EXACT DAY I received the final deal. How's that for synchronicity?

The tool also works well with life stuff. I bought a collar for a dog I did not have, months before I'd even started looking. At the NYC department store counter, the woman asked, "How big is your dog?" I held my arms up ridiculously, guesstimating about two and a half feet, "I think he will be about this big, but I haven't met him yet." Her visceral reaction signaled she thought I was one eccentric lady. But cross my heart, when I found Dash at the animal shelter, that orange leather collar fit him to a T.

This is not about conspicuous consumption. It's about reminders to self, of battles fought and won. Consider various cultures throughout the ages. Adornments varied from jaguar pelts to turquoise rings to the ornate shell breast plates of the Dahomey Amazons (Yes, this female regiment of warriors existed in Africa for more than 250 years!), but the message was the same: I came, I saw, I conquered. What we once wore were symbols of great conquests. Today this marker could be a trip to a wellness retreat, a "Go Bananas Party," chartering a boat with friends, giving the local cheese shop owner $25 and carte blanche to surprise you with triple cremes, nabbing an original piece of artwork, dunking a dozen donuts in milk with family for a taste test, ducking out of work early to head for a summertime swim, celebratory sparklers, and paper lanterns . . . whatever your baby heart desires. The women who work with me do this, too—it's a shared ritual in our little crew. My designer Marissa got a pair of very weird, but apparently hard-to-come-by boots (toe indentations and all). To each her own!

And for last-minute, mini triumphs, ALWAYS keep bubbles (alcoholic or non!) in the fridge. The point is to stop and celebrate every win, big or small. Get those brain neurons hardwired around business wins, craving more. Rewire for reward.

Now on to CONSTRUCTION$$. Business finance is the funding an owner needs to start, run, and scale her new enterprise. Before long, though, finance becomes mostly about managing in equal parts how money is made AND spent—that's the name of the game. In the upcoming BLDG Blocks, we will focus first on the best business model, so you know how to structure your business and monetize your offering. You'll then develop a number of foundational financial statements to see how successful your business model is in practice: the forecast, budget, and P&L (profit and loss statement). I'll also walk you through a simple tool that'll help you prioritize how to grow, so you can expand into places that will have a big payoff for your business.

So. Go. Get. It. Serious money. The goal here is to have that rich business and life combo platter you crave, so your crew can have rich lives, too. But for now, please place that champagne bottle back in the fridge. I need you dead sober for this next part.

The three BLDG Blocks you will get in this chapter are:

1. Best Business Model
2. 6 Money Managers
3. Future Fortune Matrix

BLDG BLOCK 1: Best Business Model

One of the top questions from aspiring entrepreneurs or those already in motion is "Should I seek out funding?" With a few caveats, unless the ONLY way to scale is through intensive capital injection, I usually reply with a blunt *no*. Raising money should be a last resort.

Here's the thing. We can generally build businesses without investors. We can bootstrap. I've never taken a nickel for any of my businesses. And for those who do? One founder I know wished she'd just done it herself. Another calls it her biggest regret. Fundraising takes up precious mental space and emotional energy. Then, managing investors is another part-time job, where usually objectives don't align (often short-term growth is prioritized over long-term customer satisfaction). Deciding not to raise capital, or even think about it, can be a powerful decision. This model runs in stark contrast to the scale-at-all-costs messaging foisted on us by the media. And it's in contrast to the predominantly male venture capital narrative that "You just need to be a founder with vision. And then you will get capital to hire your people, create your proof of concept, and branding." Right! Just go be a pre-profit founder without being cash-flow positive for years! Huh? I've yet to meet many women with that story.

The typical reality for most women entrepreneurs starting out is more like . . . worked at a loathed corporate job, started a business on the side, finally summoned the courage and became burned out enough to quit said job, used personal savings to set up the business, bubble-gummed and Scotch-taped early days, called on favors, did Google searches ("How do I start a business?") up the wazoo, asked for advice, used freelancers and digital tools to create the basics (logo, social media graphics, etc.). From there, the business became a tad profitable, which allowed for bringing on an itty-bitty day-to-day team. The result? A small business where the founder owns 100 percent of the equity.

Consider this BIG PICTURE backdrop: 70 percent of small businesses are owned and operated by a single person, without investors. Because opportunity in entrepreneurship is not equal. For underrepresented founders, there is not only systemic gender bias, there is also racial bias in funding: venture capital, traditional banks, etc. (means smaller loans at higher interest rates and difficulty getting business lines of credit). Lack of access to capital adversely impacts revenue generation and slows growth. It's outright sobering and downright infuriating. Across the board, studies show 64 percent of new small businesses are launched with less than $10,000 and microbusinesses with around $3,000 to start. And while statistics are flying around, know that 90 percent of women-owned businesses have NO employees, and most that do have employees have only one to four. Yes, you read that right![2]

Now back to funding. For the record, while I'm a staunch advocate of bootstrapping and not taking outside funding, if you want to go for others' gold, go for it. Outside investment might come from friends and family, angels in your network, bank loans or lines of credit (capital you can draw down if you need to), crowdfunding platforms, business accelerators, grants (which you don't have to pay back), or even venture capital (if you think you have a billion-dollar idea). There are experts who write about finding investors who can help point you in the right direction and step through the gauntlet I laid out. Ultimately, each funding "formula" is distinct. So whether you invest hard-earned personal savings with additional expenses floated on a credit card or tap something from the outside, it's smart to allocate a dollar amount you want to invest now as you make plans to either start or scale your business to the next level. As you make this commitment, watch parts of you scream. You'll think about the trip you could go on or the bag you could buy with that money instead of putting it into your business, the more fun things you could do. The resistance that comes up is a normal part of the process.

Seed money will go further if you keep purse strings tight. Lean and mean. And the ingredient you need most—sweat—is absolutely FREE. Persistence is also free. Creativity is also free. It's helpful to think: How could I do this on a dime? Create an inventory list of assets you have at your disposal. Walk your space, look in your closet, and open drawers. You won't believe how much you actually own. If you're in the First World, chances are you have: a computer, phone, a subway pass or car, books, hell, even pens and paperclips. This will make you focus on what you HAVE vs. what you don't have.

To get even leaner and meaner:

Start your side hustle and discreetly ramp up your business, while you have a job with stable income. It's generally best if you can stay gainfully employed until your business is throwing off enough cash for you to live safely. I created mine secretly for well over a year while working on my website and meeting with potential clients.

Seek new employment in the same industry as the product you want to launch. This accelerates your learning curve on someone else's dime where informed baby steps are taken around product development.

Not to be a wet blanket Debbie Downer, just know that while the barrier to entry is low, the failure rate is high: half of all businesses are gone by year five.[3] If you strolled down Main Street to ask owners about those abandoned storefronts and why they failed, one of the main culprits you'd find: poor business finance. Basic understanding of finances and cash-flow management. The default attitude often is "I'll tackle finances when I'm actually making a lot of money" or "It's too soon. I'll figure it out as I go." Don't get me wrong—that approach can be freeing. Initially. But there will be big, scary corners to navigate and going the distance requires diligent financial groundwork. You'll need to push to be the exception to stay afloat. But let that be a motivator, not a detractor. The odds may not be in your favor, but the business world has not met YOU yet.

So how to get at that cash money? To the actual "business" of your financial business? Start with defining your business model—one that makes money. At a high level, a business model is the way your company generates revenue and profit—it factors in revenue sources, customers, products, financing, and other operational considerations. Think of the primary levers as the cost to create and deliver your product or service vs. the price you sell it.

So what the heck are you going to sell? Your product will vary dramatically based on your type and category of business; but regardless, it's important to focus on one core offering or product to start. For a product business, you might have a prototype or proof of concept (sample of your product) or for a service, a sales sheet or pitch deck.

At this point, you just want to know *what you're going to sell* and *for what price.*

From there, at macro level, to create your business model, you'll want to start by defining your business structure.

Business Structure

B2B: Business to business (i.e., selling your product/service to other business customers)

B2C: Business to consumer (i.e., selling your product/service to consumer customers)

B2B2C: Business to business to consumer (i.e., selling your product/ service to other business AND consumer customers)

From there you'll want to think about the means of how you actually make money.

Income Types

Active Income: Income that comes in direct proportion to the effort you put in. It's usually limited to the amount of working hours in the day and requires physical and mental participation (examples: direct sales, salaries, bonuses, commissions etc.).

Passive Income: Income that can grow over time without incremental time or expense. It usually generates money while sleeping and after an initial upfront physical and mental investment, requires no more participation (examples: subscriptions, rental income, affiliate marketing, advertising etc.).

Finally, you'll want to determine your primary sales channels. There are new ways to generate sales cropping up every day, but here's a smattering of ten common ones.

Sales Channels

Direct Sales: Network of salespeople who sell directly to customers via presentation or one-on-one demo. Examples include: Avon, Dell.

Franchise: Owners purchase a stake in an existing model with a defined brand, process, and product. Examples: Marriott, Starbucks.

Freemium: Services given away at no cost with the promise of future transactions. Examples: Spotify, Audible.

Subscription: Customers pay a recurring fee for use of the product or service. Examples: Birchbox, Netflix.

Broker: Buyers and sellers are brought together and charged a fee per transaction. Examples: Expedia, Stubhub.

Advertising: Advertisers are charged a fee to target your audience with their products or services; this can also include sponsorships. Examples: YouTube, *TIME*.

Add-On: Core product has a low price, but numerous extras drive up the final price. Examples: Gillette, Keurig.

Low-Touch: Low cost and/or no-frills service to pass a low price on to the customer and drive volume. Examples: Walmart, JetBlue.

Pay As You Go: Usage is measured and customers pay only for the amount they consume. Examples: Con Edison, Verizon.

Auction: Products and services do not have a fixed price; instead, customers independently assess their value, with the final price determined by competitive bidding. Examples: eBay, Sotheby's.

Say for example, you are a real estate agent, then you would fall into the broker camp. If you are a digital marketing expert, you might make money from subscriptions. A media company? Then advertising could be how you'd likely charge. A jewelry business might be direct sales. And a rare sneaker or collectibles business might be run as an auction.

Regardless of what business model is right for you (structure + income type + sales channel[s]), you'll want to make sure you maintain as high a margin as possible, either through process efficiency or having features that drive significant value, allowing you to charge more. Price testing what the external market will allow while optimizing your costs is the name of the game.

Why does all this business model stuff ultimately even matter, you may wonder? One word: options. Something as simple as my paying for a cab ride or a dinner check could land me in a cold sweat. While others had real means. This created disparity in relationships. While it was never stated, someone else was always more powerful, and I was the one making concessions.

I've been broke; I've surfed the couch and showered at the gym to skip hotel bills. I've walked until my feet blistered to save on cab fare, switching shoes outside the building, strutting in as if my chauffeur dropped me off, fresh as a proverbial daisy. I shot twelve videos in one day, memorizing all scripts and feverishly changing wardrobes in the bathroom, because I could afford only a one-day shoot. I've been known to use coupons, manically study a credit card statement to dispute even the smallest charge, do free thirty-day trials just to watch something new or take the 6:00 A.M. flight because it's $60 less. As success mounted, threats also mounted. I once was so buried in legal bills to make a dispute go away, I resorted to acquiescing, to placating, even putting on a higher-pitched, more saccharine, sugary-sweet voice. I imagine you may have already been in similar corners. And once you've been there, you know: it's better to have, in equal parts, fly-free and F-you money.

Having money means you choose the customers, relationships, experiences; they don't choose you. Money is freedom and freedom is success, I've learned. It is the freedom to choose who you love, and when to leave if you need to (shouting, "And you can keep the furniture," as you slam the door for effect on your way out). It is the latitude to say no to a client or job you don't like. To choose what you want to do every day. And it's the ever-present knowledge that you won't be governed. It is a feeling beyond any fleeting experience or possession. That means having *dynamite* money. And I want you to have boatloads it.

Money is first about survival. Then it's about defending what you've built: your exposure, liability, and profile. To finally complete, total, wind-in-your-hair freedom.

BLDG BLOCK 2: 6 Money Managers

By my thirties, I had become a self-made multimillionaire. And it wasn't from skipping avocado toast or the Starbucks line. It was 100 percent because I broke out on my own as an entrepreneur. It was through entrepreneurship that I got to a place where I could live in a penthouse apartment in NYC with river views, buy a Range Rover all cash on the spot, reward myself with a diamond tennis bracelet for a job well done, collect artwork, take my mom on first-class trips from Cape Town to Paris. Sounds like rich, bougie spoiled stuff, but I never took investment. I F-ing earned every cent.

There are six money managers to be financially strong: three money mindset tricks (not taught in *fi-Nancee* [insert fancy-schmancy accent]) and three money skillset tools. So now for getting your financial mind right. Where the mind goes, money flows. That comes from getting real comfortable with all things money: expecting it, negotiating for it, fighting over it (when necessary), managing it, and knowing when to spend exactly how much of it. Often, the biggest roadblock is emotional. As women we often overlook or downright run away from money. But to keep your business baby alive, finances have to become your bosom buddy.

1. Identify As a Filthy-Rich, Self-Made Woman

I'm talking megawatt rich. As you look over your floor plan and think where-oh-where to stash that safe, here's a quick sidebar. A number of years ago my money coach, BUILD Inspector Barbara Huson (who charges an ungodly amount per session, but I guess that is fully on brand for, well, a money coach), said to me, "You keep chasing powerful men with money, but what if YOU were the rich one? What you seek in someone else is what you seek in yourself."[4] I guess I walked straight into that exposed beam.

It's true. I was a bit of a gold digger, because I was a goal digger (cheese-licious saying aside). It wasn't about the money per se, but what I watched it unlock. The price for that key? Owning my power. Amplification. Becoming the sort of woman who commanded money. Demanded it. Delivered value for it. Felt worthy enough to charge for it (oooff). Until then, someone else was always the proverbial powerhouse in my house, and that felt like the natural order. This went way beyond boyfriends. It was with clients, too.

That "aha" about reframing my identity would soon change everything. I *COULD* be the powerhouse. I could be rich. Driving around 90210, one of the few women who actually bought the house all cash. (Un-fun fact: up until 1974, women were generally required to have a male cosigner on all loans.[5]) So why not you? Watch your material world shift as you start to see yourself as filthy rich. As megastar Priyanka Chopra says about her marriage, "Financial independence is paramount. My mom always says that when a woman is financially independent, she has the ability to live life on her own terms."[6]

2. Welcome Awkward Negotiations

Given that most female founders operate their companies on a razor's edge barely hanging on by their press-on nails—where sickness, lack of client payment, caretaking, overextending on a purchase order, not properly sidestepping a bad deal, or something as simple as spending a few too many dollars per hour on a contractor can teeter your business over the edge into oblivion—it becomes exponentially more important to push for money upfront, so you have a reserve down the line. Men seem to have the luxury of being a bit more unbothered about money.

After I started my company, I had coffee with the ultimate vest bro and I just remember sitting there marveling at how carefree he seemed. His big plans, his lack of concern about money, his lollygagging . . . who even has time to walk that slowly?!? Fact of the matter, it's more stressful for us, as our fallback plan if our business doesn't work out isn't usually a cushy-coasty sort of thing. That's why negotiations are so critical for us. In short (and, in the short term) let them be itchy-sweater awkward. Get comfortable being uncomfortable. Stay in that messy middle. Your future _____ [fill in the blank: bank account, kid's new cleats, *Eat Pray Love* trip] will thank you.

Two tips that help even seasoned negotiators: (1) Negotiate on behalf of others. Research shows that women negotiate more assertively for others than for themselves. When I negotiate, I still find it helps with a tough ask to think about doing it on behalf of my team or my future daughter Georgia Grayce, aka Gigi, and her college fund. (2) When making an ask, let it hang in the air without justification, and then play the pregnant-pause waiting game while someone decides if you're "worth it." For a boost, channel actress-entrepreneur June Diane Raphael. She told me: "You need to ask for the money and let it sit. Pick up a pencil. Take a sip of water. Don't fill the space. Don't care about likability or seeming like a nice person." This is when insecurity and self-doubt will come roaring in. You'll think, *Do they have someone better? Did I ask for too much? Did they track down that awkward dance video of me from five years ago and I should actually be apologizing right now?* But your ask will be well informed. (Translation: even if you don't have financial fluency and are a bit tongue tied, you will be able to back that shit up.) Power, autonomy, and agency aside, if you are going to have a business, money is straight-up important, so practice the "pregnant pause."

3. Spend? Save? Find the Flow.

Everything is interconnected, as we covered in the BUILD Integrated Life Layout. The finance area is both fed and depleted by all other areas (e.g., business, relationships, environment, spirituality, passions, and health). To ensure everything stays in balance and harmony, we need money mindfulness. That means strategic saving is just as important as strategic spending.

Let's say all the profit from your business currently goes into your personal life. Which means no safety net in your business. Imagine, for example, you start killing it with your new business. Large wires start funneling into your account. And because of how exciting that is, you start spending. New car, clothes, jewelry, the "finer things." At the end of the year, the balance sheet reads net zero with nothing to reinvest back into your business, despite having done SO well. Or maybe it's more benign. Your life partner believes all of the money made in your business should go back into the communal pot, not understanding a business is not like a salaried position where technically you can spend all of your take-home pay. Neither scenario is ideal.

On the flip, you take all the money from your personal life and put it into your business. Which means no safety in your personal life. You could be so bullish on your business, you leverage your home, your kids' college fund, take out extra lines of credit, hell, sign year-long contracts with vendors, which you don't know how you'll pay for in a few months. You hear a lot of guys say, "Put it all on the line! Debt is how you build a business! You can always declare bankruptcy!" But this gets pretty dark if you only have your own uncalculated hand to blame for putting all your chips in the center of the table. Let's not play that game, either.

What to do? It's all about flow. Emotional and mental regulation. Discipline. Strategically managing the mix: spend on standard household expenses (rent, mortgage, food, etc.); reinvest a significant amount back into your business; save some for a rainy day and splurge on a shiny risk and reward.

The paradox of spending? To others (or to yourself initially), it might seem foolhardy, self-indulgent, or reckless to spend on life areas like childcare ("After all," someone might say, "you're an entrepreneur at home; you can keep an eye on the kids") or housecleaning ("You can do loads in between calls") or a massage ("Wait, what?"). But actually, trying to do it all in order to not spend money is the reckless (shortsighted) route. Because the trade-off is then you don't have the time or energy to invest in the big picture, which is what gives your business safety, security, and success in the long run.

This spending paradox also plays out in business investment. At times you may want to spend the most when you are making the least. Use a downturn to reinvest back into your business. Make decisions based on the macro forecast of what can be made in aggregate over a few years, not based on the micro of what you're making that particular month or quarter. The difference is that when you do "overspend," it's intentional. Like when you bring on a high-level contractor to tune up your brand or buy an expensive piece of equipment so you can create inventory even when no revenue is coming in. You do it judiciously. It is calculated. All implications considered and never outsized to the point where it could ruin everything.

And, given life's interconnectedness, always keep your personal finances tidy. It's helpful to make a list of what needs attention like all those unopened, unpaid bills stacked on the kitchen counter or that pesky credit card with a nauseatingly high interest rate that you have not paid off. Keep business and personal finances separate with a distinct business checking account and a business credit card. Before I had the means, I decided to get a platinum credit card to connote success when paying. And did that card ever get action! I used it to host just about everyone I could at a swanky restaurant back-to-back. Getting there bright and early, I would snag the corner "power" table, all the waiters knew my name as a regular, and for the price of my one cup of coffee and a cup for each guest, I was able to really flex, Godmother style. I also always keep $100 in my wallet. As they say, think and grow rich.

When I sat down to chitchat with Eva Longoria, she really stressed money hygiene: "What women don't realize is your credit is your passport into the financial world. And so whether it's student loans, credit card debt, or a mortgage, whatever it is, clean it up. You cannot start your business without that passport, right? Without a record of paying on time and a little debt so they know that you are actually buying and paying for things. That's the biggest mistake I see, so clean it up."

* * *

The preceding three non-MBA mindset tricks pair perfectly with the next three MBA skillset tools to get your money in order. Think of a money tree: the more time, attention, watering, and whispers of encouragement, the more your finances will flourish. To avoid losing the shirt (or bra) off your back, you'll have these technical tools to make more informed decisions, to place strategic bets, and to optimize how to manage and adjust your business to meet the market.

Specifically, the forecast, where revenue comes from. The budget, where operating costs, overhead or expenses such as crew team salaries, benefits, office space, products, hardware, etc., are tracked. And the P&L, with the profit that is left after losses are deducted. Let's start with a couple of simple definitions:

A forecast tells you **WHERE** your business is going.

A budget tells you **WHAT** you'll allocate funds to in the business.

A P&L tells you **HOW** you're tracking against your goals.

Let's dig in more.

4. Forecast Fundamentals

A forecast is an indication of where the business is actually going, its financial trajectory, and it is an input into the budget. A forecast estimates your future revenue and expenses, usually based on historical performance (if already in business) or category performance (if just starting out). The key function of a forecast is to set and monitor your business's performance, so that you can minimize shortfalls and maximize emerging opportunities. It's a fluid document, updated monthly or quarterly based on business changes.

5. Budget Basics

A budget is about smartly allocating funds to drive growth. It estimates the revenue and expenses you expect over a certain period of time, and gives you a baseline for expected revenue and expense against what you're actually bringing in. The key thing a budget enables you to do is allocate resources to line up with your strategic goals and targets. Typically you reevaluate a budget once every year. If starting out, the budget you draw up might include a website, domain name, LLC incorporation, rent, and furnishing a physical space. Over time, standard expenses include salaries, contractors, marketing and advertising, office supplies, travel, and more. If you are also working on your overall health to better support your business, be sure to set aside funds to work with a coach or trainer, too.

6. P&L Statement

A profit and loss statement (which you'll also sometimes hear referred to as an income statement) summarizes revenue and expenses for a given period and shows a business's ability to generate profit either by increasing revenue or reducing costs. It shows how you are tracking against your goals. The first real step to creating a P&L is tracking and categorizing every revenue dollar that comes in based on the lines of business you monetize, as well as every expense and cost you incur. Make sure to work with a bookkeeper and accountant to ensure your company is properly tracking everything for tax purposes and you adhere to annual state and federal filing requirements.

And if all of this financial stuff leaves you scared to start, just do it scared!

BLDG BLOCK 3: Future Fortune Matrix

Ruffling some feathers and pigeonholing various pecuniary money practices is our takeoff point for this one: Are you the ostrich . . . clueless, avoidant, your head buried in the financial sand? The peacock . . . flashy, strutting about, overspending, distracted from debt? The sparrow . . . busy (gotta get those twigs!), accumulating, never spending just nestling that egg

away for a rainy day? Or can you see yourself as the hawk . . . survey-
ing the landscape with a savvy, strategic eye to the future, diving after
targets with precision and accuracy at up to 150 miles per hour? Soaring
sky high, flying smart, carrying the fundamentals in your talons (forecast, budget, P&L) while also winging it, riding the market thermals that
ebb and flow (like what I did there?!). Spoiler alert: you want to be the
hawk. Nothing bird-brained here.

Back to those all-important financial foundations. One of the most
common mistakes entrepreneurs make early days is they focus on too
much too soon. Diversifying their businesses so they have multiple lines
of business before they have profitized one. Too many products, too many
offerings, too many messages, too many marketing channels, AND too
much BTS development before sharing anything. (I've got this last one
as a scarlet letter: sometimes toiling for years to get a product perfect
before even testing it in the market.) This means fragmentation of time,
money, and energy. Why do we do it? It's more fun to constantly be creating and also subconsciously makes you feel safer because you've got
so many irons in the fire. You know, no core offering can ever be fully
rejected because you're never all in on any one thing. It's definitely at-
tractive to follow each shiny ball, but we need to honestly ask ourselves
before we do: is my core business functioning and profitable first? Make
sure you're expanding, but at the right time.

Take Sarah Kauss of S'well who did it well, founded on the mission
"to rid the world of plastic water bottles." S'well has monetized its simple product into a varied and diverse line, appealing to customers of all
tastes, realizing that the path to growth relied on allowing their customer to express their individuality. Instead of falling into the trap many
brands face of diversifying too quickly, S'well stuck to its single product
(metal water bottles) and diversified by offering three sizes and dozens
of designs. By keeping the main technology consistent across the board,
S'well focused their efforts efficiently and, as a result, is now doing over
$100 million in annual sales with the average customer owning more
than five bottles.

Once your business is going really well and you have more active income—customers love what you're selling, you're making steady revenue, keeping costs down, and you're growing month over month—it's a good time to start thinking about where and how to unlock new growth opportunities. You do this through passive income, in other words, other lines of business that require initial upfront investment but then don't require your day-to-day involvement. Great business owners know that to be sustainable in the long-term, they can't stick with the status quo forever. They look for ways to grow revenue and reach new customers, and there are multiple ways to do that through markets and products. This is how you build real wealth.

There is a tried-and-true tool to help identify growth opportunities: the Ansoff Matrix. With it, you'll prioritize what new products to launch or what new markets to enter, and how to maximize return on investment (ROI) while minimizing risk. This matrix from business school will help you weigh the risks associated with each decision and then help you identify the best path forward. Typically, businesses use the tool annually to determine if improving or adjusting their offering makes sense.

The framework consists of four growth strategies that are measured across two dimensions: whether the *market* you're looking to grow in is new or existing, and whether the *products or services* you're trying to grow are new or existing. Considering and pursuing these paths simultaneously is the mark of a progressive business and can help ensure long-term survival.

Ansoff Matrix

Market Penetration is the least risky of the strategies and consists of selling your existing products into existing markets to gain higher market share. This strategy is commonly pursued when competition is intense, or when there is additional market share up for grabs that can be gained with low investment. A tactic commonly used to penetrate markets would be increasing marketing activities, which could generate higher sales among new and existing customers.

Product Development is slightly more risky, as it involves introducing a new and/or improved product into your existing market. You can use focus group results, trend analysis, or research and development to identify new product opportunities within your existing market. This is usually pursued when the business has good market share and a well-established customer base, and that market has reached saturation, thereby necessitating new products in order to grow (and market penetration is no longer viable).

Market Development is moderately risky and involves introducing your existing product or service into a new market, either by finding a new use for the product or service or by adding new features and benefits. This is a great strategy for companies that have a proven product or service that could derive similar value with a slightly different positioning from an adjacent customer group, geographical location, or gender where the offering is not currently competing.

Product Diversification comes with the highest amount of risk as it involves introducing a new, unproven product into a new market you may be unfamiliar with. Diversifying your portfolio requires very clear expectations and success metrics and an honest assessment of whether it's worth the risk. Diversification should be pursued when the above options have been exhausted or when you have a first-to-market, research-proven concept and a high tolerance for risk.

So how to use this tool? It's actually pretty simple as you'll see in the DIY exercises. You'll look at your opportunities, figure out how risky they are, and then chart a path forward.

Make those money moves. Go get that money, honey.

Builder Spotlight: Rebecca Minkoff

Fashion designer Rebecca Minkoff could have focused solely on her name-sake brand—trendy clothes, shoes, and handbags and her iconic Morning After Bag, which rocketed her company to success. But as she says, "Sure, it's nice to leave a legacy of a product but as I'm getting older I want a legacy that's so much greater." She cofounded the Female Founder Collective (FFC), a network of businesses led by women, supporting women. Her goal: a directory of twelve million female founders to use for shopping and services! As a cofounder the expectation is you are experiencing hockey-stick growth. So when Rebecca and I grabbed coffee in NYC, I was struck by how pragmatic and honest she was about finances. To keep her business alive, she made personal sacrifices, no matter how painful. Sometimes that meant taking a bare-bones salary. Sometimes that meant muscling through when the business was floundering. No financial risk, no reward.

On Building

... My mom recently dug through my old kindergarten paraphernalia and a teacher wrote a note, "Rebecca is a natural leader." So maybe I was born a Builder, but I've no idea.

On Breakdown → Breakthrough

... Strong women get a bad rap. Where if you're tough, it's like you must be on your period. Or be a diva. But you still have to lead with strength. It's not all about sappy, propitiative encouragement. It's a different skillset and should be admired. You must also let go of what others think of you—good, bad, or indifferent—and lead your way. If you don't, in time it will either tear you or your business apart.

On Business Model

... At Christmas one year we were celebrating "cheers to the year" with a department store for our partnerships and growth. Then they said, "There's a recession coming up. How do you lower your prices to accommodate your new customers' ability to spend?" But how do you do that and stay alive? We didn't want to take any quality out of the bags, so what were the smart things to do with supply chains, order times, lead times, and negotiations to cut out in some instances at least $200 at retail for each bag? No margin for us—not making or losing money, either. We went back to factories and suppliers and negotiated. Three months went by, and there was no change in sales. "We're really screwed," we said. But the next year we grew 546 percent.

On Money Management

... At first when I started, my salary was, "Rebecca, add up what you need for rent and your food. Good. That's what you're going to make, $23,000 a year." And then it was no bump in my salary later when we brought on our first president, because that's what was needed to grow. No bonus in six years was among the hard choices I had to make.

On Growth

... What I doubt has changed over the years. I already know what it takes to scale a business. When I started the Female Founder Collective, I struggled with how to give value to women, so it's worth their time to join. With my doubts, I had to say to myself, *Shut up. You can do this. People are excited about it. You just had a call from big business expressing interest, so get over it!*

Nuts & Bolts: What do you value in others? *Integrity.* In yourself? *Persistence.* What holds you back? *Exhaustion.* Keeps you sane? *My children.*

8

FIXTURES

Finding Your Customers

Just follow the yellow brick road.

—GLINDA THE GOOD WITCH

GET READY TO CHANNEL YOUR INNER DORA THE EXPLORER (OR DOROTHY FROM *THE Wizard of Oz*) to investigate the world around you. Daydream. Follow your curious nose. Leave that desk where you "should" be. We are not robots to be tethered to mission control stations. Technology drains. Life inspires.

A few years into my business I found myself craving more time outside. I felt cardinal-sin-level guilty each time I escaped midday to wander while emails bounced around. So much so, I'd often wear a baseball cap and big black stealth shades. When I'd get back to my desk, I'd try to spit-smooth out my hat hair. Just as I was about to buckle down and course correct, something remarkable happened: for the first time I could objectively see this "pointless" exploration was not only making me, as a founder, more creative, but my business insights were growing sharper. In turn, my business strengthened and started to resonate more with customers. So instead of ditching this practice, I decided to formalize it. Bring it out into the open. Meet your next Golden Tool. And prepare to dishevel that hair!

With the Hard Hat Golden Tool, you can step out of the expected. Explore. Anytime. Hell, 11 A.M. on a Monday. Take a hike under the furious red-oranges of a winter sky. Eat at a restaurant where the owner longingly talks about the origins of her spun-clay-pottery place settings. Peruse a Georgia O'Keeffe exhibit, the simplified dresses with white trim she designed while painting stark desert landscapes. Drive "aimlessly" for a half hour before work, blasting country music and daydreaming (don't forget the road!). Or embark on a remote, solo "think retreat." Just the other day, the GM of my company told me she'd rather go for a walk outside than return to the office to just think. To get out into the world, you'll need to give yourself permission to be unrealistic, unavailable, and unproductive.

It may sound self-indulgent (like someone looking for an intellectual alibi to validate ADHD tendencies), but out-of-the-box exploration— that is, casually exploring the world OUTSIDE your business—helps inform what's going on INSIDE your business. This process is similar to what the art world calls "process painting," which celebrates the process itself, the act of discovery, not the white-knuckle "outcome painting" most of us learned in elementary school. Trend lines come from strange places. New insights happen when things bang up against each other, at the intersection of ideas.

Take fashion designer Stacey Bendet, who told me that she's most influenced by artists. She's constantly releasing collaborations using images from painters like the late Keith Haring and Jean-Michel Basquiat (think street-art wearables like graffiti leggings). Forget only being a subject matter expert in one category; think mass exposure to other fields for cross-pollination.

This immersion into art, food, music, nature, books, and beyond is where you make contact with what is happening in culture at large, category dynamics, and lives outside your own insular existence. The more you can plug into both the pain points and the places where people want to go and grow, the greater the chances your business can serve and lead. Meaning you understand what people want and so can take them where they want to go, to the promised land. The real reason for all this exploration is to get to know your customers. Taking an expansive, wide Grand Canyon gaze will help identify which customers will want your product or service. From there, you can position your brand to speak to your target customers' exact wants, needs, and desires, then reach them in all the right places. You can also incubate new business ideas to match new customer demands.

And here's the bonus: this focus on customers will just flat-out make YOU a more interesting creature. The breadth and depth of your lived experience often determines the quality of your circle (including customers). Chances are, people don't want to know all that much about your business. They want to know about you as a founder. What do you like to do (hobbies, habits), what do you believe (values, vision, inspiration), what have you learned (theories, facts), where do you like to visit (places). In nature, this would be the difference between being a fractal fern—the same identical pattern repeated over and over again—vs. a murmuration of tree swallows with thousands of birds flying together in a whirling, ever-changing pattern. Sky painting. Doesn't the second just sound like more fun?

In the previous chapter, you learned how to make and manage your money; but to even have money you need . . . customers. Customers who buy from you! This will give you a solid framing from which to build the rest of your business. It really sets the stage. Coming up you can expect a bit of a roundabout journey to look at trends and competitors, with the end goal (aka the most important part) of identifying your business customer. Things here will really start to take shape in terms of what is happening in culture, your business category, and with those all-important customers. So you can see how to stand out from your competition and emerge with a clear picture of your target, which will vastly simplify developing a product or service, creating a brand, then marketing and selling it.

Simply put, you'll eat, sleep, breathe what's up in the world, up in culture, and up in customers' lives. You should even try talking to strangers, something your momma once warned you to never, never, ever do!

The three BLDG Blocks you will get in this chapter are:

1. Trendspotting: The 3 C's
2. Competitive Assessment
3. Customer Target

BLDG BLOCK 1: Trendspotting: The 3 C's

For trends, to seek out the three C's—culture, category, and customer—let's imagine this scenario: you're dropped in rural Maine, hard hat in hand, to open a restaurant. To get the general fixtures in place for your new venture, you might want to first dive into *culture*, everything from the current state of the economy to employment. To get a sense of the *category* you are operating in, in this case food, you'd visit some local farms, find out what's in season, what's not represented but special to the state (like lobstah and fiddleheads), and research dining trends (is spending projected to grow or flatline?). Finally, get to know some potential *customers*. You might head to the farmers' market, or set up a pop-up meal in an Airstream, asking questions like "How do you want to feel when you go out to eat? What would you pay for dinner? How many courses?" Some might suggest dishing out a totally new menu of beer-battered cod with a chilled IPA. Others, relishing the last blissful bite of tiny, wild just-picked blueberries and crème fraîche, might tell you not to change a damn thing. (Hint: these are your people!) From there, *Beautiful Mind* style, you reflect on all you've learned. A juicy customer target profile starts to emerge: a forty-something, high-net-worth female foodie living in an urban city who seeks farm-to-table seasonal ingredients and longs for connection so badly she would travel hours just to eat at a restaurant that feels like a best friend's kitchen.

Through this sort of trendspotting, you get a general understanding of what's happening in the world at large (culture), which leads to getting an understanding of what's happening in your market (category), so finally you can drill down to what's happening in the lives of real people (customers). Along the way, examining trends both qualitatively (insights/opinions/themes) and quantitatively (numbers/data, no more library Dewey decimal system, thank you internet). You'll find the last two categories below—competitive assessment and customer target—covered in the next two BLDG blocks of this chapter.

In short:

Cultural trends show **WHAT** is happening in the world.

Category trends show **WHAT** is happening in your category.

Customer trends show **WHAT** is happening in the lives of customers.

Competitive assessment shows **HOW** your business can stand out.

Customer target shows **WHO** will purchase your product or service.

Let's take a little field trip to further explore the 3 C's:

Stop #1: Cultural Trends

Overview

High-level view of the world using IRL observations (your Google Earth view).

Directions

General exploration of the world. This is about taking the temperature of the world in real life, seeing what the media is writing about, what stories are being covered, what the country is moving toward and away from. Is it a time of change? (People spending, chasing down dreams, courageously moving to new cities, embracing unconventional lives.) Or is it a time of fear? (People saving, deferring parenthood and home ownership, overwhelmed by the stressors of modern life like inflation, rising cost of goods, layoffs, election cycles, etc.).

Points of Interest

News, media, books, art, food, nature, politics, religion, economy.

Destination

You emerge with a general feeling without drawing any conclusions or making direct connection points to your business. Think input without output.

Stop #2: Category Trends

Overview

Midlevel view using digital research (i.e., Google Traffic).

Directions

Analysis of your category. To do this market research, you'll define what specific market you're operating in (like hair care, beverages, consulting, fashion, content, etc.) and then examine the trends within it. This is about understanding the forces that are driving change in your industry, such as innovation, new market entrants, increased (or decreased) regulation, and changing tastes. Where do experts predict the category is heading? What are competitive brands in your category doing? What seems broken in the category?

Points of Interest

Category reports on future market trends (i.e., Mintel), data forecasts, market research databases (re: market size, growth rates), industry trade reports, annual reports (from a company's website under investor relations), analyst reports, press, past advertising, and thought leadership from key opinion leaders.

Destination

You emerge with a detailed, well-informed, evidence-based perspective.

Pro Tip: If you have not started your business or are a bit unsure about whether you are even in a viable category or if you uncover headlines in your category research like "Dying industries include _____ [<name of your category>]" or "_____ [<your category>] is expected to decline X%," you might want to take a pause. Seeing words like "dying," "decline," "volatility" are not good indicators. Your business is rarely the exception to the category. It moves with the market. So best to pick one trending up to ensure your business is on terra firma.

For help validating, you might want to do these two market-sizing exercises:

TAM (total addressable market): This is the revenue available in the markets and sales channels you're operating in. You'll also want to know the total market size, which is all revenue available in your market segment as a whole (this will be bigger than the TAM) and the total revenue opportunity will be the share of the total market for which you can realistically compete (this will be smaller than the TAM). To find information on growth rates, you can use market research databases or trade publications in your industry. Also use what you know about the industry's prices, distribution, and units sold, especially for the biggest competitors in your market.

Market Lifecycle: This helps you determine if you are in an emerging, growth, mature, or declining industry. As a rule of thumb, an emerging industry is a very new, young industry growing at less than 5 percent per year; a growth industry is one growing at over 5 percent per year; a mature industry is one where growth has slowed to less than 5 percent per year; and a declining industry has had negative growth for a prolonged period. The ideal case is to be in a market that is growing, doesn't have that many competitors, and low barriers to entry.

Stop #3: Customer Trends

Overview

Close-up view using a hybrid approach: IRL + digital (i.e., Google Streetview).

Directions

Deep dive into the lives of your potential customers. This is specific research into what your target customers are seeking in terms of product, price, and positioning. Hone in on what they want, why they want it, and what they would be willing to pay for it. (Without leading the person, seek brutally honest, unbiased feedback. It will save you in the long run.) What are the pain points with their current product or service? What do they think about your product? What would make them trade one for the other? What would they like to pay? Do they even want what you are going to sell? The best brands are constantly doing consumer research, getting feedback on new product ideas, marketing campaigns, and even piloting small batches of product with testers to tweak things before production. This is not a one-and-done process. The insights you glean are an ongoing part of product market fit.

Points of Interest

One-on-one interviews, blind taste tests, focus groups, ethnographies (watching people in their natural habitat use your product), or maybe even ask strangers you meet in line for coffee. Supplement with desk research like social media threads, blogs, Reddit boards, internet polls and surveys.

Destination

You make contact with your ideal customer to the point that they go full technicolor dreamcoat on you. They divulge insights that can inform all facets of your business, including the unique strengths to lean all the way into. What emerges is a clear picture of who will buy what you are selling.

To find your customers, you might put your idea up on social media and see if you can find twenty people who are interested. Then really go down the rabbit hole to get a sense of their profile (who they are, what they follow, who their friends are, etc.). If you can get them to engage with you even more, like each other's content and send messages, maybe they will even become your early adopters. It seems daunting, but remember, all you need is to get a clear picture of the person who is likely to buy from you. It only takes a few to get started!

To double down, customer trendspotting can also really help drive new product development, as well as refinement of existing products. In testing a small batch of product in the market, you can see if people actually want to buy it or what they would want to change (around formulation, etc.). Say, for example, you're selling a lip gloss kit. If you produce a small batch and it goes in twenty-four hours, you know you are on to something. Time to produce more. This research helps you optimize the price, the target, the product, everything. The more distinct you can

make your product through customer insights, the better. It just needs
to be a minimally viable product (MVP) to test and learn.

Examples of MVPs tested with customers:

- Shoes: Tamara Mellon had bespoke cobbler Jimmy Choo create
custom shoes
- Cookies: Tate's Kathleen King, age eleven, baked cookies for her
father's farm stand
- Shapewear: Sara Blakley cut feet out of pantyhose for Spanx
samples

For a well-known, REAL example to bring all three trends home, I
learned in speaking to Jessica Alba that she used this trends approach to
launch The Honest Company. As a new parent, her priority was "making
a happy, healthy home for loved ones . . . a need that wasn't being met."
She began with a hard look at a common problem in society: the use of
chemicals in household products. After meticulous research, speaking
with scientists, sizing up competitive offerings in the market, studying
customer behavior, and looking at recent trends both in home products
and adjacent industries, her company was launched. She and her team
had two fundamental insights: using products with clean, safe ingredients isn't inherently expensive; and driving larger-scale environmental
change can work by lowering the price point on clean products. Just
think: these trends, backed by data, rocketed The Honest Company into
a billion-dollar business.

If you take nothing else away from this BLDG Block other than the
more information, the better (osmosis!) and that some of your best "doing" will come from just "thinking," that's a win. Through exploration,
you gather as much information from as many distinctive vantage points
as possible. Unique ideas come from allowing yourself the freedom to
roam, have conversations with strangers, and sometimes ditch out on
work just to walk the earth.

BLDG BLOCK 2: Competitive Assessment

"My product is so groundbreaking, I have no competition." WRONG! Everyone has competition. Now that you have a thorough handle on the market (culture, category, customer), it's time to key in on what makes you different, what sets your business apart, so you can "go hard in the paint" highlighting those strengths. And identify weaknesses. Sometimes if you can't fix something, it's smart to feature it (for example, instead of apologizing for being small, you might say, "We are intentionally small. If you want a mighty giant, we are not for you."). See what we did there?

Customers make decisions based on a unique combination of factors, including price, location, service levels, and product features. And not every customer chooses alike. This is why competition exists. Knowing your competition and being able to assess competitors' strengths and weaknesses will allow you to develop a strategy to gain that all-important competitive advantage, seizing that white space. How can YOU fill in market gaps? You'll want to be aware of competitors but not distracted by them. Put those blinders on, never look to your right or left, and never, never, never speak ill of or even acknowledge them as a means to sell. It's tacky. It's trivial. It's low energy.

To start, let's identify your direct and indirect competitors so you can consider ALL the ways that customer needs can be satisfied.

Direct competitors offer similar products or services and target the same exact customers and market.

Examples:

- *New York Times* vs. *Washington Post*
- Nike vs. Adidas
- McDonald's vs. Burger King

Indirect competitors offer slightly different products and services that satisfy similar needs. These are also known in business as "substitutes."

Examples:

- *New York Times* vs. *Vogue*
- Nike vs. Converse
- McDonald's vs. Sweetgreen

Once you compile a list of direct and indirect competitors, you'll want to perform a SWOT analysis, which shows strengths, weaknesses, opportunities, and threats. Not exactly an art project, but paper and pencils (they can be colored) are required. This is a framework for identifying internal and external factors that can impact the viability of a product or service and assess competitive strengths and weaknesses across positioning, marketing, price, location, availability, offerings, customer service, and product features.

SWOT Example (Imaginary Business)

Strengths: Growing adoption of products. Alignment with recent customer trends.

Weaknesses: Only one product line. High price point is prohibitive for general market customers.

Threats: Low barriers to entry. Readily available access to resources with low differentiation.

Opportunities: Target high-net-worth customers. International expansion.

The goal is to identify what competitors' objectives are in market, and what strategies they're using to achieve them. You can look at their recent actions, including: marketing (how and where they market can reveal a lot), product portfolio, targets, revenue, profitability, growth, pricing, and market share. A few potential areas to examine: What is their messaging and what marketing channels are they using? What are common themes they talk about? What sort of content are they putting out? What is the tone? Look and feel? What seems to be performing well? Are they trying to maximize short-term gains or seem patient for longer-term profits? Are they innovative? Are they trying to be top dog in one market or are they developing new markets for existing products? Are they reducing prices to quickly gain share, or giving customers a reason to pay a premium? What is their distribution? Does it seem like they are preparing for a market shift? What's their long-term play (growth, acquisition, merger, IPO, etc.)?

Once you know what your competitors are doing, you can hone in on how you're different, how to outperform and charge into those white-space areas where you see growth opportunities. A SWOT analysis is especially helpful when you want to dive deep on one competitor (to either replicate their strategy or go head-to-head). Some patterns will emerge that point to the brand's strategy and key drivers, so you can counter with your own strategy or, better yet, use it to catapult or leapfrog your company as a smaller brand to where they are already headed. Usually a bigger brand's strategy is based on lots of market research (aka trend-spotting across culture, category, and customer), as well as lots of costly trial and error in the market, which means it's probably more informed and proven. When you are starting out, there is no shame in a bit of a copycat strategy; over time you'll evolve to a place that's unique to you.

Soon that dream headline will be yours: "_____ [<name of your startup>] Takes on _____ [<category leader>] in the Ultimate David and Goliath Story."

BLDG BLOCK 3: Customer Target

Working in advertising, I was taught to think of customers as nameless, faceless data points aggregated to exploit. Talk at them en masse. Make them feel like they need you, couldn't live without you. But we are going to flip that script. Customers can be so much more than cardholders. They can feel like friends whose lives you want to make easier, richer, more frictionless, more inspiring, more abundant: ultimately, you want to help them take up space in the world, so they can become their highest, best selves. What they want, need, desire, and seek is to be seen and heard. Create with them at the center. For this, they will love you. Be loyal to you. Weather ebbs and flows with you.

It's a living hell (or shall we say a vague, gray, murky place to be) when you don't know who your customers are on the other side. If you stand for everything and everyone, you stand for nothing and no one. It's the difference between having no idea who's in the room and making a generic pitch vs. knowing exactly who's there, tailoring a very specific message so they don't just walk, but run to purchase when given the CTA (call to action).

Your customer guides all decisions and allows you to be laser-light focused in your product design, brand strategy, and marketing. You'll want to understand not only every nuance and detail of who they are, but where to reach them (in what channels) and what matters to them. The better you understand who you're targeting, the more you will fulfill unmet needs, and the faster you'll see growth. They should feel real enough to where their 3D hologram can weigh in on everything from a new product formulation to a marketing campaign to social media copy (a bit creepy, but!). At a certain point you'll be so in sync with your customers that they will love nearly everything you create for them.

So let's nail down who it is that you're trying to sell to, whether that's people (B2C) or businesses (B2B). Likely, you'll need to focus on only one of these, but in some cases, you'll have both targets (B2B2C), in which case, look at both. Every business has a primary target, which is the group of people or businesses most likely to buy your product or service. They should be easy to locate, be willing to try your product with little marketing, and help you generate enough sales to meet targets and turn a profit. For illustration purposes, we try to give a lot of dimension to bring this target to life, but of course not everyone in the target will share everything in common. That's A-OK.

Do you have a B2C business? If so, who is your customer?

If you're targeting people (B2C), start by understanding basic demographic characteristics. Like age, gender, household income/employment, geography, race, and education (i.e., millennial, female, making six figures, grad degree, NYC-based, etc.). You then can layer on psychographic characteristics like personality, attitudes, values, interests, and lifestyle (i.e., what they like to do, use, follow, buy, wear, watch, someone who owns a dog, considers self a trendsetter, prefers organic, etc.). This will help you develop a robust image of who will buy from you.

Do you have a B2B business? If so, who is your business customer?

If you're targeting businesses (B2B), the same tenets apply in figuring out your target, but the attributes are a bit different. You'll start by understanding basic characteristics of the businesses you're trying to sell to, including company size, industry vertical (specific niche), function (activities carried out by the industry) and geography (national, regional, or local footprint).

Once you have your target group, you may want to give them a name: the Everyday Athlete, the Health Maven, or even an actual pet name like Daisy. Just a shorthand so you can speak less clinically and more familiarly. You'll also want to double-check your target has enough scale (you won't make money if your target is so specific that only one hundred people are left). At the end of the day, your ideal customer will usually reflect you as a founder. So if it feels personal, deeply personal, all-the-way personal, that's a good sign. This shared connection will foster a sense of intimacy between you and your customers, and in doing so, enable your business to flourish.

Builder Spotlight: Tina Brown

I first met Tina Brown when I was a delegate at her Women in the World Summit. At lunch I sat between DVF and Queen Noor of Jordan. Because that's normal! Tina has always struck me for her ability to see trends before they happen and her unapologetically competitive nature. That's mis-

sion critical in cutthroat media where, if you're not first to break a story, you're last. Tina has had an award-winning career championing women on the frontlines of change, as a journalist, author, and editor-in-chief (of Vanity Fair, The New Yorker, and the Daily Beast).

On Building

. . . I am a born Builder and often get bored when the job is done, and I feel I am becoming a steward.

On Breakdown → Breakthrough

. . . It was tough for me when *Talk* magazine closed. I felt many talented people had followed me to the promised land, and then I couldn't bring it home. I broke through by returning to my roots as a writer with *The Diana Chronicles*, which became a #1 *New York Times* bestseller.

On Trendspotting

. . . Among my greatest risks was leaving *Vanity Fair* when it was super successful to edit *The New Yorker* when it needed a revival. Another risk was leaving the *Daily Beast* to launch Women in the World in my late fifties.

On Competition

. . . What keeps me going and building is what a friend calls my "deranged vitality." I have always lived life to the overcrowded fullest.
. . . Doubt is my way of life. Courage is overcoming it.

On Customers

. . . I know it's time to leave someone or something when the light goes out of my eyes when I talk about them or it. And when I feel my vitality sapping at the prospect of seeing them or doing something.

Nuts & Bolts: What do you value most in others? *Tenacity.* One thing you're afraid of? *Asking for money.* What is your biggest vice? *Spending it!* Something you wish you would have stopped sooner? *Sugar in my tea.*

9

FINISHES

Positioning Your Brand to Stand Out

The difference between a good product and a good brand is emotion.
—Jen Rubio

THERE WILL BE TIMES—WHETHER YOU ARE STARTING AN APPAREL LINE, MEDIA agency, or the latest, greatest innovation in skincare—when your business mission will seem hauntingly, dauntingly impossible (even if your idea aced the Heart Test). But trust, as the saying goes, that you are a match for your mountain. There is a knowing inside you, a calling, that will carve out a suitable space based on your aptitude, capacity, and capability. Our purpose on Earth, among other things I believe, is to first find that mission and then go about the business of living it. That is the real business we are in.

So now for a semi-jarring story to demonstrate what a powerful mission can do (hope you're not eating) . . .

The Fall. It was two A.M. on the fourth night in my new home in LA. My new company's brand mission "to put women at the heart of business building"—to spotlight self-made women with agency in all their multidimensional glory—had landed me here. I'd decided to go all in: put my money where my mouth was to self-fund my new business, then ante up a bit more by buying a home in a place where I barely knew a soul until this mission was realized. Not exactly part of my life plan at forty. But I digress . . .

Back to that night. My stomach seized. You know that comedic food poisoning bit where you broker with the devil, offering up your first-born? Somehow, in an impressive demonstration of force as I fainted (vasovagal syncope), the full weight of my body managed to unhinge the toilet seat. When I went to get up, I hit my head on the porcelain underbelly, which knocked me out again, my head now bleeding. When I finally found my feet, it was 911 to the ER. I was proud that in my bleary state I was able to negotiate bespoke stitches over staples for my head wound. Released (alone) to recover (alone), I returned to what looked like a *CSI Miami* crime scene. Smears of blood on my freshly painted China White walls. (Not the walls!) After meeting with a neurologist for an evaluation that eclipsed the SATs, it turned out I had an acute traumatic brain injury (TBI) that had impaired my prefrontal cortex, which manages "CEO" executive functioning. Long of the short, I lost my brain for a bit.

The months that followed were bizarre. Like an astronaut in space, I watched my brain in a suspended state of animation, struggling with language, moods, sensory overload, ear ringing, seeing stars, searing headaches, crushing fatigue, and at times the inability to even understand what people were saying. Physical exertion has nothing on cognitive fatigue. All sorts of quirky irregularities, too:

I sent a pillow to the wrong address since I forgot where I lived (my bare-bones new home was more like a monastery than a recovery oasis).

I went to a barre exercise class and did every move opposite.

I was honked at to "walk faster" and told the two-hundred-pound guy to F-off and that I'd knock his lights out. He recorded that lovely exchange.

I would stare for terrifyingly long stretches of time at inanimate objects.

Here's why I'm telling you this crazy story: Had the brand mission for my new business not been as strong as it was, I would have taken my little SOLD sign and flipped it back to FOR SALE. I had the perfect excuse to tuck my cotton tail between my wobbly hind quarters and hop right back to the East Coast. But surprisingly, the accident only fortified my resolve around this mission. I even force fed my neurologist a professional bio and speaking reel, so he could understand my "baseline." "You have to get me back. I have important work to do," I said. This mission of mine pulled me through at record speed. A complete recovery.

The fall was a call. I watched myself fight for myself, fight for my business, fight to make a comeback. That's what a powerful business mission can do. But it doesn't have to be this extreme. A compelling mission can simply make you pop out of bed first thing Monday morning feeling like you've got the Energizer Bunny's battery.

Imagine finding something you care enough about that you want to pick up a damn metaphorical sword and fight for it. And make others want to fight alongside you.

You've learned about finding your ideal customer. Now it's on to creating a brand customers love, so they pick your business over the millions of other options out there time and time again. In this chapter, I will help your business become a brand, a beacon, which means it will stand for something that is distinct and meaningful in their minds. Here we will polish up the key elements that form a brand: mission, strategy, and campaign. Once you have a brand, you will have erected something much bigger than yourself. And that's pretty wild!

The three BLDG Blocks you will get in this chapter are:

1. Brand Mission
2. Brand Strategy
3. Brand Campaign

BLDG BLOCK 1: Brand Mission

What's intangible, amorphous, can't be seen but can be sensed?

A brand. A business becomes a brand when customers identify it as something unique, when it feels distinguished from other products or services, when it becomes "known" for something. Brand signals value to customers that gives them a reason to pay the price you're asking. Without a brand, you are just a product, a commodity, a thing. Or at best, a random assortment of logos and slogans.

Brand development is the process of creating a distinct identity for your business while keeping in mind your target customers so it can be easily communicated and marketed. Now for simplicity's sake (and believe me, my brand-building training was much more nuanced—gnarly, in fact), here's a streamlined process for startups. At the most basic level, a brand consists of three things: a mission, a strategy, and a campaign. Those brand elements are then driven through every aspect of your business: voice and tone, storytelling, visual identity (logo, color, etc.), product, personality (key traits), packaging, pricing, marketing campaigns, sales materials, customer service, you name it. That experience is consistently reinforced across every touchpoint. Consistent reinforcement leads to consistent sales. Everything works synergistically.

For the first part of the brand, let's start with your mission. It involves a mother-daughter dynamic but with all the best elements of that dynamic. Remember how you created an all-encompassing vision supported by your Integrated Life Layout, which included seven life areas, including a business—all sharing the same purpose, intention, and values? Well, the brand mission for your business is basically Vision's daughter, birthed from and born out of the same DNA, always looking up to Vision for direction. Vision is the guiding light, the destination; every step your business takes brings you closer to that full life you seek. This Vision is the holistic dream of the future, of tomorrow, that you want to work toward. To get closer to realizing it, your Brand Mission guides your business actions in the present. Brand Mission can accelerate your vision faster than any of the other life areas because of everything it tangibly provides.

The secret? *An enemy.* To get at a big, ownable enduring meaningful mission requires a big, hairy nasty problem to push up against and take on. A mission should seek to fight something back, some injustice, wrongdoing, area of bad governance. Think about a wrong that needs to be made right. What are people not getting that they deserve? What needs to be changed? Who or what is taking advantage? Problems have very sharp edges; they are relatively easy to define and generally carry real discomfort for people. The pain of the problem has urgency, because customers want problems solved rather than lightweight opportunities addressed.

Ideally, your business becomes the Joan of Arc heroine fighting against this given problem. It seeks to become an equal and opposite counterforce. Interestingly, the bigger the foe, the greater the likelihood you'll become a big business. For it takes might to meet might. Think about that final scene in *Star Wars* where the Jedi Rey must use her white lightsaber to repel Kylo Ren's dark light. So let's find that enemy of yours and call it out!

Enemy Examples
- Unrealistic beauty standards
- Toxic household products
- Machines taking over human jobs
- Dropped phone service when people need connection
- Performance athletic training without recovery
- Multiracial women not represented in fashion
- Mental health wait times
- The outlandish cost of eyeglasses

You get the drift. Once you have an enemy identified, you can craft your BUILD Mission Statement, which defines the purpose of your business. A mission is a moon shot. It's the internal promise your business makes, its stated reason for existence. Articulating what the business will be, create, go, and do. It's a commitment to company culture, employees, and partners. And in return, it's the creed by which those who work for or associate with your brand govern themselves. In the best case, your business will provide so much meaning it will exist a hundred years from now. Actively protected, defended, and reactivated when it dims. A legacy that will outlive you.

To craft your brand mission, think about what your company will do to make the world a better place—and in doing so, provoke and combat the enemy you identified. What would be your internal facing declaration? It should be inspirational as hell, goose bump–inducing, while also being something you can authentically own and work toward. Clear, direct, muscular, strongly opinionated, decisive, articulating the truth as you see it without caveats or posturing. If it doesn't make you uncomfortable, push it further. Above all, it should make you come alive.

Oh, and one sentence is all that's needed for the Brand Mission!

Brand Mission Examples
- BUILD (my company): To put women at the heart of business building.
- Google: To organize the world's information and make it universally accessible and useful.
- Netflix: To entertain the world.
- Starbucks: To inspire and nurture the human spirit—one person, one cup, and one neighborhood at a time.
- Airbnb: To create a world where anyone can belong anywhere.
- Casper: To awaken the potential of a well-rested world.
- Disney: To create happiness for people of all ages, everywhere.
- TED: Spread ideas.
- LinkedIn: Connect the world's professionals to make them more productive and successful.
- Dove: Help all women realize their personal beauty potential by creating products that deliver real care.

Let's bring this BLDG Block full circle with an e-commerce shoe company example:

- Enemy: Bad shoes. People are born with healthy feet and develop painful foot issues because the shoes they're wearing are often too small, too narrow, or have heels that are too high.

- Brand Mission: Foot health. To share our heartfelt belief that comfortable, healthy footwear is important to everyone because it can contribute to happiness and well-being.

Note: You'll find me citing big brands as examples a lot—you know, Fortune 100s this and that—it's because I think it's always best to learn from those who've created enduring, successful legacies and because it's the brands I have the most experience strategically unpacking. That said, out of respect for my clients' privacy I've used brand positioning examples that are in the public domain. You'll also notice startups are not really included in this book because niche brands are not universally familiar, and I wanted to make sure the examples register.

Know you landed on a powerful mission when it elicits polar extreme reactions. It means you've tapped into the light. Some see the change you want to make, and it resonates because it exposes the dark. Some see the change you want to make and find it threatening because they like the status quo.

Powerful Missions

1. *Please people.* You will see giddy hand clapping.
2. *Piss people off:* You will be sighed at, scoffed at, sneered at.

The mission for BUILD was enthusiastically embraced. One woman was so inspired she quit her job and launched her own agency practically overnight; another moved from Brazil to the US to scale her work. It was also vehemently rejected. On social media my fire created fury: "Why limit yourself and alienate men?", even the odd threat that I should be "hogtied" . . . One industry leader called my proposition "uninvestable," adding: "Just google me. You can watch videos of me talking about where the market is heading . . ." Practically pinching my cheek with his smug thumb and index finger as he left the room.

At the end of the day, as a leader, your main job is to protect the mission. The soul of the company. No matter the noise.

BLDG BLOCK 2: Brand Strategy

Now for a look at brand strategy. This is where we figure out how to position your company externally. Here we think customer-centric. Customer, customer, customer. Your brand positioning will be the space your company owns in the mind of a customer and how it is distinguished from competitors. To gain customers, especially in a saturated market, your brand will need to take a unique position relative to the competition: this is how to set your business apart. Brand strategy is directly linked to developing customer loyalty (i.e., which customers stick with you through thick and thin), brand equity, and purchase intent by being perceived in customers' minds as differentiated, meaningful, and authentic. In the long run, these are the brands that have market traction. Your connection with customers' minds (and hearts) drives the positioning of your company.

So you've already got a business mission statement for your brand. Great. Now for brand strategy, which describes *what* your business will provide for your customer and what key differentiators your product or service has from your competition. To turn this into a positioning formula, you'll have a single customer-facing statement about what you do best, supported by three competitive differentiators (unique selling points) that resonate with the customer.

These unique selling points (business school abbreviation = USPs) are also known as value propositions, reasons to believe, or points of difference. These are the *emotional* and *functional* differentiators of what your business does better than your competitors. To emotionally connect: what do you want people to feel after every encounter? What makes you different? How are you making your customers' lives easier, better, more fulfilled? And what are those functional, tangible claims around unique features and benefits you can make? How does your product or service work faster or better, longer or stronger (i.e., a fully turnkey solution, a lower price, a better customer experience)?

The research you gathered in chapter 8 will help inform how best to pull away from the competition so you can see those white space opportunities and what your target customer wants. So now for pulling it all together in the form of a brand strategy.

Brand Strategy Formula

Single Statement of Value (What your customer wants)

Supported by Unique Selling Points (What your company does best relative to competitors functionally and emotionally)

Example, BUILD (my company)
- Brand Mission: To put women at the heart of business building.
- Brand Strategy: A business is the vehicle to your highest, brightest life.
  - Bold content
  - Heart-led community
  - Practical tools

Example, E-Commerce Shoe Company
- Brand Mission: To share our heartfelt belief that comfortable, healthy footwear is important to everyone because it can contribute to happiness and well-being.
- Brand Strategy: Shoes that are a home for your feet.

- Durable
- Sustainable
- Perfectly handcrafted

Example, Electric Car Company
- Brand Mission: Accelerate the world's transition to sustainable energy.
- Brand Strategy: The only stylish car that can go from zero to one hundred in three seconds without a drop of oil.
  - Quickest acceleration
  - Longest range
  - The safest cars ever

Example, E-Commerce Company
- Brand Mission: To be Earth's most customer-centric company. Earth's best employer and Earth's safest place to work.
- Brand Strategy: Find and discover anything you might want to buy online.
  - The lowest prices possible
  - The best available selection
  - The utmost convenience

Brand Strategy Self-Check

Differentiated: Will this positioning set your service or product apart, allowing you to drive a wedge between your company and competitors? Differentiation allows you to reframe the conversation and compete on your own terms.

Meaningful: Is this positioning something customers actually care about? Make sure it's meaningful based on the trends identified and what customers want.

Authentic: Can your company continue to own this position over time so it's not on shaky ground and does it allow you to embrace your core brand essence? To endure, the new brand position must be defensible.

Even if your existing brand strategy feels rock solid, try fine-tuning it at least once a year (same goes for brand campaign, which is up next). The more pointed and precise you can be, the more effective you'll be at becoming a brand that people come to know and love.

BLDG BLOCK 3: Brand Campaign

Whether you can spend $25 or $25,000, you will still likely be competing with a brand shelling out $25 million to win over the exact same customer. What helps you take on the big boys? A brand campaign rooted in a BIG Idea.

Nike. Apple. Coca-Cola. Patagonia. Disney.

Here's the thing about a campaign: the most iconic brands never talk overtly about their product or the competition (even though their strategy was informed by that info). They tell a story about what they stand for in the world. Nike isn't focused on the air cushion they innovated in their sneakers or the fit of their sports bra relative to Under Armour. Instead they celebrate a BIG Idea: athletes and anyone who moves their body . . . Enter the slogan "Just Do It." Apple isn't focused on their computer. Instead, their BIG Idea focuses on the concept that those who believe they can change the world actually do . . . enter "Think Different," one of the greatest campaigns of all time. There are no product shots, no talk of the computers' best-in-breed technical features, no talk of price at all. Instead, the campaign focuses on historical figures who famously dared to think differently, those who, had they been alive, would have used an Apple: Albert Einstein, Martha Graham, Rosa Parks, and Pablo Picasso. The campaign is powerful because of the emotion it conveys. It was not a transactional advertising call to action, but a call to creation. A brand campaign, pure and simple, that transcends selling.

A campaign brief should answer one question: What does your business stand for in the world?

- Dove: Real Beauty
- Coke: Share a Coke
- Always: #LikeAGirl
- Google: Year in Search
- California Milk: Got Milk?
- De Beers: A Diamond Is Forever
- Procter & Gamble: Thank You Mom

Now to bring branding together with all three—mission, strategy, and campaign.

- Brand Mission: To put women at the heart of business building.
- Brand Strategy: A business is the vehicle to your highest, brightest life.
  - Bold content
  - Heart-led community
  - Practical tools
- Brand Campaign: Build. Back. Better.

- Brand Mission: To share our heartfelt belief that comfortable, healthy footwear is important to everyone because it can contribute to happiness and well-being.
- Brand Strategy: Shoes that are a home for your feet.
  - Durable
  - Sustainable
  - Perfectly handcrafted
- Brand Campaign: Ugly for a Reason

Example, Electric Car Company

- Brand Mission: Accelerate the world's transition to sustainable energy.
- Brand Strategy: The only stylish car that can go from zero to one hundred in three seconds without a drop of oil.
  - Quickest acceleration
  - Longest range
  - The safest cars ever
- Brand Campaign: Forward Without Footprints

Whether it's with this brand campaign or with marketing, social media, or a pitch down the line, everything you do as a brand is really about storytelling. People don't just buy what you create; they buy why you created it. If it solves something for you, chances are it will solve something for someone else. The three most important words in brand building are customer, storytelling, and, of course, profit.

For a peek behind the curtain of brand campaign development, in the early days of my own business I had grandiose illusions of being Meryl Streep in *The Devil Wears Prada* where someone would roll out gorgeous campaign mood boards for me to choose from. But it went more like this: I'd get out a whiteboard or sheets of paper (the bigger the better) and markers (the more colorful the better) and messily brainstorm with someone from my crew (you can also do this solo). I'd feverishly throw out all the random ideas I'd been chewing on. Then sheer panic would set in. "This is a mess. I've got a million things on the wall. How will I boil it all down?" (The best campaigns are also the simplest.)

So I'd keep working it, distilling it—more clarity coming while walking down the street or in the shower—until eventually I'd hit pay dirt. From there I'd share the thinking with friends so they could weigh in (big brands use focus groups and take months to do this work), before bringing it out wide. One such campaign for my own business mentioned above was called "Build. Back. Better." It was intended for anyone who wanted to make a comeback after feeling knocked on their tush (the product I was selling was a digital course). Note this same down-and-dirty process works for mission and strategy crafting, too.

Basically, your brand campaign is a powerful slogan and a summary of your BIG Idea—in essence, a one-line rallying cry, a call to arms, along with a general description to bring the idea to life. The campaign statement could be your brand strategy one-liner tweaked to customer language or perhaps something more timely, related to what is happening in the world (i.e., "Just Do It" or "Think Different"). And the summary is the story of what your brand is solving for and stands for in the world (i.e., this campaign will celebrate everyday athletes or those who had the courage to think they could change the world). It can speak to the positive impact your product or service will make. If you want it to grab people's attention, you might poke at a cultural problem or that enemy you identified earlier. Think *heart over head* and get creative. A brand campaign is all about enrolling your customers in a highly emotional narrative that is big enough to create a movement.

If you are impatiently tapping your toes thinking, *What a waste of time, why bother, I'm just a single person starting a company,* well, frankly, you need a brand anthem more than anyone.

When you can't outshout, outspend, outdo, you need to outsmart.

Being an underdog and having a sharp POV makes you stand for something in the world, which helps you punch above your weight. A brand campaign puts your company's message out there and in doing so increases brand awareness. And the best part is no one sees you coming. There is a reason the biggest brands in the world are constantly optimizing brand campaigns based on new trends and customer preferences: it's to stay relevant. They invest A LOT of time and money here. (I know, because they've hired my firm to the tune of beaucoup bucks!) This F100 tool is also one of the unique things I can give you that very few other startups will have, and that's another edge.

For your own brand campaign, think about something you want to get proud and loud about.

Builder Spotlight: Jenny Baik

Jennie Baik is the former CEO and cofounder of Orchard Mile, a company that enables busy women to shop their favorite contemporary, luxury brands all in one place, online. A next-gen retail strategist, Jennie once headed strategy for Burberry. As for Orchard Mile, it is like a digital shopping street with over 220 designers' sites, and with My Mile, shoppers have the tools to curate their shopping experience, updated real time with new arrivals and sales.

On Building

. . . I have always been a Builder, but in the past preferred to go it alone. However, the biggest lesson in my career is that most of the time you can't do it alone. You need other people. Not only do they bring their talents, time, and energy but also they look out for your blind spots—and push you to be a better Builder.

On Breakdown → Breakthrough

. . . I remember coming out of undergrad post 9/11, and it was hard to get an internship. I got turned down by nearly every iBank on the street and ended up crying at an IHOP over pancakes in front of my dad. But then after knocking on a few more doors, I did eventually land one. Now raising funds for a new company, I find that talking to venture capitalists is kind of a similar experience. Sometimes it's just not a fit, but rather than taking it personally now—of course, sometimes I do feel a little bad—I just shrug and think, *Well, your loss, buddy.* My bravest moments are when I think my number is up, no more cards to play. I've stayed up nights wondering how I was going to pay my team. I've kept my cool when disagreements have happened among our team. I've gone on stage to talk about Orchard Mile in front of thousands of people right after a deal fell apart and was told, "You will never make it."

On Mission

... At a startup you're making a bet that this new thing you create will be better than a job you could find out in the market. And there's no truer test of one's resilience than trying your hand at building something.

... Personally and professionally, you need to be truly committed where there is no easy escape hatch. Whether it's a startup that you're bootstrapping or deciding to get married, those are all "risky" endeavors.

On Strategy

... Most entrepreneurs, despite popular lore, do doubt themselves ALL THE TIME. It's hard not to, as some other person is raising more money, getting better partners, etc., etc. You have to stop comparing yourself to stories that may not be true anyway. The inside story may be very different. There's a lot of overpositive fluff in startup land.

On Campaign

... If you teach someone something, that's the most valuable use of your time.

Nuts & Bolts: What do you value most in others? *Optimism, kindness, discipline.* One thing you're afraid of? *That a little more effort would result in an exponentially better outcome.* One thing you'd change about yourself? *Becoming more comfortable asking for help.*

10

LANDSCAPE

Digging into Marketing

Delivering a service that consumers feel truly connected to . . . and love to organically share and talk about is the most effective form of marketing I know.
—KATRINA LAKE

REMEMBER THOSE EASY-BAKE OVENS FROM GROWING UP? THEY WERE A GATEWAY drug of sorts, teaching us we could make just about anything, by way of super rudimentary tools like hot light bulbs and premade mixes. Well, if your creations were enough to make another five-year-old squeal with delight, the same should be true for us grownups. With the Bake & Take Golden Tool, you can prebake, premake just about anything. Create a visual feast for the eyes, leaving virtually nothing to the imagination. An undeniable spread of delicious proportions where folks are salivating so hard they need to eat what you've whipped up. Right. Now. You don't ask potential eaters to pay for your ingredients or the time it takes you to throw around that flour to whip up that pie. You invest your own cash and sweat equity to come to the table with everything already done, so all they have to do is take a baked goodie. Think sidewalk bake stand.

While this tool works especially well for marketing, the applications are endless! To break it on down, the Bake is the content you create, and then another party Takes it to use. The secret sauce: you do ALL the work upfront, the concept is fully baked, so ALL someone else needs to do is just take it off the "shelf." For you the baker, the benefit of "giving" your content away is you might get some additional marketing or PR exposure, greater distribution, etc. Which results in more sales and money. For the taker, the benefit of "taking" content is they can put it to use in a variety of ways without having to take on any risk. Like distributing something new and different on their existing media platforms. Given the proliferation of content, businesses just straight up need to feed the beast.

When you have a great idea, you don't wait for permission. Who cares if you don't know what will come of it! Potential partners are blown away by this tool because it demonstrates your belief that what you create will be in the world, with or without them. This combination is as disarming as it is appealing. And if they don't demonstrate real hunger for it, you'll take your easy-baked goods to someone else.

Ultimately, it's not that what you create is all that unique or even special. It's just that humans are super busy, burned out, inundated to the point of near drowning and everyone has a hard time envisioning . . . well, most anything. We all do better seeing ideas in living color. Anyone will be all ears if you've put in the elbow grease upfront to develop an idea, it's already in the can, produced, a fait accompli, and all they need to do is hit release. And light it up!

Some of my Bake & Takes have been voraciously consumed. For a business magazine I created a fully turnkey digital course (including video lessons with downloadable worksheets). Because I had already done the upfront heavy lifting, they agreed to market my course to their audience of twenty million readers and in doing so helped my course reach 125 countries. On a smaller scale, I served up a dinner series to Google with a built-out theme, location, and guest list. They underwrote and marketed that series (my logo next to theirs was worth its weight in gold). For Nike, I took a major financial gamble to deliver an entire brand strategy for free. Even rush-ordering hard-to-source female-founded products for the pitch meeting. It moved the conversation from "Do we want you?"

to "When can you start?"—a new business win I was able to tout on my website. That's the magic.

Another example. In Hollywood, I saw that an opportunity existed to fund, produce, and distribute content vs. waiting years for a distributor to greenlight a TV series. So I proactively shot a pilot—which involved securing locations, talent, and scripts—that was then scooped up by Universal Studios. Beyond those marketing partners, this is how I teamed up with the likes of *Fortune*, *Forbes*, *Adweek*, NBC, Vice, Bacardi, Hugo Boss, and more. I did this. Often alone. Thanks to the Bake & Take. And you can, too.

The caveat, y'all? Since you are using your own dollar bills and time is money, it usually means creation ain't Fergie's glamorous, "flossy flossy" video. Sometimes you have to shoot a dozen assets in one day for production efficiency, memorizing all scripts with back-to-back takes because you need a clean read that won't require cuts or post production ($$). Sometimes it means doing ten outfit changes for a photo shoot all while pretty much holding the light for the photographer. Sometimes it means recruiting film students, interns (all paid), or your mom, to even have a team. But that bootstrapping process can also be wild and fun. Way beyond what you can even imagine.

Now that you have an unforgettable brand in your mind's eye, it's time to plan how you want people to experience it! Getting those crucial customers talking about how great your business is, wanting to share it with everyone under the sun. Besides your positive mindset as a founder, marketing is the single most important activity for your business. Marketing is what launches your business into the stratosphere. If there's a lack of it? You're flat on the ground next to thousands of other options. In this chapter, we'll go through how to approach marketing, the customer journey, and the various marketing tools at your disposal, so you can form a Go-to-Market Plan. The great news? There are more marketing tools than ever. And women especially are consuming more media—reading news, checking email, catching up on blogs and podcasts—managing multiple devices. The bad news? There are now more marketing tools than ever. You are a company, competing with every entertainment property for attention, and so it's important to pick smart. But with the Bake & Take Golden Tool and what follows, you can be the one who gets the big ol' gold ribbon at the state fair.

The three BLDG Blocks you will get in this chapter are:

1. Marketing Approach
2. Customer Journey
3. Go-to-Market Plan

BLDG BLOCK 1: Marketing Approach

From minimum wage to overnight millionaires. Well, almost overnight. The past few years with everyone glued to their devices 24–7 had aspiring entrepreneurs marketing everything online: vintage clothing, 3D printing, nail art, coding courses . . . you name it, sky's been the limit. Meet Rachel Drori, who went from a pregnant smoothie maker to the creator of a healthy plant-based frozen food delivery service, Daily Harvest.[1] From an on-the-go college student to co-creator of an online design software tool . . . Meet Melanie Perkins of Canva.com. From a lonely high school teen to cofounder of myYearbook, a digitalized yearbook . . . loaded with friends.[2] Meet Catherine Cook of MeetMe.com.[3] And the digital marketing experts who helped them? They became one of the fastest growing millionaire segments, too.

Marketing is BIG B Business, because it has the power to magically open up pocketbooks from a remote one-stoplight town in Kansas to the flashing lights of Hong Kong. A digital-first brand can have a message reach around the world and back again, if it's catchy and clever enough. The internet is truly the number one vehicle for women. So let's harness that pure potential to make your brand presence known. Officially stated, marketing is the activity of promoting and selling a product or service. Marketing is what tells the world you exist . . . from building awareness of your products to converting customers to helping them buy (*ka-ching*).

So where to begin in an endless, overwhelming sea of emerging marketing tools and tactics? A shorthand that's helpful is to think KISS: Keep. It. Stupid. Simple. You're not stupid, but the simplicity of your plan should be, meaning one message reinforced in a few marketing channels at a time. One of the most common mistakes entrepreneurs make is they try to focus on too many messages, in too many marketing channels, too soon. Like one person creating and executing twenty different marketing tactics. How do you know what is working and what isn't? And more importantly, how do you not exhaust all your energy and spend all your money chasing down those shiny marketing channels popping up . . . like every day? Prioritization is key. As is not overspending.

Engaging, emotional storytelling is the hook that helps bring people in to experience your brand. You do that by taking your brand campaign and bringing that BIG Idea to life in a few select places. Once you've shared your macro message, you can support that with smaller micro growth-driven marketing campaigns. You know, topical, new news that's ever-changing, highlighting those USPs (unique selling points). For example, you might feature price, product differentiators, new product releases/features, seasonal themes like back-to-school, customer testimonials, partnership announcements, or press hits.

Now to measuring marketing, by first defining what success looks like: What are you trying to achieve? Are you looking for a certain number of paying customers? Are you trying to hit a general revenue target? A certain velocity of growth? Measure what matters to get that treasure trove of data going, so you know where you're generating the most leads or sales. The secret is a consistent set of key performance indicators (KPIs) that track how customers move. For example: reach, impressions, number of searches, website views, blog mentions, social media likes/comments/shares, engagement rates, product reviews, subscribes, average basket size, repeat purchases, recommendations, etc. To figure out standard benchmarks, you can research average metrics based on your marketing channel and industry. One of the beautiful things about simplifying your marketing plan is that you're able to test and learn.

Because you have fewer levers in the market, you can find out what is working well and what really isn't. You'll want to track and optimize at least weekly, especially at the beginning of a campaign, optimizing your marketing efforts toward the best performing channels based on the outcomes you set.

The payday? As covered generally in Construction$$ and the Bake & Take Golden Tool, it's sometimes about playing a long game. This might mean your ROI (return on investment) isn't there initially. You might spend $5,000 creating a new content series or hosting a dinner without getting paid a cent. But that "thing" you created may one day produce marketing value that's way beyond your investment. It might yield organic attention and media impressions via PR or word of mouth or referrals (not paid), resulting in many new customers. The trick is when you do place a strategic, long-term, nontransactional bet, you don't expect an immediate payday. This has been one of my greatest secrets to success. It's what catapulted me early into the big leagues.

As the saying goes, marketing is equal parts art and science. A blend of creativity and analysis. Intuition and data. And my form leans heavily on the art part. I believe that once you've really mastered the rules of marketing, it gives you a lot of latitude to experiment and act more like an artist. But you can't skip the rigor of getting those fundamentals down first.

BLDG BLOCK 2: Customer Journey

If you feel like all roads seem to lead back to the customer in every chapter, you're right. When in doubt, just think, *What would my customer want?* The customer journey (also known as the customer purchase funnel) shows the path a customer takes to discover, consider, buy, and share (hoorah!) or return (ugh!) your product. Plotting this out helps you super-serve customers every step of the way—and ensures no steps are derelict or dilapidated.

The customer journey is the traditional path a customer takes. The journey starts with *awareness,* the first time someone becomes aware of your product or service. Next comes *consideration,* as that person thinks about your brand helping solve a problem where they decide if it's better than competitors. That hopefully drives to *purchase,* showing positive interest/intent to buy and then taking action to acquire your product or service. Followed by *loyalty,* the all-too-often-overlooked final step in which your customer comes back again to purchase—while recommending it to others, advocating on your behalf.

Taught in business school, the customer journey is a helpful tool to frame marketing activities: prioritize marketing channels, structure a Go-to-Market Plan, and measure marketing effectiveness. Different marketing channels are good at driving behavior at different stages of this customer journey. To double-click further:

The Stages

1. **Awareness** is focused on larger, movement-making, attention-grabbing messaging that makes someone stop and take notice or at least become curious. Marketing channels include: print, PR, TV, partnerships, internet search, paid media, etc.

2. **Consideration** is a period of deeper storytelling, rich education, providing credible social proof, and highlighting unique selling points or benefits that make someone see the difference in how your product could fill a need, leaving them inspired. Marketing channels include: influencers, content marketing, newsletters, events, etc.

3. **Purchase** is all about converting a customer with hypertargeted, frequent communications, clear pricing, de-risking trial, final nudges, or reassurances based on search or browsing history, so they convert. Marketing channels include: website, text (SMS), email, etc.

4. **Loyalty** is the final step, all about superior customer experience through continued personalization, proactive complaint solving, gauging satisfaction to drive retention, and referrals so your customer feels committed to your brand. Marketing channels include: social media, email, etc.

There is no hard-and-fast rule about which marketing channels go at which stage of the customer journey. But the simple rule of thumb is to think bigger, grander messaging goes at the top and more specific, granular messaging goes at the bottom. Naturally, some channels are better suited than others at carrying those types of messages. It's a good idea to structure your Go-to-Market Plan to heavy up on whatever stage in the customer journey you're trying to optimize (i.e., whatever is most important to your business right now). For example, when I was just starting out, it was really crucial to have a basic footprint. The main necessity was a website, a place where new business leads could contact me, leading to *purchase*. Midstage, to make my business presence known, I was focused on driving top-of-funnel *awareness* and PR. To scale up later and extend my reach, I really focused on *loyalty* by way of social media and expanding my community. You'll always want to have all four stages going, but at any given time you'll likely double down on a certain part of the funnel, based on your business goals.

As you can see, even with the simplest plan, a lot of effort goes into getting someone to become a customer. It's a lot less expensive to keep customers happy, coming back for more (loyalty) than it is to acquire new ones (those who "try and buy," never to return again). Customer service is key to maintaining customers and reducing customer acquisition costs in the long run. Plus, it's just the right thing to do. Ultimately, this is about creating a humancentric approach, customizing the journey, so it feels high-touch, highly personalized every step of the way.

BLDG BLOCK 3: Go-to-Market Plan

When I started in marketing, I used to think *rinse and repeat*. Essentially, bonk a customer over the head with the exact same message in every channel, ad nauseam. What I learned is that great marketing is about having one idea with strong connective tissue that's elastic enough to be told many different ways. What's neat about a brand campaign is you can really bring it to life differently by channel. People like multifaceted storytelling.

To bring some dimension, here's one of my favorite case studies. In the early 2000s, when waif-thin, airbrushed models circulated and percolated in just about every beauty campaign, Dove decided to do things differently. It took on a formidable enemy: The fact that only 2 percent of women globally described themselves as beautiful. So was born the brand campaign "Real Beauty," rooted in a BIG Idea that beauty can come in different shapes, shades, and sizes and that our differences should be celebrated. What's worth noting is that each marketing channel unpacked that campaign in a different way. TV and print profiled real women who didn't meet traditional beauty standards to catch people's attention. Social media was used to drive community, calling on everyday women *personally*, asking that they upload long-form videos on YouTube using the hashtag #mydovemessages. Those soul-baring stories were then curated on the Dove website. PR released research reports to provide deeper, data-driven storytelling.

This brand campaign was so powerful it became a decade-long pursuit. More beauty taboos were broken around age—as in old (wrinkles, age spots, gray hair) and young (partnerships added as a marketing tactic included teaming up with the Girl Scouts as anxiety about looks kicks in at an early age). Dove was able to evolve the idea into new channels and deepen storytelling, tweaking and refocusing the effort. When you execute smartly, not only is the financial upside striking the global impact can be enormous. Dove doubled the number of women who consider themselves beautiful and eighty-two million young people were reached with self-esteem education.[4]

To get started on your Go-to-Market Plan, pull forward your brand campaign one-liner and the summary of your BIG Idea from chapter 9. Think of them as the head of an enchanting octopus. From there to bring this BIG Idea to life, you have unique tentacles, in this case different marketing channels and creative assets. The guiding principle of choosing channels should be *where are my customers consuming media?* And in developing your creative, *what will make customers stop and take notice?* Then to get them to move down the purchase funnel, you'll want a range of tactics at each touchpoint in the customer journey.

Need a boost when creating your marketing plan? Below is a base plan; it's a four-part combination of channels I've seen work well for a small brand with limited capital that pairs well with the development of creative assets. The goal here is really to develop or expand a customer base and lay the groundwork for future growth. These four channels focus heavily on earned media (vs. paid) and default to digital (as online tools have never been more accessible or inexpensive). This is more of a grassroots, movement-based model where you can organically grow an audience of true brand advocates.

Go-to-Market Base Plan

1. **Awareness: PR**
   The plan starts with driving awareness, putting a stake in the ground announcing a big, bold brand campaign. PR drives curiosity and credibility, using unbiased, third-party endorsements to serve as social proof exalting the product or service. Trusted by the customer, these placements educate people on the brand campaign and other key brand efforts, and position you, the entrepreneur, as a thought leader on the future of this category. It's about quality over quantity. Once you've gotten coverage, you can put some paid media behind the article for greater reach.

Pro Tip: To secure PR, which I have always done myself (saving tens of thousands of dollars in publicists), I write the press release ahead of time for the outlet with the "newsy" end in mind, including quotes, images, research, and stats to bolster the piece. I write the exact coverage I want. I then share it with reporters of major publications. Bake & Take makes it easy. You just go and do virtually all the work. From there create a hit list of around ten target publications and dotcoms, along with the editors who cover business or lifestyle beats (for example, someone who's focused on product releases or funding news, not celebrity gossip). Editors welcome pitches, so usually their contact info is readily available. Ideally you'd invite and get them to launch, that way you can share your pitch and ask if they have interest in covering on the spot. Within twenty-four hours follow up with that press release you already wrote. Try to cultivate PR relationships on an ongoing basis, so you don't always have an active "ask."

Focus: customer stories, category stories, ingredient stories, influencer stories, trend stories, stories by interest area, expert interviews, conference panels, meet and greets.

KPIs (Key Performance Indicators): reach, traffic, community growth, revenue.

2. **Consideration: Influencers**
   Tapping influencers to share inspirational content with their audiences promotes consideration and reinforces credibility. Micro influencers are culture mavens; credible voices that use your product or service, share their superlative experience, and tell others to follow suit. They are aspirational, with smaller audiences, but highly influential and trusted among their communities. Typically, they create content that they will post in their own social media, but you can also repost in your brand-owned and-operated channels (i.e., social media, website, PR, etc.).

Pro Tip: Create a target list of influencers and try to pick those with niche, highly engaged followings (ten to thirty thousand) in the key markets your business operates in. Decide what you can offer them (usually when you start that will just be a free product or service, eventually you might pay top-tier influencers for formal promotion). From your business social media account, send a direct message with your offer. Assuming they say yes, in the gift box you send to their home or office, it's best to include a personal handwritten note asking them to share if they like it, along with your social media handles. Ideally, you will form a relationship with them to move just beyond one single post, to where they regularly post on your behalf. Again, think Bake & Take. The more turnkey the package you give them, the more likely they will be to share it.

Focus: product "unboxings" to reveal a new launch, product or service demonstrations (i.e., why this product or service is better than others on the market), experiences (i.e., follow me behind the scenes).

KPIs: reach, traffic, community growth.

3. **Purchase: Website**
   A robust website experience helps drive purchase. This is the flagship for your brand, storefront, or digital shingle. It can be a real workhorse. You'll build an experience that serves the curious via content, the prospects via seamless purchase, and the users with easily accessible accounts to maintain connection. It is a dynamic destination that should always be optimized to provide an optimal UX (user experience) looking closely at these areas: customer conversion, top-notch security, data protection (security protocols to keep collected data secure, i.e., payment info, etc.), personalization features, seamless connections to other sales channels, etc.

Pro Tip: If you're just starting out and haven't done so already, you'll want to think about getting brass tacks in place: First, securing a domain name (URL) from a hosting service. Then creating a DIY website on a turnkey platform (drag-and-drop simplicity). It's never been easier to snag one of the many beautiful websites already out there. You do not need a customized site, anything that requires coding or even design or development support. Just make sure the one you pick has the functionality you want already baked in (i.e., you can buy products or take courses, etc). E-commerce brands will need a bit more selling functionality.

Focus: company genesis story, products or services for sale, founder bio, team, testimonials, partners, press, case studies, email lists, blogs, FAQ, user accounts, customer support, contact information.

KPIs: traffic, time on site, revenue, conversion rates, retention rates.

4. **Loyalty: Social Media**
   From there, social media fosters sharing and loyalty. It is the primary community platform with ever-changing entrants (i.e., Instagram, LinkedIn, TikTok, Facebook, etc.). Directly engage your audience with conversation and content, where they already spend half their phone time (two or more hours per day).

   Pro Tip: First you'll want to claim social handles across all social media platforms. If your company name is taken, just pick something close enough, and set up social media accounts for not only your business, but also you as a founder (people are going to want to follow you too and will like it when you post on your brand page!). For social media use and just about everywhere else, you'll want to design a logo and create a brand style guide (consistent branding look, tone, and feel; color palette; packaging, etc.). This does not need to be done by an expensive Parsons School of Design graduate with a fine arts degree. If you're artistically inclined, you can do this your-self or ask your roommate, best friend, sister-in-law, if they have the skills! Once that's locked, turn to platforms where you can do your own graphic design to generate individual static graphics (e.g., Canva) and then schedule posts for social media. While it's nice to have unique strategies for each social media platform, at the on-set it's more important just to post on a consistent basis (multiple times a week). To cut down on workload, you can use the same con-tent across all platforms. For the hour after posting, try to cultivate connection and engage with your audience through the comments section (you should respond to everyone even if it's just an emoji).

Focus: lives, guest takeovers, comments, direct messages, polls, quizzes, Q&As, customer features, social proof (press mentions, influencers), hero-brand moments, product USPs (unique sell-ing points), and product demonstrations.

KPIs: reach, engagement, followers, traffic.

There is a laundry list of other marketing channels you can choose to activate, augment, replace, or supplement your base plan. These include partnerships, events, retail, print, out of home (OOH), TV, direct mail, podcasts, paid social, paid search (SEO), email, newsletters, blogs, text (SMS), webinars, customer service, referral, and loyalty programs. If you want to go deep on any of these tactically (i.e., learn how to set up a lead-generating campaign, write a press release, optimize an e-commerce website, connect to Shopify, set up an Amazon storefront, etc.) there are useful SMEs (subject matter experts) for that and lots of online help, too. Lawyers can double-check any product claims or taglines.

Go-to-Market Creative Assets

Which brings us to the jazzy, artsy part: creative. The creative assets you actually push out in the marketing channels you've selected. This is the final step in the Go-to-Market Plan. For creative development, take your brand campaign one-liner and the description of your BIG Idea and start brainstorming all the marketing "moments" you could create, including at least one creative asset for each core marketing channel. (That would be four if you went with the base plan.) No idea is a bad idea in a brainstorm. Go hog wild.

A creative asset usually consists of content and copywriting. It's a one-two punch! Content can be a still lifestyle image (original or sourced), quote, infographic, short sizzle film, individual video, product demo, interview series, audio recording, podcast, or really any other audiovisual form. Copy usually accompanies that content. It can be anything from a catchy, short slogan to a very detailed, long-form press release, product write-up, manifesto, hot tips, shortcuts with your product, you name it. No matter the form, it helps to always speak "customer first" (Shave *your* legs easier with these razors) and product second (Our razors are 10 percent sharper). A good rule of thumb is to use a voice/tone that is relatable to your customer and sounds like a friend. That should nearly always lead to a CTA (call to action). This is you asking a customer to DO something. Where you get them off of the platform where they saw your creative and bring them to your platform (website, retail store, etc.) where you can convert the visit to a purchase ($).

Before sharing creative, it's always good to slow down for quality control. Would this creative make someone stop scrolling? Would they want to learn more, buy, or share? Creative is endlessly enticing because it taps into human psychology. Sometimes what you think will strike a chord doesn't, while ideas you think are flat take off like a fast-rising helium balloon. Look to beauty line Glossier for inspiration. The company's creative consisted of tight shots that highlighted natural, skin-enhancing ingredients—suggestions that surfaced from their blog readers. The creative helped Glossier catch fire off the back of 90 percent word-of-mouth sales and only 10 percent paid marketing. Or take a fashion brand that irreverently starred Sicilian *nonnas* in their creative campaign. It lit up all the blogs. And if you think that all worked because beauty and fashion are sexy categories, take a look at the luggage category. It doesn't get more pedestrian than travel bags, but startup Away generated over $125 million by focusing their creative on the journey you embark on and the memories you get from a trip, not the box with wheels you happen to have in tow. This is all to say that when women like a brand, they'll talk about it.

Oh, there are so many ways to get your brand out there. Just start high with the brand campaign that becomes an organizing idea, a springboard for all marketing activities. One that delivers the right messages, to the right customers, in the right places. Use a simple plan. Don't be afraid to make a few strategic bets on channels and creative. Balance effectiveness with patience for brand-building (this takes time!). And keep the faith that if it doesn't work this time, you can always try new incarnations and incantations.

Builder Spotlight: Shay Mitchell

On a chilly, sun-drenched morning, I met with actress and lifestyle entrepreneur Shay Mitchell to discuss her love of travel, motherhood, and creating the travel accessories line Béis. We'd been meaning to do this for months; and like a boss, she made it happen despite being in NYC for only a whirlwind twenty-four hours. Frankly, I thought she might just be another influencer who slapped her name on a product line. I prejudged a bit, but Shay struck me as fixated on manifesting possibility, shifting the gray into focus, speaking about what she wants to create, and being deliberate about the way she languages what she's marketing. Our words, she conveyed, hold so much power. As for acting, her breakout role came in Pretty Little Liars *and she starred in the female-led comedy series* Dollface. *"The sky's the limit," she said frequently, a meaningful reminder about how far we can go.*

On Building

. . . I have always been somebody who wants to put the pieces together. And even now, in a different space producing shows, that's kind of building, too. I've always had that in me since I was little. I completely love it.

On Breakdown → Breakthrough

. . . Do I have fears? Do I have breakdowns? Sure, but so does everybody, and it's how quickly you pick yourself back up that sets you apart. For Big B, I'm not married, so there will be no divorce.

On Marketing

. . . I started Béis, a travel accessory and luggage brand, simply out of my love for traveling. I realized that there was a lack of chic, affordable, and functional travel [gear] out there in the space. So we created it. But I've created a few things where at the end of the day I was like, "I don't like the color of this." We've already made them, but we're not going to launch them because, for me, if it's not a bag or a product that I'm proud to carry myself, then it shouldn't go out there. This isn't a collaboration. This isn't me endorsing somebody else's brand. This is my company. So, for me, every single thing that we put out there has to be something I am proud to talk about, and not just today, but for a long, long time.

. . . I always want to be a little uncomfortable. I love putting myself in situations where I'm like, "How the hell did I end up here?" I didn't go to business school. I didn't go to design school, but I know what I'm talking about because it's coming from the seed of my passion.

On Customer Journey

. . . All these products I've really created selfishly for myself, but especially after becoming a mom. I was doing a lot of research prior to having Atlas, and I just didn't find anything that was exciting in the diaper bag category. And I thought to myself, *Why does this have to be so depressing? Why do I have to get something that looks like there needs to be breast milk spilled on it?* No. I wanted to create something chic, and that I could take with me to a meeting and nobody would know what I had inside of it. And that's really how this company is run. Any of us on the team present ideas for things that are actually needed in our lives.

On Go-to-Market Plan

. . . I had a major anxiety attack the night before [launching] because I'm a bit of a perfectionist. For anybody who is putting something out in the world that people don't expect you to be doing, that can be a little nerve-racking. And for me, it was like, "Oh my gosh, is the website good enough? Are our products good enough so people are going to like this? What am I doing?" But again, my whole belief is if other people can do it, then so can I. In a month we sold out of our estimated six months of product. And that was my initial "this is what it's like to own a business" moment. We were really successful right off the bat.

. . . So what's the risk? Okay, so it doesn't work out and people don't like my bag, well, great. I'll have a bunch of free samples. At the end of the day, I'm like, *I took that chance and that's pretty awesome.* What scares me the most is dying and wishing that I would have done something. That's what terrifies me.

Nuts & Bolts: What do you value most in others? *Passion.* In yourself? *Empathy.* What holds you back? *Nothing.* One thing you're afraid of? *Rodents.* What is your biggest vice? *Pizza and reality TV.* What keeps you sane? *The gym and hot sauce.*

11

STAGING

Hammering Away at Sales

I'd get kicked out of buildings all day long; people would rip up my business card in my face. It's a humbling business to be in. But I knew I could sell and I knew I wanted to sell something I had created. I cut the feet out of those pantyhose and I knew I was on to something. This was it.

—SARA BLAKELY

MEET MY—AND SOON TO BE YOUR—FOREMOST SALES TOOL. IT'S MADE ME LOSE often, but when I do win, win BIG. No evil genius stroking a white cat backstory, either. It began as an impulsive trial balloon released from desperate hands (employees to pay without a single customer) connected to numb arms (no goose bumps, tingles, or hair-raising excitement of any kind).

Say hello to my little friend: the Outrageous Ask Golden Tool.

An Outrageous Ask (OA), otherwise known as an unreasonable request, is a basic ask ramped up to the tenth exponent. It's a provocative way to start a conversation. A quick way to network and build out a pipeline of potential partners. An overreach to get something you want that normally wouldn't be available. It's akin to the difference between serving a dry graham cracker vs. jumping out of a human-size Milk Bar birthday cake (which they don't make, so I'd first have to convince founder Christina Tosi). Here's the secret: your willingness to take outrageous action, stick your neck out in the form of egoic sacrifice, public humiliation, extreme effort, or obscene creativity makes your ask maybe, just maybe, get answered. The mistake nearly everyone, *and I mean everyone,* makes is they ask without giving a personal demonstration. It is precisely your willingness to go above and beyond, do WHATEVER it takes that makes someone stop, take notice, and feel like they want to contort themselves to catch you. The ask is simultaneously that ridiculous and inspiring.

Think of Outrageous Asks as amplification's hyperactive handmaiden, working tirelessly on your behalf as you move through the world so you can live an amplified life. These OAs all hang in the ether, like Easter eggs waiting to be discovered.

You know it's an OA when it makes the person receiving it think:

1. Who does she think she is?
2. Is she crazy?

You would not pass the reasonable person of sound mind test. When making an OA, you should feel like an absolute, overentitled nutcase. (But if you know you are delusional, doesn't that actually make you sane? I digress.)

Some examples: While on a plane watching the documentary *Becoming Warren Buffett,* I emailed Warren Buffett's office to ask if I could fly to Omaha to share a business idea with him during his morning Egg McMuffin drive-through run. No added time to his day, just five minutes to share a rapid-fire pitch. I was told that Mr. Buffett got a kick out of my chutzpah and gave a "not now," which isn't a no and wasn't a never. When kicking off Build Like A Woman, I blindly, wildly fangirled Jessica Alba to do our interview series. Well, more like I contacted the Honest Company's PR firm (this is always a good way in), who then looped in someone from the brand's internal marketing communications team, who then raised it up the flagpole to Alba. Ultimately, she said yes, which helped other Builders follow suit. Early in my career, at an event hosted by Sheryl Sandberg, I made a promise (to my mom) that, no matter what,

I wouldn't leave without summoning the courage to say hi. Three years later, I used a selfie of us snapped that day to "infiltrate" Facebook. I outrageously asked if I could pay my own way for the opportunity to introduce Sandberg at an event in France. Surprisingly, they agreed.

OAs also work outside of business. To find love, I sent a note to perfect strangers asking to be set up. It read, "In the words of Amal Clooney, I started to resign myself to the idea that I was going to be a spinster . . ." And then a part of me shouted, "This isn't a good idea!" Blind dates followed suit. For fun, I dared World Cup (and Olympic) alpine skier Lindsey Vonn in a social media post to ski with me for a day in exchange for a donation to her foundation. Still waiting on that one. And to meet my idol, the queen of media herself, Oprah, I had my designer photoshop a picture of us for her interview series, which sealed the deal in my being chosen by her producer. This sit-down went viral (at least with my people)!

From time to time, I also get OAs from strangers. A woman named Kirstie was a rising senior at my alma mater. Over a twelve-hour period, she had her marketing club post unignorable comments across every one of my social media platforms on why Kirstie was a superstar and needed my mentorship. I was so moved that this many women would go to bat for her, I not only agreed to mentor her, I offered her work. She helped with research for this book. Even celebrities lob out OAs. At an advertising event I planned, photographer Annie Leibovitz snapped client photos and then followed up, asking if we wanted to buy the camera roll. It was too steep a sum to say yes, but I liked her chutzpah. For other OAs, I've known women to ask to shadow a business exec for the day, fly with a potential client just to have face time, or attend a conference for free as "media" to dodge a seriously steep ticket price.

Fire those suckers out. Bing. Bing. Bing. For a potential BOOM.

But heads up: An OA should be so outrageous it has a 99 percent rejection rate. It's like a lottery ticket. But those odds are worth it because one yes can put you and your business on the map. Overnight. Literally, it just takes one. The ability to implement change in your life can happen like a switch, in a single moment. Change can take place in a mere minute. Not playing it safe, playing outrageously, is littered with rejection: no, never, deafening silence, outright scoffing. Those "losses" show your reservoir of resilience and the power of persistence. I practice OAs sometimes just to shift energy when I'm feeling stuck. To this day, I'm struck by how few people use them, which is what makes one cut through ice like a hot rod.

You'll get a lot of momentum from the work you just did in marketing, but within the broader marketing umbrella, partnerships are worth taking a magnifying glass to because of what can be incrementally generated. In this chapter, you'll delve deep into partnerships as a way to supercharge business, learn the art of the perfect pitch, and, at the end, close all those sales. Sales is so much more than just getting a deal done or someone signing on the dotted line. Consider sales as a type of transformative energy. Magnetizing new opportunities and people to you, people you otherwise would not have known. It's also the pursuit of putting yourself out on that tightrope. That feeling of electricity as you pitch and that giant exhale when you close.

The three BLDG Blocks you will get in this chapter are:

1. 3 Partnership Pillars
2. 5 Pitch-Perfect Principles
3. 15 Pro-Presentation Practices

BLDG BLOCK 1: 3 Partnership Pillars

Well, howdy, partner . . . One of the fastest ways to scale up is to use OAs to bring in strategic partners and lasso in deals. Partnerships are one of the single most effective business-building techniques. I remember my third year in business being dreadful as we pitched and pitched and did not win a single client. Not a one. Payroll was high, so the obvious thing to do would be to cut staff, but instead I reallocated everyone's salaried time to help me develop and activate a partnership with a major magazine. Amazingly, inbound clients started rolling in. When I asked where they had heard of my company, they said, "Hmm, don't know. We've just heard of you." While I can't draw a straight line from that partnership to those client sales, I believe the magazine's credibility and reach are what made them happen.

Marketing, as we covered earlier, really requires methodical organization and planning. I love that partnerships are a bit of a marketing outlier, steeped in possibility. It's a flexible channel where you can play more fast and loose. Once you've sold to individual customers, you can expand and partner with brands to drive even more sales. And when it comes to sales, more is more is MORE. That means aligning with a large partner that has a complimentary offering in an adjacent category, which helps you tap into an established audience (instead of building a new one from scratch) or a physical retail/distribution footprint (that you don't have). In turn, you bring something to the table. Like an incremental revenue stream outside their core line of business, special content, or a new audience (yours), brand cachet (business "dinosaurs" need the cool factor). It must be a mutual win-win where the sum is greater than the parts.

Simply put, partner with major, mighty brands (this is something small businesses don't do nearly enough) that have qualified, established audiences and a larger footprint. If you run into roadblocks, you can still make it happen by going after smaller, more accessible brands that have less red tape. Look to your existing network for leads and lean toward cocreation and shared ownership. Create bespoke programming and collaborations based on everyone's unique assets. Activate digitally to start (less expensive) with a heavier focus on live activations and deeper integrations once the partnership signals success.

Partnership Sales

- **Partnership Types:** Events and activations, digital programming, wholesale or retail distribution, and other cobranding opportunities. No official rules on what you can create here!

- **Sales Models:** Revenue shares, brand sponsorship splits (based on lead gen), trade or barter (exchange services or products without exchanging money), affiliate (commission for each sign-up or sale), finder's fees, and more. Most models can sync with any partnership type.
  - *Example, granola bar:* Partner with fitness studios where they physically distribute your product on site (revenue share) or with other cool "better for you" brands in adjacent categories like lifestyle, apparel, or nutrition (affiliate commission).
  - *Example, sandal:* Partner with well-known fashion designers to create limited-edition collaborations (revenue share).
  - *Example, strategy agency:* Partner with a creative agency where you promote their service (finder's fee).
  - *Example, financial consultancy:* Partner with a media property that distributes and markets your content: interview series, digital course, podcast, byline, etc. on their platform (paid on media impressions or brand sponsorship split).
  - *Example, skincare:* Partner with a design studio where you give jars of your miracle cream in exchange for label creation and packaging (barter).

3 Pillars for Powerful Partnerships

1. **Core Values.** Align in values. A mutual mission and similar core values are vital. (These values should be similar to what you established in your BUILD Integrated Life Layout in chapter 4.) Lack of alignment can hurt your brand with followers and make you feel personally out of sync; but if right, will fit like a glove. Ultimately, who you partner with is just as important as who you decide not to partner with (and be aware that a bad partnership can get litigious).
2. **Clarity.** Define what success looks like from the outset. Like any

good relationship, you want to have clarifying conversations early and often to develop a shared understanding of where you are mutually headed (similar to what we talked about in crew, chapter 6).

3. **Contribution.** Capture the "give-get" of what each party is going to contribute (i.e., you give x and get y, and vice versa). Spend time brainstorming what each party can uniquely contribute. Partnership agreements should be formally drawn up outlining the exchange (i.e., deal points around who does what, who owns what, what success looks like and by when, how sales will be split, and how the partnership can be dissolved, if need be) so you can put that pretty pen to paper!

Once you have a partner (woo hoo!) and move into execution mode, you'll want to move fast. Startups are speedy at prototyping and two-week sprints. This sprint model should also apply to partnerships, with the goal of hitting new milestones in rapid succession, allowing partners to be involved earlier on vs. waiting for things in a black hole, which could be all the way wrong. Moving swiftly also helps the partnership get activated while things are still red hot.

BLDG BLOCK 2: 5 Pitch-Perfect Principles

ABC . . . as they say, **Always Be Closing.** The first rule of thumb is you never know who you are standing next to, who might be your next partner. Whether it's a brand director, local chamber of commerce intern, city mayor, business reporter, or heck, the person behind you in the ice cream line, you should always be sharing. A pitch that's tight and together, carefully prepared (no tied tongue like a Twizzler). Jessica Rabbit with jazz hands. Laughter, tears, heartstrings played. At the end, everyone should basically want to give a standing ovation and go change the world with you. It should get weird.

The format of a pitch is that of any good story. Always start from a broader place and don't start with YOU. A pitch goes super high (inspirational, which at a three P.M. Friday meeting can make you seem a little cray cray) and down low (practical brass tacks). It skips the middle filled with generic platitudes (which is what most pitches do). Truth is, folks really just need inspiration with a little information. Your pitch becomes this invaluable tool that tells your story and makes a potential partner want to take action. With you! No matter how big your company becomes, you always need a good one.

A killer pitch tells an enticing story visually and verbally. It usually consists of a deck and spiel. See and say. Some learn visually and some aurally. Think of a TED Talk, stand-and-deliver style. For the deck, heavy up on high-impact images, charts, and graphics, and go ultra-light on text. Punctuate with a compelling voiceover (V/O). It should be short and sweet. Practically everyone has some variety of ADD, ADHD, or distractibility (thank you, social media!), so by condensing information you have a better shot at holding your audience's attention. And don't sweat it if you're without a deck on that ice cream line. You can just give your spiel sans materials to show it's that IN you . . . no need for words on a page to guide you.

5 Principles for a Perfect Pitch

1. **Identify a Problem You're Solving.** Speak bluntly and directly to a broad, cultural problem your business is trying to solve in the world (this is the enemy you ID'd in brand strategy) and WHO has that problem, which will tee up the customer your business is targeting.
2. **Include Key Stats or Trends that Substantiate the Problem.** Highlight one objective, data-driven stat or one undeniable trend line. You can pull from the cultural, category, and customer research you uncovered in trendspotting (chapter 8). You'll want lots of information in your back pocket, but in this case,

more is not more. People get overwhelmed when you give them TMI (too much information).

3. **Expand on the Macro Opportunity for Solving the Problem.** Show the market opportunity and how the market is growing. Describe any businesses attempting to solve this problem, with a nod to why they are falling short for the customer.

4. **Introduce Your Solution.** Explain what makes your product or service uniquely suited to solve that cultural or market problem and why this solution will bring about better results for easing a customer's pain points. With the main issue now solved, everyone can make money. Believe it or not, this is the first time you even talk about your business!

5. **Demonstrate Proof Points and Ways to Partner.** Include any differentiators around what makes your business special and credible (i.e., press, past partners, testimonials, and case studies). This is where you reinforce that you are a reliable bet. From there share a high-level summary on how you propose working together—essentially, the give-get.

In this particular instance, the pitch we are crafting is for partners, but you can use this information for just about anything and tailor this template for other prospects: crew recruits, investors (i.e., include information on valuation, projected growth, and where investment would go), and potential clients (i.e., replace give-get in step 5 with work-for-hire terms and fee structure). There is no one "right" way, but when starting out, this proven structure should deliver results.

Once your pitch is done (deck and spiel), it's time to put it to use.

Targeting

Identify target partners. First, create a lead list with brands you want to go after. For ideas, look at who competitors or adjacent brands are teaming up with. Then search online to track down a key point person for each brand prospect with contact info. Look for titles like: business development, marketing, or partnerships. A director or VP level is generally best, so it's not someone too junior without power or someone so senior they don't have time.

Outreach

Make that OA! Use something unconventional to get their attention and stand out from the crowd. When you reach out, include details on why you'd like to meet (and make it as personal as possible). While blind outreach works, a warm intro from a shared connection is best. As women, we have an advantage here as we tend to have stellar interpersonal skills. One of the best uses of a founder's time is establishing partnerships (again, let someone else be your busy bee). Set up a quarter of the year where you do nothing but get to know all the players, find out what they need, and become a lean, mean pitch machine.

Mindset here is key. It's a numbers game. Go in expecting R-E-J-E-C-T-I-O-N. Counterintuitively, know that rejection is good, because it brings you closer and closer to your goal. Every NO brings you closer to your YES. But don't just take my word for it. For reinforcement, I'm calling in BUILD Inspector Arlan Hamilton, the kick-butt founder of Backstage Capital (the venture capital company she established that invests in women, people of color, and the LGBTQ community, all started while she was homeless). She says, "I'm going to get ninety-nine no's for the hundred asks to get the one. It's going to happen. Inevitable. So I need to ask one hundred times, one hundred people, for the thing that I want in any given situation."[1] For me, when I am rejected personally, which happens a lot, in that same moment of rejection and frustration (or rage-induced fury on ego days), I just shoot the same ask back out to someone else. Within the hour. I may tweak it based on feedback, but instead of saying to myself, *Oh, it must not be meant to be,* I think, *Too bad they don't get it. I'll find someone who does.* I channel that energy right back out into the world where it belongs. OA style. Volley that sucker back!

BLDG BLOCK 3: 15 Pro-Presentation Practices

That first vital impression? It happens in less than seven seconds flat, I'm told. Having a pitch down is only half of what you need to succeed. The other half? Presenting it in a way that makes a strong first impression and seals the deal. I've seen pitches go sideways and good brands get overlooked because the founder did not present well: revealing tank top, withholding financials, caginess when answering direct questions, inappropriate R-rated artwork in the Zoom background (yes, that happened), making people wait . . . you name it. When presenting, there are simple "hacks" that signal you're a total pro. No amateur hour over here. Over millennia, to deal with the uncertainty of not knowing people, humans learned to communicate quickly, which is what leads to those fast first impressions. The main qualities people are evaluating? Trustworthiness. Competence. Confidence. Authority. Likeability—all instant data points. Then confirmation bias steps in. People ignore information that contradicts their initial belief (give the benefit of the doubt) or try to prove out their initial hunch. Partners are either positively predisposed to buy what you are selling . . . or quite the opposite.

For a strong start, your presentation needs to demonstrate respect for the other party. Everyone assumes this is you putting your best foot forward, so if you are late, if you look like a hot mess, if you have spinach between your teeth, they are going to expect that normally you are even worse off or can't be bothered to even try for them. Even if your daily baseline is a "one," mismatched sweats with a bird's nest for a topknot, for this you want to be all the way turned up, a "ten." Full volume. On blast. Go on . . . surprise even yourself! As my Irish nanny always said, "Better to be overdressed than underdressed." That applies to everything including . . .

PREPARATION. You'll see that pro performance requires being overly prepared. Advance planning. Making it look easy is actually hard work. Take Ina Garten (aka the Barefoot Contessa) with her signature catchphrase "How easy is that?" So it seems—but that's all thanks to loads of advance prep for her TV show: having every ingredient pre-minced, every movement choreographed from chopping block to stovetop. The title of her cookbook, *Make It Ahead*, could just as well be used for your work, too.[2] Distractions on "game day" are minimized by prep. As women, we're in our heads all too often ("Is my outfit OK? Should I do a wardrobe change real quick? Did my voice sound too shrill?"). Because you've worked through everything in advance, you are not only the most together person in that room, you are not "in your head," easily thrown off your game. Preparation allows you to charge into spaces. Pitch bigger, march bigger, activate bigger. Amplified.

A while back I was asked to give a company-wide presentation to a Fortune 500 company. Think profit in the billions. Employees in the tens of thousands. So I prepared like a pro. Memorized all my talking points. Created a spiffy deck. Confirmed A/V equipment. Flew my assistant to HQ with me. Arrived hours before I was set to go on stage to do a dry run and sound check. Even got a jumpsuit that matched the brand's signature blue. Fast forward. It just so happened to be International Women's Day, but instead of burning my bra, I lost mine. Onstage. In front of the entire company. The mic's power pack had somehow managed to unhook the back, straps simultaneously sliding down both arms; the front, well . . . not "Janet Jackson at the Super Bowl" bad, but close. But this wardrobe malfunction was laughed off (because of all the other ways I'd shown professionalism) and I was not derailed (because I'd prepared). Unexpected things are bound to happen. There are always variables outside your control, but if you can get positive data points stacked in your favor, you'll still win the day.

15 Practices to Present Like a Pro

Pre

1. **Stalk.** Think about what intel you would pull before going on a first date. Create what I call Business Backgrounders: dossiers, bios, basically CSI files on who you are meeting (where they

have worked, the projects they have spearheaded, how they sound, what they look like, who they are married to, etc.). Know everything you can about who's in that room.

2. **Flex Bigger.** Pull in crew members. These are extra hands who can help with scheduling, joining a presentation to take notes, supporting with tech or follow-up emails, so you present bigger. Enlist an entry-level number two, a student who is working for college credit or, if you want to get wild, create a bevy of email aliases that you manage . . . Hello, Georgia from PR, Reonna from Sales, and Kara from Accounting!

3. **Set the Agenda.** Break the meeting into carefully allotted chunks of time with presentation roles and responsibilities. Leave at least one-third of the meeting for conversation. Share it with your partner at least a week in advance and invite feedback so you are already on the same page going in.

4. **Style Your Space.** Curate a backdrop with flowers, books, art, or found objects if presenting remotely. Make sure you are centered in frame, at eye level with your camera. And don't forget your ring light! If hosting live (but don't have a dedicated space), call in favors to borrow a friend's conference room or rent one.

5. **Dress to Impress.** Wardrobe is armor. Serve different looks based on the audience (channel Michelle Obama). Potential partners luh-luh-love it when you wear their brand colors and reflect their style (Remember the Spice Girls? Sporty? Serious? Premium? What's the brand's persona or lewk?). Rent clothes or shop your own closet. And the most important part: killer shoes! Invest in your own version of Dorothy's ruby slippers. With three clicks of your heels, begin to walk in the shoes of the future you.

6. **Hit Your Marks.** Never reschedule a meeting!

7. **Rehearse, Rehearse, Rehearse.** Do as many dry runs as you need to get it right. Memorize your pitch (deck and spiel). In front of your mirror, while in bed, in the shower. From your brain into your body, until it's muscle memory.

8. **Prepave.** You've got this Golden Tool already under your belt, so use it. The night before, in your mind's eye, imagine the ideal meeting outcome.

During

9. **Be on Time. Wrap on Time.** If you're not early, you're late! Few things trigger a busy, senior person more than being late or letting a meeting run over (it also infers you must not be successful if you are lollygagging around). So arrive fifteen minutes prior to start. Pretest the tech. Get the best seat in the house at the middle of the table. Stick to the allotted time.

10. **Posing and Posture.** Set the tone. Strike a few power poses in the room. It exudes confidence. Then mirror others' posture throughout the meeting. Really! This subtle technique helps create a sense of familiarity (ergo, likeability).

11. **Find Common Ground.** Open with human connection. Thread through common interests or points of connection based on your background research. Let them brag. People love to talk about themselves and rarely have an outlet.

12. **Tango.** Yup, tango! Just like dancing with a partner, both can't lead at the same time. Know who is the lead and who is not. Take turns. This meeting should feel collaborative, like a jumping-off point. Not dictatorial. When glazed-over eyes suddenly switch on, brainstorm on the fly what could be possible, and magic enters the room. That's when you know you've got them. That's nirvana!

13. **Stay on Script.** Stick to the agenda. Switching it up feels like you are trying to pull a fast one. Catfish.

Post

14. **Follow Up.** This might be Emily Post common sense, but those personal follow-up notes of thanks are remarkably rare. So write one and stand out.

15. **White Glove Onboard.** When (not if!) the partnership gets

greenlit, you will want to put on your client service hat and roll out a tight onboarding process (i.e., partnership agreement, team briefing, roles and responsibilities, time line, asset transfer including logos, brand guidelines, etc.). This really sets a powerful tone for the partnership.

You've got closure. That energetic feeling that you wouldn't have changed anything, because you hit the mark jusssssttttt right. Sealed the deal. Drove something to completion. Pushed it over the line. It's one of the greatest feelings of all time.

Builder Spotlight: Karla Welch

Called one of "the most powerful celebrity stylists" by the Hollywood Reporter, *a true tornado of taste, Karla Welch works with people like Karlie Kloss, Pink, and Oprah ("the best day of my life," says Karla). Actress Judy Greer, another client, said of Karla, "She's the most self-confident woman I've ever met." With Justin Bieber she created the fashion line x Karla (named after how she signs her emails) and more recently Wishi, an online styling app. Not only that, but with shoe designer Tamara Mellon she partnered to design a workboot that can be used, as Tamara says, "to go to the polls or a protest. These are boots to get sh*t done in." And another partnership with The Period Company helps provide menstrual equity worldwide—with absorbent and inexpensive period underwear that can last five to ten years. I sat down with Karla in LA in between her taking care of her kids and jetting to a last-minute styling appointment (this woman is busy with a capital B). We discussed her activist spirit, unshakable sense of self-confidence (she has a voice and is not afraid to use it!), and global ambition.*

On Building

. . . I was a born Builder, which is probably annoying to say. Even when I started styling, I only assisted a tiny bit because I felt so confident that I had the skills to do it, and I was never afraid to ask for help or ask questions so I'd always find someone way smarter than me, way more experienced, and pick their brains and then just really work at it.

On Breakdown → Breakthrough

. . . I probably have more of those Little b breakdown to breakthroughs than anything. I think realizing what it means to be the leader is major. This happened at the restaurant I ran in Vancouver with a staff of thirteen people. When this was happening in my mid-twenties I suddenly realized, I'm kind of like, for a lack of a better term, the man. The boss. And when the shit goes down, it's on you. And when people have sh*t to say, it's usually about you, and so developing thick skin is an important part of being a leader.

On Partnership

. . . My new app Wishi and the clothing lines, other projects, have all been fed from creating a really strong foundation. You know, build a house that won't crack, and then realizing I wanted to flex more of my own creativity and brain, and to see where it could go organically but also deliberately.

. . . My husband, Matthew, who is my creative partner, always says to me, "Make sure you are giving yourself to the right people because you still have to come home at the end of the day and give to us. And when you give to the wrong stuff, you don't have anything left to give to the stuff that matters."

On Pitching

. . . I had no idea how much work was gonna go into x Karla, started with only a white T-shirt. I was on set, and this incredible entrepreneur doing hair, Jen Atkin, is like, "Just remember this day 'cause this is gonna be the easiest day of your life." People from the outside can think, "Oh, my god, you're doing so many things. Oh, it's so great." And it's like yeah, but I don't sleep and it's a constant stress and every facet of you gets so stretched. That's hard.

On Presenting

... I was a kid that had a loud voice, probably getting me in a bit of trouble, but I think what I was standing up for was always my moral compass.

... I work with directors and am kind of lower on the hierarchy of our work, in service. I want to be at the top of the totem pole. But it takes, like, I don't want to say balls 'cause you know it takes a lot of vagina to say, "Yeah I'm gonna do that" and not be afraid of someone saying, "Well, she doesn't know what she's doing." And so I'm fortunate that I found mentors, and sometimes they're side-by-side mentors. It can be a peer. Your best mentors are right beside you.

Nuts & Bolts: What do you value most in others? *Kindness.* In yourself? *Kindness.* Something you wished you had kept doing? *Family therapy.* What keeps you growing and building? *To make my parents proud.*

12

SHOWCASE

Making IT in the Real World

If there's one thing I'm willing to bet on, it's myself.

—BEYONCÉ

AT THE END OF EVERY INTERVIEW, ALL BUILDERS ARE ASKED A SINGLE QUESTION: "Knowing what you know now, was it worth it?" The answer might surprise you.

This business-life blueprint is now IN you. At a cellular level. Digested. In section I, you started this process eyes-wide-open around the *state of women* and how to face your *fears*. You learned to see a *breakdown* as a good thing, knowing a *breakthrough* is coming. A bold *vision* and thoughtfully designed *Integrated Life Layout* turned *amplification* all the way up. Your wellness *framework* took many forms, from sweat to silence to sustenance. Foundational. For. Every. Single. Day. *Mindful leadership* revealed your unique style. Creating a *crew* called in reinforcements and helped eliminate anyone whose energy felt like a *Scream* painting. The *60-Second Pause* gave you time to think about what you want to say.

Section II revealed the *best business model* and how to make smart moves around *money,* honey. You went *trendspotting* and found your *customer target*. You then forged a brave *brand* from *mission* to *strategy* to *campaign. Marketing* had you form a *Go-to-Market Plan*. You widened the *sales* aperture via *partnerships* and *pitching*. Along the way eight Golden Tools: *Prepaving* lets you visualize what you actually want. *Outrageous Asks?* That's the magic that enables you to ask for outrageous help. *The Bake & Take, AID, Heart Test, Nailed It, Hard Hat,* and *Risk & Reward* . . . mandatory treats, preferably with sparkle! You now have all the building blocks to a killer business and better you.

This BUILD blueprint has mindset and skillset working in perfect harmony. The beauty of having done this business and life-strategy work simultaneously is that you have no division and therefore no fault lines in your foundation. You know there is no business without life and no life without business. Everything is integrated and interconnected. This is where every concept and tool we've gone over in the book comes together. It all coalesces. Gels. And I'm telling you, you've got it. You've been a student. You are educated. You're now good to go. It's time to ladder up—move from internal planning to execution. Jump into action. Shift that gaze external. With an eye to making this real in the real world.

Fast-forward to another question . . . this one being the number one regret on people's death beds? The answer: "I wish I'd had the courage to live a life true to myself, not the life others expected of me."[1] Fifty percent of women give up on their dreams. Fifty percent! Half of all women. So now to the most terrifying and exhilarating part: living for yourself. In life, there are generally two wildly different paths. Talk, talk, talk. Ruminate without taking action. Then die. Or wake up to the fact you can act, act, act. Go for an unconventional life. Elbows scuffed, knees knocking in fear, but wide-toothed grinnin' as you skid into home base (and—spoiler alert—still die . . . but content as hell).

So you chose. This is your moment. Not mine. Not Aunt Sue's. Yours. And yours alone.

Do you want to be the person who dares to dream and does it now? Or defers it? Do you want to level up if you've got something already going? Amateur or pro? Do you want to listen to the "commonsense" refrain from that fear-mongering naysayer in your head that asks, "But what if the business fails, what if I don't have what it takes, what if I lose money?" But what if the business soars, what if you do have what it takes, what if you do become filthy rich? Don't you want to insist on building your dream your own way? Don't you want to bet on yourself?

You, a Builder!

You get a business. And if you've already got one, a bigger one! The second you take a single action, you become a Builder. An entrepreneur. You join the ranks, enter a new realm. Because you are now doing IT. By the sheer process of you even *attempting* to build, your spirit is unleashed. Having the courage to roll up your sleeves, get on the site, and say, "I'm waiting for no one and nothing. I'm going to break ground. It's time to build." The part of you that watches you reach for something outside your comfort zone and current consciousness is going to fight for you and whatever magic you are trying to put into the world. You, bravely imagining something that doesn't exist and then putting it out into existence, as only you can see it. Being able to point at something and say: "This wasn't here before I got here. I did *that*. I made *that*." How unreal is *that* when you really take it in?

Much of the satisfaction in building (which is really what you are after) is to be experienced IN the building. It is in doing that the JOY of building is to be found.

Think about it. Actually playing in the dirt is way more fun than thinking about playing. Actually figuring out how to make it out of the mud is way more interesting than never having stepped in the mud at all. We think it's about the end result, but the feeling that comes from seeing the final house is fleeting. A day or week or month, if you are lucky. The real joy is in the building, on site. The creative process of finding your vision, losing it, and then returning to it over and over again. Without consistent action, your dream will remain a dream and not a building. So build a new life. Don't live someone else's. Build one.

Today you are joining twelve million other women in all of their multidimensional glory who seek to find their own definitions of success. Women with agency. Women who don't fit in a neat, little itty-bitty box. For if we don't show the world what we are made of, capable of, who will? Imagine the massive collective impact we would have if every woman on this planet considered herself a Builder? If, instead of giving up or feeling like a victim of circumstance, she rolled up her sleeves, went to work. Built a new future. What a world we could live in!

This chapter asks you to finally step out of theory, out of planning, to actually get into the market and create in the real world. You have gone from talking to thinking to planning to building. If you don't have a business, launch one. And if you already have a fully functioning business, think new heights, y'all. This is all about making your dream real in the world. What you do in this chapter doesn't need to be pitch perfect; this is your moment to start creating something tangible, an actual business (or your 2.0, new and improved one). It's the grand unveiling, the showcase.

Simply put, this chapter is about unleashing your dream. Who do you want to be? What do you want to do? And from there, share it!

As to how those female founders I interviewed answered the question, "Was it worth it?" I was knocked over. An unequivocal yes. They wouldn't trade this experience, they all said, for anything in the world.

The three BLDG Blocks you will get in this chapter are:

1. Be Amplified
2. Break Ground
3. Broadcast Out

BLDG BLOCK 1: Be Amplified

Lights, camera, action. Shimmy those shoulders back. Chin and chest up. Elbows out. Turn all the way up and ON. Time to assume center stage, a glint in your eye as you readjust to reveal that heel and move like a woman who's got places to go, things to do, and people to meet. Fret not if you didn't make the high school rendition of *Rent*; this is just about you sharing amplified you. Know the greatest asset of all in your tool-box? YOU. YOU unleashing YOU. YOU are the star of this show!

Retrenching here . . . amplification is the X factor to any woman's success; we know this in theory from earlier in the book. Now to the juicy part: actually putting it into practice.

What makes being a Builder so fun is you can lead an unconventional, unique, unorthodox life. Be a whole lotta woman. This stepping into the fullest expression of you happens when you've integrated life with work, the personal with the professional, combining your vision, values, and habits with business practices. Looking at your whole world holistically and intentionally. Looking at your foundation to ground your work AND life. *Then taking things a step further,* using that work-life base for total unleashment. Once you are completely, unapologetically integrated, amplification happens. The brightest, highest, fullest, tallest, truest expression of you emerges—all collective potential and possibility. Without reservation. This is the path to authentic power. And it is a widely propulsive force.

What you are creating now is truly the safest, most certain way to build because it is bespoke to you. Your specifications, preferences, style. No one can completely show you the way, because it's tailored to you and your unique life. You decide your home. To some it may initially look like a crazy, hot mess of demolition, with exposed boards and beams. But don't be fooled: a perfect-looking Potemkin village facade is usually just covering up rooms of echoey nothingness. And sadly, sometimes the people you love most will also react most negatively, because your expansion casts a spotlight on what they have never given themselves . . . the permission to do. Your light frightens them, exposes them, and showcases all that they never had the capability or courage to chase down. Either way you'll have neighbors leaning over the fence at a ninety-degree angle like, "What the hell is she building over there?"

So take a spin on the unconventional wheel of life. You've got your Integrated Life Layout across seven life areas (business, money, relationships, environment, spirituality, passions, health). You already know the puzzle pieces that feel right to you. To step into this newfound positive state of being, where you vibrate higher, feel exuberant, here's a final dose of inspiration. What follows are real things that *real* women, your entrepreneurial sisters—some you've heard of, some you haven't—are doing in business and life.

Demonstrations of total amplification:

- Rent a hotel room to write (or do business planning) without distraction. It might include card games to occupy the "Little Mind" for when the writing "Big Mind" needs a break.[2]
- Sneaker up for a brain-oxygenating "walk and talk" with a coworker to unlock creative business ideas.
- Overnight a bright red lipstick—gotta get that swagger back—to a friend going through a rough patch.
- Office closed! Take off every Wednesday for R&R. Or Tuesday. Or Friday. Reject the idea of a traditional "weekend."
- Celebrate a business mentor by bringing her favorite people together to speak about her impact. Or invite a top teacher to attend a celebratory Broadway play with you, twenty years later.
- "ThinkTreats." A quarterly retreat (accompanied by french fries + massage) where you don't think about practical business issues, only creative ideas.
- Give homemade bread to new clients.
- Freeze your eggs, treating your mom to designer ballet flats at the end of it, to become a single mother by choice.
- Buy a home without a cosigner.
- Open a leadership academy for girls with "tenacity, charisma, and smarts." Five hundred graduates.[3]
- Work only six months of the year.
- Corner the cashier to pay for another woman's lunch.
- Launch an "Imagination Library" that mails free books to kids from the day they are born until age five.[4]
- Thrill employees with two first-class airline tickets and $10,000 in

cash, announced, in this case, at a party celebrating the majority
sale of the company.

So many amplified women doing things their way!

On the flip side, big swings for an amplified life mean big misfires and
missteps. Failures and fallouts (more here from *real* women):

- Sued by someone with claims of stolen IP
- Ousted from one's own activewear company by the board while
  on maternity leave
- Walked out on by a life partner, on the greatest professional
  night of her life
- Received cease-and-desist letters
- Watched a dog seizure after a stressful, drag-out work tussle
- Fined by the FCC for a "too-explicit" Super Bowl performance

To stay amplified and push forward when you feel like you're falling
down a bit, it's good to keep in mind:

Imposter syndrome is roaring for good reason: Imposter syndrome is
defined as feeling your success isn't legitimate or deserved. You may feel
like an imposter, because you are, actually, perceived as an "imposter."
It is in the air. It is not a syndrome, but a signal. It isn't anything for
you to regulate or shush. Contrary to what culture pronounces, there is
nothing for you to work on or get over. It is your body's natural, intui-
tive, very real reading of how the outside world views you. Our society
in business *does* believe you to be an outsider. An imposter who should
not hold power. This IS the terrain. All of this is, of course, infinitely
worse for BIPOC women who speak to needing to code-switch and shift
behavior to navigate the dominant white culture.

This imposter concept can be more overt and easier to get a handle
on when you think about experiences you've had in other countries. It's
just the feeling of not belonging because you are, in fact, different. I once
flew all the way to Dubai—6,836 long miles away, nearly thirteen hours

sitting in coach, across nine yawning time zones—to speak at a creativity conference. Once there, I was sequestered in my hotel for days working on part of my presentation that had been rejected due to violations of Sharia law. When I went to speak, it was encouraged that I be accompanied by a male escort and wear a fake wedding band. Clearly, a cultural imposter. While more oblique at home, you get the idea.

The feeling of extreme imposter syndrome comes up for anyone in business. But we as women are uniquely qualified to handle it, because we've experienced it more, named it for what it is, and now are claiming something different: our power.

Inward is the way out: Naturally, there will be times when you lose your way, your joie de vivre. When you need affirmation to keep going, turn inward. Get out of your head and back into your body as soon as possible. When nagging questions or worries creep in—like "What the f*&% was I thinking starting this business? Should I shutter up shop?," handling everything from daily operations to spending life savings to having to shoulder decisions alone, etc.—chances are you've slipped up on your grounding habits and rituals. Dropped what centers you. And that's when stressors and doubt creep in. From there things go sideways and you start to spiral out. You fall out of your power and lose motivation.

If you feel this way, the best first question to ask yourself is, "What do I need in this moment?" Mother yourself. Slow shit down. Restabilize. The sooner you can drop into your daily 60-Minute Prime (sweat, silence, and sustenance) to shift your mindset back to baseline, the better. From there, ask yourself, "Where can I turn to for inspiration?" Things like nature, music, art, and cooking will help you elevate into a more positive space to where you then feel energized to keep going. Back to this book. Back to women who inspire you. To ignite your light again.

Just know if what you start isn't firing for you, you *always* have a right to change it, move it, shift it. Try different. It's a series of stop-starts.

Sucking is the price of admission: I encourage you to be brave enough to suck at something new, as the saying goes. Embrace the suck. Embrace the judgment as you thrash around in the deep end. My first appearance on a national morning show sucked royally. I spoke on a subject I couldn't hate more (hamburgers) and had only an hour to prep (my sound bites were as dreadful as my hair). The first of anything is always awful. So better to get firsts out of the way!

Innumerous things will ONLY be in your life because you were willing to embarrass yourself initially. Start a business, launch a digital course, take equity in a startup, get paid out for said equity, negotiate partnerships and rights positions with some of the world's biggest brands, trade stocks, give a speech onstage to thousands of people, join a board, teach at a college, get a book deal (all my things). For your version, you will know not a drop about them when you start. You are like a baby, a novice, at every new thing you try. Would you expect a baby to be able to drive a car? For starters, their arms and legs are too short. Give yourself the grace of being a big ol' baby with the pedal to the metal. Actually, expect to be swerving all over the road, scuffing doors, taking out car side mirrors, and bursting fire hydrants (you'll be fined for that, by the way).

Women take it so personally when there is a failure, as if you yourself failed. No, your business failed on that day. An idea failed. Not you. The most powerful, confident people I've met are comfortable routinely embarrassing themselves because they are always trying new things. In going after moon shots—those outsized risks that also have the potential for outsized returns—you must welcome failure, expect it. You are learning. Getting new information. Being nudged somewhere else. A new, better direction. It's the richest form of life teaching us how to move through the world.

Just do your best to learn something, contribute something, flounder around at something. That is a rich life. Roll those windows down, let the music blare, and just keep driving forward no matter the shit you hit. The quality of your life is determined by your willingness to stretch into this uncharted territory. So doesn't sucking seem like a fair price of admission?

Magic, possibility, and creation reside in you. Anything you can dream, you can DO. Trust yourself. You have the power to create the exact life you want . . . winking at that picture of you as a little girl on your bookshelf as you go. Know that once found, you can't lose her. And you never know, maybe just maybe, her pilot light will ignite others, too.

BLDG BLOCK 2: Break Ground

Breakdown → Breakthrough → Break Ground → Breakdown → Breakthrough → Break Ground → Breakdown → Breakthrough → Break Ground → Breakdown → Breakthrough → Break Ground.

Git 'er done! This is an ongoing process of breaking and building and tinkering and sharing and scaling. The greatest business strategies in the world—if they don't translate into action—mean nothing. So how to take deliberate action? A breakdown directs you to what needs to be changed. A breakthrough shows you what to build next. And breaking ground is how you actually do it. This is the final distinction and step. Set that vision, minimize the noise, maximize the action. I want you to give yourself, here and now, PERMISSION to break ground. And if you won't give permission to yourself, I'm doing so. Now.

Everyone has a million-dollar idea. Everyone. Ideas come easy. So many good ideas languish and never leap into the real world. Because here's the rub: people lose precious time overincubating an idea or wanting to get it just perfect before telling anyone. It's all about execution. Activation. Action! We all know that person who secretly tinkers away endlessly. Let's face it, that's the equivalent of a gorgeous, single woman thinking, *When I lose weight, I'll start dating.* Just know what you're doing is buildable. It's buildable. It's buildable. Now.

So it's time to break ground in the real world. If you don't have a business, you might want to start with establishing a basic footprint. If you are up and running, relaunch your business. Here's a grab bag of goals you can take action on next:

- Register your business (LLC, S corp, partnership, etc.) with an online provider or a lawyer.
- Develop a proof of concept and find a formulator willing to produce samples for your new line.
- Launch a new brand marketing campaign.
- Start selling a new product or service.
- Send outreach emails to your top prospects and establish your crew.
- Create a killer pitch deck and start pitching potential partners.
- Set up your first website or optimize your existing one.
- Get a work space. The leanest option for your business type. A lot of people overextend with long-term leases, which creates overhead and, in turn, *pres-sha*. Maybe a coworking office, coffee shop, library, conference room, communal commercial kitchen, or just carving out a dedicated space on your kitchen counter.
- Host a popup event.
- Implement the 60-Day Challenge with the 60-Minute Prime (three Anchor Habits done daily) and 60-Second Pause.
- Get childcare.
- Move to a new state that is more friendly to your business type.
- Set up a project-management system to save time and complete more projects.

And don't forget to shine up your Golden Tools along the way. Applying the Nailed It Golden Tool, for instance, for a business deadline as you keep your word to yourself first and foremost and then to others. If something changes, rebroker the plan. Make a wildly ambitious Outrageous Ask. Create and fund one Bake & Take Golden Tool opportunity, without permission. In advance of a big meeting or important activity, use the Prepave Golden Tool, writing out how you want it to go. What is the overall feeling anticipated? What might this potential other person say? And don't forget to consider: What is the desired outcome? Write out that darn script.

They say a goal is a dream with a deadline. Whether launching or relaunching now, write a laundry list of macro and micro actions you want to take next. Not practicing, but actually doing these things. Don't you just love making a good list? Take radical action. Make everything trackable. Once these goals are complete, load on more.

Breaking Ground Goal 1
- Goal:
- Timing:

Breaking Ground Goal 2
- Goal:
- Timing:

Breaking Ground Goal 3
- Goal:
- Timing:

BLDG BLOCK 3: Broadcast Out

Sound the sirens. Tune the trumpets. Drop the bass. Get loud. On blast. It's time for you to start sharing anything and everything when it comes to building. Make everyone a little annoyed. Get a little too big for your britches. A mouthy, haughty, saucy, self-important broad.

Sharing your journey is not just about the mountaintop times, but the valleys and in-between moments. The high highs AND the low lows. Taking us along for the climb. Not just the peak ten years from now, but the pits when it's pouring cats and dogs and you still put one foot in front of the drenched other, singing to yourself, "Dreams can come true."

Those moments. The mini successes (or stumbles) each time you build—acquired that business credit card, registered your LLC, got approval on a trademark, negotiated your first contract and signed on the dotted line, pitched and didn't get the business, fired your first employee, hired your first employee, had a business shout-out in the press, got sued, revamped your website, launched a brand campaign, got slammed legally—what nearly took you down, where you overcame, those who stood to close doors . . . or open them. The good times and, courageously, the not so good ones, too. Push out this new amplified you and business. In meetings, social media (especially social media—tag me!), presentations, negotiations, with your crew.

Why can't I keep all this building to myself, you might ask?

Sharing is for your business, first and foremost. People need to know about your business to buy your products or services, for you to make money.

Sharing is to help other female founders. We all need community. On tough days other founders, perfect strangers, will be emboldened watching you. That means you're sharing everything from the emotional to the tangible to the informational.

Sharing is for the world to break cultural chains. The braver you feel to call out injustices and the people who get in your way, the less possible mistreatment becomes.

As we all know by now, the world doesn't really want us to build new systems, structures, services. Us, taking things into our own very capable hands, building the products, programs, and platforms that we have sought as women but have not been able to find. The world wants us to stay small. Because it serves them. Feeds them. Clothes them. Pleases them. Institutions and people in power will do everything to keep us in our place for daring to defy the system. Truth is, you won't have language for a lot of what you will experience. You will feel weirdness, closed out of rooms, not taken seriously, frustrated that the bro, who started at the same time and you outwork, makes more money. It just won't quite add up. But part of what has kept women financially anemic, feeling lonely, and at the mercy of behind-the-scenes aggressions or discrimination is that we build in *private*. They bank on us not telling anyone. Not calling things out. The more vocal we are the less this can exist.

Summon courage. When a person tells you to get back in your box, that you've got "a basic idea that will never go anywhere," that "you're a bitch for leaving drinks early," or that "your product is subpar," instead of losing your voice and getting small, even if that happens temporarily (I still shrink as a default response), broadcast out.

Every time you fall down, lose your spark, may you, as the saying goes, "Rise as the whole damn fire." May the earth tremble, hearts palpitate and others be unleashed as a result of your doggone defiance. Your stubbornness. Your persistence. Your unwillingness to accept what you were handed. Not a victim, not a survivor, but a thriver. And may you feel called to expand. Take up even more space. Break even more ground. Build back even better.

Now it's time to wake up the whole neighborhood for the big reveal, the showcase. Light that sucker up. Turn all the high beams on. Bang some pots and pans real loud. Let those prying eyes know you've got the hottest house on the block. Bedazzle everyone with the magnificent business and life you've built with your brave, bare hands. Celebrate with those nearest and dearest. Country music on, champagne in mug. High, low, whatever celebration looks like to you. Breathe in all that you have done and become to . . .

BUILD LIKE A DAMN WOMAN!

CLOSE

WE ARE IN THE DREAM BUSINESS.

While most see barriers, we see possibility. What must be built. What must be ushered from the unseen into the seen realm, no matter the cost of crazy. Living intentionally by design, not default. We know that building is not to be found in the physical building, but in the build itself. And that the deepest form of that building comes from transforming a breakdown into a breakthrough in order to break ground. We are for those who get off the floor every single time. Who, when the world barks, instead of folding up shop, bark back, "You. Won't. Break. Me." To BUILD again. And again. And again.

Deeper, wider, stronger, taller, taller still, never smaller, smaller.

Building the life and business you dream of against the wretched, gorgeous backdrop of being human will have you wondering if you can at times. But that's when you'll dig real deep and try again. A new habit, a new hire, a new partner, a new ponytail, a new pitch, a new coffee cup, a new city, a new meditation, a new measuring stick, but always back to that same amplified YOU.

A life by your own hand, from your own pen, and of your own choosing.

Having a business will break you, test you, defy you, elude you, confuse you, excite you, tempt you, and . . . transform you. To go the distance, use whatever you have inside you. It was put in there for a reason.

Don't judge it—the light, the shadow, even the rage, especially the rage. Let it become you. Use the nasty things you've been called by others and those quiet things you've whispered to yourself. Summon it all. Channel it all. Harness it all. Wield it all. These are your tools for mass creation.

Let the world come to know the force in your fingertips and the force multiplier that is us when we come together.

I hope you have mornings filled with folds of sunlight, garden greens, and pausing to plan what speaks to your soul. Where you can then do focused, meaningful work. Experience joy in being a part of a team. No longer lone-wolfing it. Lingering to daydream at droplets accumulating on the olive trees. Taking a month or a summer off when you need to rest, just because. Where you have walk-away wealth. Where you call the shots. Connection in words exchanged with strangers, time to listen and linger, not hurried. Having the ability to field anything in business without absorbing it in your tissue, triggered. An authentic life that you don't have to run from, numb from. Centered. Where you can simultaneously hold fragments of the woman waiting for you on the other side with tendrils of you in the here and now.

And one day when you are well on your way (because there really is no end, is there?), in a quiet, utterly insignificant moment, probably under unflattering fluorescent light, may you experience that flash in the mirror that finally, for the first time, you would not trade places with another person on this planet.

Your life, so perfectly imperfect, perfectly yours.

DIY

(DO-IT-

YOURSELF)

EXERCISES

These drills and exercises will help you brainstorm and create some initial thoughts and ideas for your business so that you're prepared to turn thought into action. If you need more space, grab a notebook and write away.

1. PLOT:
Understanding the Lay of the Land

DIY 1: State of Women

Despite all the headwinds women currently face in business, like struggling to find funding, be taken seriously, you name it, what is it about this time that excites you? Jot down your thoughts.

_____

_____

_____

_____

_____

_____

_____

_____

_____

_____

_____

_____

Of the three obstacles that hold women back from starting a business, what stands most in your way: is it lack of support (not having the financial, practical resources, or mentorship)? Is it doubting your own leadership (not feeling like feminine skills are valued)? Or is it lack of confidence (you don't believe in your own ability to start a business)? What is the biggest obstacle?

_____

_____

_____

_____

_____

_____

_____

DIY 2: 12M + You

What are some of the innate brand-building skills and superpowers you (and other women) entrepreneurs have? What motivates YOU? Examples: I want to pursue my passion. I want to be my own boss. I want freedom to be in control of my schedule. I want financial independence. I want to make a change in my community. I want to feel more alignment between my work and my life, etc.

What are your brand-building superpowers?

_____

_____

_____

What is your motivation to start your own business?

_____

_____

_____

DIY 3: Fear Means GO!

How can you change your relationship with fear and how can you engage it so it no longer drives your life, your choices, your future? Consider for a minute what scares you the most. Peel back the layers beyond something like, "I'm afraid of failing." Is it because you hate rejection? Are afraid of uncertainty? Keep getting negative feedback? In spite of this fear, how can you launch to new heights? Is it through setting a goal, practicing, practicing, practicing, and analyzing the risk—those tricks that great risk-takers use? And remember not to run away from it. Write down your reflections.

_____

_____

_____

_____

_____

_____

_____

_____

2. DEMOLITION:
Breaking Down to Break Through

DIY 1: "Big B" and "Little b" Breakdowns

Use the AID Golden Tool—Acknowledge, Identify, Declare—to help you identify a professional breakdown. These will then be combined to form your BUILD Statement. Note: If you cannot pinpoint a breakdown, skip those steps and just declare what you are building. As stated earlier, not all businesses come from a breakdown. And if what's top of mind is a personal breakdown, try to link it back to business as that is the basis of this book.

1. **Acknowledge your breakdown:** This is about awareness. What is the breakdown you are experiencing? Denial will block any form of progress, so accepting and acknowledging what is happening is always the first step. Give it a name (Big B or Little b). And don't forget, not only is the breakdown OK; it is, in fact, good.
   Example: I am having a Little b breakdown in in that I feel burned out at my corporate job.

   _____

   _____

   _____

   _____

   _____

2. **Identify where you want to break through:** This is about a perspective shift. What is your breakdown's root cause? What familial, cultural, or professional forces played a role? What did you invite, allow, ignore, or tolerate (we always have a part,

even if it's small)? Try to take radical personal accountability for what happened. The more you can see yourself as part of the problem, the greater your power will be in seeing yourself as the solution. Identify what has shifted inside you, the new insight or perspective. There is no better time to understand what you do want than when you are right in the middle of what you don't want.

Example: The cultural belief that one should grind 24–7 is messed up, but I allowed it (so fatigued I'd need to catnap under my desk). I want to break through to a state of empowerment, with more flexibility in my work and more free time.

_____

_____

_____

_____

_____

_____

3. **Declare . . . your BUILD Statement:** This is about taking action. What business or professional undertaking are you going to break through to build (i.e., BUILD Statement)? The key step that empowers your breakthrough is stating what you are building next. Note: declaring this intention can feel delusional at first.

Example: I am going to build my own marketing consultancy.

_____

_____

_____

_____

_____

Pro Tip: What is the worst thing that could happen if you move forward? When we play out the worst-case scenario and know we can live with it, it frees us!

DIY 2: From Victim to Victor

So much of our work is actually a shedding, a lightening, an unlearning process. Letting go of all the cultural expectations and personal insecurities that impact you, while embracing that you are good enough exactly as you are in this current moment. Below, write down one "not enough" and one "do more" force and one area where you are "good enough." With this mindset shift, transformation can be immediate:

One "Not enough" feeling that you can let go of (i.e., being prettier, skinnier, smarter, etc.):

_____

One "Do more" expectation that you can let go of (i.e., working harder, longer, stronger, etc.):

_____

One "Good enough" acknowledgment that you can embrace (i.e., being a good enough mother, businesswoman, financial steward, partner, etc.):

_____

DIY 3: The Heart Test

It's time now for the Heart Test Golden Tool. To pass the test, you run the idea for your business—what you've just declared you want to build (or are already building)—through your heart. As you consider your business idea, what does it do? Circle the verdict.

1. Breaks your heart
2. Sets your heart on fire

You likely passed. Wunderbar. If not, if you feel flatlined, think about another issue you want to solve that breaks your heart or is an opportunity you can run at that sets your heart on fire.

Finally, consider a name for your company. Once you have a name, you can do a quick Google search to make sure it's not used elsewhere. Then think about legally incorporating your entity (registering your business as an LLC, S corp, partnership, etc. with an online provider or a lawyer).

Business name:

_____

3. VISION:
Imagining Your Future

DIY 1: Play It Forward

It's time to create your B-I-G BUILD Vision. On a scale of 1 to 5, how do you feel about conjuring this up? 1 = not comfortable and 5 = extremely comfortable: _____

To make room for your BUILD Vision, write down anything or anyone that limits your ability to think BIG: an unproductive environment, a voice that tells you to be more realistic, a toxic person hell-bent on cutting you down to size—anything that will diminish or chip away at the vision for your business moving forward.

_____

_____

_____

_____

_____

_____

_____

_____

Now imagine destroying your ties to those people, places, or things. In your mind's eye, take the list, cut it up, throw it away, burn it, or put it in a balloon that floats away. Use whatever mental technique works for you. At the end, make a promise to distance yourself from anything limiting, so you can focus on what you want to build.

DIY 2: Dig It Deep

Bring in your BUILD Statement from chapter 2—what you want to build and go do. Now list the five whys that go along with it to get to your business's reason for being and your true motivation. Keep drilling down until you hit bedrock.

My BUILD Statement:

_____

_____

Why?

_____

_____

Why?

_____

_____

Why?

_____

_____

Why?

_____

_____

Why?

_____

_____

DIY 3: Feel It Real

Now, for ten minutes, close your eyes and imagine a detail-filled vision for your business. Not what someone else wants or thinks is "realistic," but what you would architect if you could create anything. What does your vision look like? Sound like? When people talk about it, what do they say? Why does it matter to you? Who do you serve? What problem do you solve in the world and why does it matter? For this last touchy-feely part: How do you FEEL as you realize this vision, once it is REAL? Your vision should create a strong feeling in you. Are you energized? Can you feel joy, peace, or excitement?

☐ Completed visioning exercise

Once imagined, write down the BUILD Vision Statement conjured up just now (for your eyes only). It should be about a paragraph long, chock-full of detail and in the present tense. Written as if you have already built your business and reached your goal. Write the vision as if it's a movie, with you bringing it to life and loading it with emotion. Feel it real, and it will become so.

BUILD Vision Statement

_____

_____

_____

_____

_____

_____

_____

_____

_____

_____

_____

_____

_____

_____

_____

_____

_____

_____

_____

_____

After writing your BUILD Vision Statement, do a quick scan to double-check that it does the following: solves a why; is crisp and juicy as hell; is long-term focused; is in first-person perspective, and helps you relive how you rocked it in the past. Lock it in. Read your BUILD Vision Statement every morning. Whatever you need to do to keep it front and center as a daily North Star.

4. DESIGN:
Amplifying Yourself for Authentic Power

DIY 1: Integrated Life Layout

It's time to start working more intentionally on your BUILD Integrated Life Layout, building out each of your Seven Areas of Life. Begin by dropping in your BUILD Vision Statement for your business from chapter 3. From there, create "lite" visions across the remaining six life areas, including some notes on what you want and ideally see for yourself—all the unique, individual facets of life that matter to you. What would bring more fulfillment? This doesn't need to be as built out as much as your business vision.

Rank from one to ten on how well you are currently doing or feeling in each area, where 1 = not satisfied (i.e., breakdown) and 10 = extremely satisfied (breakthrough). And for any areas you identify as anemic, deficient, or suffering (i.e., those Big B or Little b breakdowns), there's no judgment. It's just asking: how could you create a vision that gets you closer to what you want?

1. BUSINESS: Ambition, vision, mission, and contribution

   Rank: _____

   Vision: _____

   _____

   _____

2. MONEY: Overall wealth, business income, spending, and saving

   Rank:_____

   Vision Lite: _____

   _____

   _____

3. RELATIONSHIPS: Partner, parents, siblings, children, friends, teammates (crew)

   Rank:_____

Vision Lite: _____

_____

_____

4. ENVIRONMENT: Home, geography, living and working conditions

   Rank:_____

   Vision Lite: _____

   _____

   _____

5. SPIRITUALITY: Purpose, connection, religion

   Rank:_____

   Vision Lite: _____

   _____

   _____

6. PASSIONS: Travel, entertainment, social life, community projects, learning, pets

   Rank:_____

   Vision Lite: _____

   _____

   _____

7. HEALTH: Physical and mental well-being, exercise, meditation, self-talk, self-expression, nutrition, sleep, energy, appearance, personal accountability

   Rank:_____

   Vision Lite: _____

   _____

   _____

Pro Tip: Every few months go back to each area and rank how satisfied you feel. This is a great way to get a quick temperature read on your current level of integration.

It's time to bring all life areas together in one holistic picture to form your BUILD Integrated Life Layout! Wrap up with a summary paragraph that lays out your total life, by combining a sentence or two from each of the prior Seven Areas of Life.

Build Integrated Life Layout

_____

_____

_____

_____

_____

_____

_____

_____

_____

_____

_____

_____

_____

_____

_____

_____

_____

_____

_____

_____

_____

_____

_____

_____

_____

_____

_____

DIY 2: Value Values

What are the top three values that you intend to bring to your integrated life and all that you do? Here are some ideas:

authenticity	freedom	open-mindedness
caring	friendliness	patience
charity	generosity	performance
collaboration	grace	persistent
commitment	gratitude	persuasiveness
community	growth	purposefulness
connection	happiness	reliability
consideration	honesty	resourcefulness
courage	hope	respect
creativity	humility	responsibility
curiosity	humor	service
dedication	idealism	simplicity
dependability	inclusivity	speed
diligence	independence	spontaneity
efficiency	ingenuity	strength
empathy	innovation	style
enthusiasm	integrity	sustainability
equanimity	joyfulness	transparency
fairness	kindness	trust
faith	LOVE	vulnerability
flexibility	loyalty	wisdom

1. _____

2. _____

3. _____

DIY 3: X Factor = Amplification

When you are integrated, you start to feel unleashed across ALL aspects of your life and become amplified! Give an example of a situation in the past month or two when you were amplified. If it hasn't happened for you yet, just make a note to pay attention when it does.

_____

_____

_____

_____

_____

_____

_____

_____

5. FRAMING:
Creating an Actionable Plan

DIY 1: 60-Day Challenge

At the end of sixty days, which is the optimal period for habit formation, you'll have new practices in place. As you've learned, the smallest of consistent micro daily actions enables you to do the biggest macro things in the world. What excites you most about the 60-Day Challenge? Check the most significant:

- ☐ Knowing at the end of sixty days I will see tangible results
- ☐ Maintaining a daily commitment to myself
- ☐ Looking at health not as an indulgence but a necessity
- ☐ Seeing some momentum
- ☐ Getting more personal alignment in place
- ☐ Feeling less frustration by putting myself first on my to-do list

DIY 2: 60-Minute Prime

Consider one activity you do that is already a healthy habit. Share a sentence or two about how it makes you feel.

_____

_____

_____

_____

_____

Write down three Anchor Habits you want to do daily for sixty days, for sixty minutes per day. For example, thirty minutes of exercise, twenty minutes of meditation, ten minutes of extra nourishment (vitamins, green juice, etc.) supplemented by walks in nature and positive affirmations.

1. _____

2. _____

3. _____

Extra credit: Here's Dr. Amishi Jha's Three-Step Mindfulness Exercise for your toolkit:

1. *Focus:* Put your mind and its flashlight of attention on breath-related sensations. Choose a target, like the coolness of the air as it enters your nose, and hold your attention there.

2. *Notice:* Pay attention if your mind has wandered away. Are you thinking about lunch, or a conversation, or a sad memory? Whatever it is, notice where that flashlight is actually pointing.

3. *Redirect:* If your attention is not on your breath, redirect it. That is the mental push-up: focus, notice, redirect. Start by doing this for a minute daily and work up to twelve minutes.

DIY 3: 60-Second Pause

For the 60-Second Pause, practice the art of protecting your time and energy. Jot down three things you want to say YES to. And also three things to say NO to, that are distracting you from reaching your full potential or living life on your own terms.

YES	NO
1)	1)
2)	2)
3)	3)

6. CREW:
Leading the People Around You

DIY 1: Boss Up

Mindful leadership starts with the awareness that you want to lead differently in your own unique way. Start off by describing in a few sentences what your style of leadership would ideally look like.

My mindful leadership style would be described as:

_____

_____

_____

_____

Once you are committed to lead in this way, it's helpful to know yourself inside and out, making peace with ALL of you. To bring more of you to the surface, list your five best and five worst traits (for your eyes only):

My best traits:

1. _____
2. _____
3. _____
4. _____
5. _____

My worst traits:

1. _____
2. _____
3. _____
4. _____
5. _____

DIY 2: Nailed It

Nothing to write here, just remember the two aspects of the Nailed It Golden Tool (below). This tool will have an impact on the deadlines you've committed to for work and life; your morning habits, like exercise, healthy eating, and meditation; the promise you made to your kids, etc. Soon you'll add this practice to your daily life.

1. Keep your word to yourself. Just do what you say you are going to do.
2. Don't give up when it gets hard.

DIY 3: Dream Team

What is one area of your business or personal life that makes you feel alone, or where you could use more support?

_____

_____

_____

_____

_____

_____

Check the group within your crew that you are least confident in building out:

☐ Core group
☐ Day-to-day team
☐ Subject matter experts
☐ Advisors

What is most important to you to consider when building your crew? Rank from one to seven, where 1 = most important and 7 = least important.

☐ Complementary skillsets
☐ Affordability
☐ Strong work ethic
☐ Self-awareness
☐ Relevant experience
☐ Likeability
☐ Passion for the work

Soon you will recruit and build out your dream crew and get everyone on site! So identify the three people you want per group. If you don't know the name of the person yet, that is A-OK; just write down the role you want them to play (or the type of expert or the skill set) you seek.

Dream Team Roles

1. Core group (example: friend, family):

_____

_____

2. Day-to-day team (admin, social media, project manager):

_____

_____

3. Subject matter experts (lawyer, accountant, financial planner, coach, marketing expert):

_____

_____

4. Advisors (executive, celebrity, entrepreneur):

_____

_____

Now that you have a target list, share the compensation you can offer each!

Crew Compensation

1. Core group (experiences, reciprocal business advice):

_____

_____

2. Day-to-day team (monthly retainer, salary, hourly rate):

_____

_____

3. Subject matter experts (project fee, hourly rate):

_____

_____

4. Advisors (gifts):

_____

_____

Now write an enrolling note you could send to a day-to-day teammate, SME, or advisor prospect to get them onboard. Think about what you are creating and what you can offer!

Outreach Note

_____

_____

_____

_____

_____

_____

_____

_____

_____

_____

_____

_____

_____

_____

_____

_____

_____

_____

_____

_____

_____

_____

_____

_____

_____

_____

_____

7. CONSTRUCTION$$:
Cashing In on Your Business

DIY 1: Best Business Model

To get your business airborne or launch it to new heights (the 2.0 version of your company), write down a dollar amount you are committed to investing into your business and where this money will come from (personal savings, friends and family, a loan, existing revenue, etc.):

    $Amount: _____

    Source(s):_____

What is the business model that makes the most sense for you? List core revenue streams and sales channels that you could monetize.

    Business Structure (B2B, B2C, B2B2C):

_____

_____

_____

    Types of Business Revenue (Active and/or passive):

_____

_____

_____

    Sales Channels (Subscriptions, advertising, broker, auction, franchise, freemium, direct sales, etc.)

_____

_____

_____

DIY 2: 6 Money Managers

Do you identify as a rich, self-made woman? If not, could you reimagine your identity to see yourself in this way, starting today? _____

   Do you struggle with awkward negotiations? What might you do differently in the future?

_____

_____

_____

_____

_____

   Spend? Save? Find the flow. In general, do you find your money moves more toward your business or to the rest of your life? Does it feel balanced? If not, how could you be more mindful? If you have outstanding financial debt (credit cards, overdue bills, unpaid student loans, etc.) list them and start to clean them up.

_____

_____

_____

_____

   At a high level, and to use as inputs for the more technical financial tools coming up (Forecast, Budget, P&L), you'll want to identify the various revenue categories for your business. Time to figure out the estimated revenue for each.

REVENUE CATEGORY	ESTIMATED REVENUE ($)
1	
2	
3	

What are the main categories of expenses associated with selling the products you make or services you offer, and with operating the business? How large would you estimate those expenses to be?

EXPENSE CATEGORY	ESTIMATED EXPENSE ($)
1	
2	
3	

You will start by completing your forecast, which will have many of the inputs you'll need to create your budget. Then on to your budget, which will give you the baseline for comparison vs. actuals in the P&L. You'll then set up your P&L. Note there are software tools that provide an easy way to do this systematically and can even link to your bank account.

To create a FORECAST

1. Select a tool to track and manage your Forecast, like Excel, QuickBooks, etc.
2. Define a time frame for forecast (typically one year by month, and the following two to five years annually), plus assumptions.
3. Forecast revenue

   Key inputs include price and unit sales, which can vary based on marketing, staff, innovation, etc.

   Use market and customer size to estimate revenue (i.e., X industry is $2M growing at 5% year over year and at X price, so is Y revenue reasonable?).
4. Estimate fixed expenses (i.e., rent, loan payments) and variable expenses (i.e., utilities, supplies) and cost of goods sold, ideally by averaging past expenses per line item. Be ambitious but realistic.
5. Combine numbers into one-to-five-year projections. Enter into budget.

To create a BUDGET

1. Select a tool to track and manage your Budget, like Excel, QuickBooks, etc.
2. Define time frame for budget (typically one year), plus assumptions.
3. Enter forecast revenue from Forecast.
4. Based on expected revenue, estimate and allocate budget fixed expenses (i.e., rent, loan payments) and variable expenses (i.e., utilities, supplies), ideally by averaging past expenses per line item.
5. On an ongoing basis, track the difference between estimated and actual in the P&L.
6. Investigate drivers of difference—fix the problem or maximize an opportunity—and revise allocations as needed.

To create a P&L

1. Select a tool to track and manage your P&L, like Excel, Quick-Books, etc.
2. Define time frame for P&L (typically once per quarter).
3. Calculate all revenue that came in across all business units during that period.
4. Calculate all expenses incurred across categories during that period, like operating expenses and salaries, and costs you spend on making goods you sold ("cost of goods sold," or COGS for short).
5. Find profit (or loss) by subtracting costs and expenses from total revenue.
   Interpret the results: Are your expenses higher this quarter? Why? Did spending more generate additional revenue? Is revenue flat? Why? How might you be able to spend more to generate additional income? Are there other changes you need to make to your operational plan?

DIY 3: Future Fortune Matrix

Using the Ansoff Matrix, brainstorm one or two options for each growth strategy. Then step back to evaluate and prioritize opportunities. Think about the opportunity size ($) and evaluate the opportunity/strengths vs. the upside/risks. Weigh all the factors associated with each option. At the end, identify and circle the main growth strategy you want to pursue next (but only once you have a core product or service offering down).

MARKET DEVELOPMENT	DIVERSIFICATION
New geographics, new sales channels, new customer segments, new ways of positioning	New unproven, first-to-market products or services in new unfamiliar markets

MARKET PENETRATION	PRODUCT DEVELOPMENT
New marketing strategies, pricing, promotions/coupons, loyalty programs	Line extensions, related offerings that complement offering, launching similar offering

Based on the growth opportunities and strategies you've identified and evaluated above, assuming successful execution of the targets you've laid out, what revenue do you want to be at this year? In three years? In five years?

This year:

_____

In three years:

_____

In five years:

_____

Extra credit, Risk & Reward Golden Tool: What is one risk you want to set your sights on and one reward you will treat yourself to when the goal is accomplished? Remember, celebrating wins even when they are small has been proven to not only strengthen your psychology but also strengthens ties with your crew.

One risk:

_____

_____

One reward:

_____

_____

8. FIXTURES:
Finding Your Customers

DIY 1: Trendspotting: The 3 C's

What are the three biggest trends that relate to your business? To identify trends, use observations in the world, desk research (industry trade publications, news sites, blogs, annual reports, etc.), and talk to customers. Write down what you discover in the table below.

TREND

Cultural:	
Category:	
Consumer:	

Extra credit: What thought leaders exist in (and outside) your industry who can help you keep up with trends? Write three names below. Sign up for their newsletters or other content and follow them on social media.

Thought Leaders

1. _____
2. _____
3. _____

DIY 2: Competitive Assessment

Let's talk about competition. Who are the three direct competitors who keep you up most at night?

1. _____
2. _____
3. _____

What are the main characteristics or attributes you think you'll compete on (i.e., price, product, positioning, etc.)? Brainstorm a list of five ideas.

1. _____
2. _____
3. _____
4. _____
5. _____

For your #1 competitor, complete a SWOT analysis (strengths, weaknesses, opportunities, and threats), with three to five points in each.

COMPETITOR (NAME): _____

Strengths:	Weaknesses:
Opportunities:	Threats:

What is the biggest white space opportunity (those unmet customer needs) for your business? What unique gaps can you fill? On what basis can you compete and win? Jot down some thoughts on how you're different.

_____

_____

_____

_____

_____

_____

DIY 3: Customer Target

Based on what you know about your market and the current state of competition, who is your target?

Target name (descriptive name to call your customer):

_____

General description (paragraph explaining who they are):

_____

_____

_____

_____

_____

Now list as many demographic characteristics, as well as psychographic attributes to paint a detailed picture of your target!

Target Details (B2C)

Age: _____

Gender: _____

Household income: _____

Geography: _____

Occupation: _____

Education: _____

Lives: _____

Does: _____

Uses: _____

Follows: _____

Buys: _____

Wears: _____

Watches: _____

Target Details (B2B)

Company size: _____

Industry vertical: _____

Function: _____

Geography: _____

Extra credit, Hard Hat Golden Tool: Think about where you can explore next for a mini cultural excursion.

9. FINISHES:
Positioning Your Brand to Stand Out

DIY 1: Brand Mission

Jot down what you think is your business enemy. What cultural conflict or tension are you attempting to solve for customers? (Example: toxic household products)

_____

_____

_____

_____

Now jot down your BUILD Mission Statement. What do you want your business to stand for in the world? What is the commitment or promise your brand is going to make? What space will your brand fill in the market? (Example: To create a world where anyone can belong anywhere.)

_____

_____

_____

_____

DIY 2: Brand Strategy

To develop a strong brand strategy, you'll want to think about a couple things: your competitor's SWOT (strengths, weaknesses, opportunities, and threats), what makes you unique (white space), and your customer target (all pulled from chapter 8). Equipped with that information, think about the single statement of what your customer most wants, supported by three unique selling points that will meet the specific needs and desires—both functionally and emotionally—of your target customers. What will your brand contribute that will improve the lives of your customers (functionally)? How do you want your brand to make people feel (emotionally)? Now pull all of these elements into your brand strategy.

Brand Strategy

Single Statement of Value (What your customer wants):

_____

_____

Unique Selling Points (What your company does best relative to competitors-between functional and emotional. Pick 3 attributes total.)
Functional:

_____

_____

_____

Emotional:

_____

_____

_____

Final check: Does your brand positioning check these three boxes:

DIFFERENTIATED?	MEANINGFUL?	AUTHENTIC?
☐	☐	☐

DIY 3: Brand Campaign

Write down a BIG Idea for a brand campaign. This should be a real rallying cry for your brand. Ultimately, it's a single statement, a slogan, a powerful one-liner (example: Just Do It), followed by a general summary (example: this campaign will champion everyday athletes). This really is an exercise to unleash emotion, so have fun with it, come up with a few iterations, and, above all, think big and brave!

_____

_____

_____

_____

10. LANDSCAPE:
Digging into Marketing

DIY 1: Marketing Approach

From the top of your head, quickly write down five media channels that your target consumers likely enjoy, magazines they are likely to read, newsletters they subscribe to, influencers they may follow, content they like to watch, accounts they follow in social media, events they are likely to attend, or other engaging media.

1. _____

2. _____

3. _____

4. _____

5. _____

DIY 2: Customer Journey

From the four-step customer journey (from awareness to consideration to purchase to loyalty), have you cared for brand actions and guiding your customer along in the way? Identify any stages in the journey that are missing.

_____

_____

_____

_____

DIY 3: Go-to-Market Plan

A Go-to-Market Plan identifies the channels you will use to reach customers. You know how you want to position your brand and who your ideal customer is. Now you'll need to shout that out so potential customers come running. To create a simple Go-to-Market Plan, fill out the information below. You'll insert a goal for each channel (i.e., $50,000 in revenue, twenty-five thousand new social media followers, ten subscription signups, five new PR hits, etc.). Then list the channels—such as PR, influencer, website, social media, partnerships, direct mail, etc.—and include an activation idea or creative asset for each. That means how you will bring the brand campaign to life in this channel and what you want to do. And finally, timing. Feel free to customize based on how you'd like to roll out your brand campaign!

BRAND CAMPAIGN NAME: _____

STAGES	AWARENESS	CONSIDERATION	PURCHASE	LOYALTY
Goal				
Channel(s)				
Creative Asset(s)				
Launch Date				

Extra credit #1, Measurement: As they say, what gets measured gets managed! When you launch a marketing campaign, a tracker can help you measure channel performance weekly and inform strategic decisions around where to allocate or reallocate your marketing budget. If that's too labor intensive, when the marketing campaign wraps, try to identify which channels contributed most toward the goals you set.

Extra credit #2, Bake & Take Golden Tool: Plan to create and fund one idea. Without permission.

11. STAGING:
Hammering Away at Sales

DIY 1: 3 Partnership Pillars

Write down three partner targets. What could you create to make them strike a deal?

	PARTNER	IDEA	GIVE-GET (DISTRIBUTION, INCREMENTAL SALES, AUDIENCE)
1			
2			

3

DIY 2: 5 Pitch-Perfect Principles

Now for the pitch. Let's start with a high-level outline. Think less than ten slides, no longer than twenty minutes, and a font size of thirty. This will be a skeleton, which you can use later to turn into your deck and spiel.

Pro Tip: Pull information from trendspotting in chapter 8 and brand mission in chapter 9 to answer these questions.

1. What is the problem or enemy in the world that you're trying to solve for and who has that problem?

_____

_____

_____

_____

2. What data or trends substantiate this problem?

_____

_____

_____

_____

3. What is the market opportunity? Expand on how the market is growing, what currently exists in the market that is

attempting to solve that problem, and why those businesses are falling short.

_____

_____

_____

_____

_____

4. What is YOUR solution? Explain what makes your business uniquely suited to solve that cultural or market problem and why this solution will bring about better results for a client or customer, easing pain points.

_____

_____

_____

_____

5. What are your proof points and how do you want to partner? Include any differentiators around what makes you special and credible (i.e., press, partners you've worked with previously, testimonials, and case studies) and a high-level summary on how you propose working together. The partnership give-get.

_____

_____

_____

_____

Lead list: Now for targeting and outreach, develop an actual list. You can use the following template as an example of what information to include and how to track outreach. Remember: you can search online looking for titles like: business development, marketing, or partnerships.

PARTNER	LEAD POINT OF CONTACT (NAME/TITLE)	CONTACT INFO (EMAIL)	OUTREACH / OA STATUS (FIRST CONTACT, FOLLOW-UP, PRESENTATION DATE, FINAL MEETING)
1			
2			
3			

DIY 3: 15 Pro-Presentation Practices

Don't forget your checklist before your next big pitch or presentation. You may want to make a copy for easy reference.

Pre

☐ *Stalk:* Create Business Backgrounders or bios on who you are meeting (where they have worked, the projects they have spearheaded, how they sound, what they look like . . .). Know everything you can about who's in that room.

☐ *Flex Bigger:* Pull in crew members. Extra hands who can help with scheduling, join a presentation to take notes, support with tech or do follow-up emails, so you present bigger.

☐ *Set the Agenda:* Break the meeting into carefully allotted chunks of time with presentation roles and responsibilities. Share it with your partner at least a week in advance.

☐ *Style Your Space:* Curate a backdrop with flowers, books, art, or found objects if presenting remotely. If hosting live (but don't have a dedicated space), call in favors.

☐ *Dress to Impress:* Wardrobe is armor. Serve different looks based on the audience. And the most important part . . . killer shoes!

☐ *Hit Your Marks:* Never reschedule a meeting.

☐ *Rehearse, Rehearse, Rehearse:* Do as many dry runs as you need to get it right. Memorize your pitch (deck and spiel).

☐ *Prepave:* You've got this Golden Tool already under your belt, so use it. The night before, in your mind's eye, imagine the ideal meeting outcome.

During

☐ *Be on Time. Wrap on Time:* Arrive early and stick to the allotted time.

☐ *Posing and Posture:* Set the tone. Strike a few power poses in the room. Then mirror others' posture throughout the meeting.

☐ *Find Common Ground:* Open with human connection. Seed common interests or connection points based on your background research.

☐ *Tango:* Know who is the lead and who is not. Take turns. This meeting should feel collaborative.

☐ *Stay on Script:* Also known as the agenda.

Post

- [ ] *Follow Up:* Send personal follow-up notes of thanks.
- [ ] *White Glove Onboard:* When the partnership gets greenlit, put on your customer service hat and roll out a tight onboarding process.

AND THAT'S A WRAP. NO MORE DIY HOMEWORK!

NOTES

Punchlist

1. Victoria Williams, "Small Business Facts: Women Owned Employer Businesses," *Small Business Administration Office of Advocacy,* August 2021, https://advocacy.sba.gov/wp-content/uploads/2021/08/Small-Business-Facts-Women-Owned-Businesses.pdf.

2. Andrew W. Hait, "What Is a Small Business? The Majority of U.S. Businesses Have Fewer Than Five Employees," *United States Census,* January 19, 2021, https://www.census.gov/library/stories/2021/01/what-is-a-small-business.html.

1. Plot

1. Andrei Cimpian and Sarah-Jane Leslie, "Why Young Girls Don't Think They Are Smart Enough," *The New York Times,* January 26, 2017, https://www.nytimes.com/2017/01/26/well/family/why-young-girls-dont-think-they-are-smart-enough.html?_r=0; Lin Bean, Sarah-Jane Leslie, and Andrei Cimpian, "Gender Stereotypes About Intellectual Ability Emerge Early and Influence Children's Interests," *Science,* Vol. 355, No. 6323 (January 27, 2017): 389–91, https://www.science.org/doi/10.1126/science.aah6524.

2. Amanda Marcotte, "The XX Factor: Parents Ask Google If Their Sons Are Geniuses and If Their Daughters Are Fat," *Slate,* January 21, 2014, https://slate.com/human-interest/2014/01/parents-ask-google-is-my-son-gifted-and-is-my-daughter-overweight.html.

3. "Just 24% of News Sources Are Women. Here's Why That's a Problem," *World Economic Forum,* March 2, 2020, https://www.weforum.org/agenda/2020/03/women-representation-in-media/.

4. Jaime Ducharme, "Social Media Hurts Girls More Than Boys," *Time*, August 13, 2019, https://time.com/5650266/social-media-girls-mental-health/; Elia Abi-Jaoude, Karline Treurnicht Naylor, and Antonio Pignatiello, "Smartphones, Social Media Use and Youth Mental Health," *Canadian Medical Association Journal*, February 10, 2020, https://www.ncbi.nlm.nih.gov/pmc/articles/PMC7012622/.

5. Statistics," *NSVRC (National Sexual Violence Resource Center)*, https://www.nsvrc.org/statistics; "Victims of Sexual Violence: Statistics," *RAINN (Rape, Abuse & Incest National Network*," https://www.rainn.org/statistics/victims-sexual-violence; "Violence Prevention: Fast Facts," *Centers for Disease Control and Prevention*, June 22, 2022, https://www.cdc.gov/violenceprevention/sexualviolence/fastfact.html.

6. Carrie Blazina and Drew Desilver, "A Record Number of Women Are Serving in the 117th Congress," *Pew Research Center*, January 15, 2021, https://www.pewresearch.org/short-reads/2021/01/15/a-record-number-of-women-are-serving-in-the-117th-congress/.

7. "The Data on Women Leaders," *Pew Research Center*, January 29, 2021, https://www.pewresearch.org/social-trends/fact-sheet/the-data-on-women-leaders/#fortune-500-ceos.

8. Stacia Damron, "There Are More CEOs Named David Than There Are Women CEOs," *OneModel*, September 26, 2018, https://www.onemodel.co/blog/davids.

9. Lila MacLellan, "70% of Top Male Earners in the US Have a Spouse Who Stays Home," *Quartz*, April 30, 2019, https://qz.com/work/1607995/most-men-in-the-top-1-of-us-earners-have-a-spouse-who-stays-home.

10. "Fast Facts: Women & Student Debt," *AAUW (American Association of University Women)*, 2021, https://www.aauw.org/resources/article/fast-facts-student-debt/; Melanie Hanson, "Student Loan Debt by Gender," *Education Data Initiative*, July 16, 2023, https://educationdata.org/student-loan-debt-by-gender.

11. Katty Kay and Claire Shipman, "The Confidence Gap," *The Atlantic*, May 2014, https://www.theatlantic.com/magazine/archive/2014/05/the-confidence-gap/359815/; "The Confidence Gap in Work Performance Reviews Between Women and Men," *The Wharton School*, January 3, 2020, https://www.wharton.upenn.edu/story/the-confidence-gap-in-work-performance-reviews-between-women-and-men/.

12. "Melinda Gates Q&A: A Billion Dollars for Gender Equality," *Harvard Business Review*, October 4, 2019, https://hbr.org/2019/10/melinda-gates-qa-a-billion-dollars-for-gender-equality.

13. "Women in the Labor Force: a Databook," *BLS Reports*, April 2017, https://www.bls.gov/opub/reports/womens-databook/2016/home.htm; Mitra Toossi and Teresa L. Morris, "Women in the Workforce Before, During, and After the Great Recession," *US Bureau of Labor Statistics*, July 2017, https://www.bls

.gov/spotlight/2017/women-in-the-workforce-before-during-and-after-the-great
-recession/home.htm.

14. Gené Teare, "In 2017, Only 17% of Startups Have a Female Founder," *TechCrunch*, April 19, 2017, https://techcrunch.com/2017/04/19/in-2017-only-17 -of-startups-have-a-female-founder/.

15. Joedy McCreary, "Study: Diversity Remains Low in Sports News Departments," *APNews*, May 2, 2018, https://apnews.com/article/a45d1d2abc7746aaa4 dbeaa7f7987923; "Gender Distribution of Full-time Law Enforcement Employees in the United States in 2021," *Statista*, https://www.statista.com/statistics/195324 /gender-distribution-of-full-time-law-enforcement-employees-in-the-us/; "Share of Shuttle Drivers and Chauffeurs in the United States from 2020 to 2022, by Gender," *Statista*, https://www.statista.com/statistics/1086933/share-taxi-drivers -chauffeurs-united-states-gender/.

16. "Half the World's Women Have Given Up on Their Dreams: Kids Challenge Them to Dream Again," *PRNewsWire*, June 21, 2016, https://www.prnewswire .com/news-releases/half-the-worlds-women-have-given-up-on-their-dreams-kids -challenge-them-to-dream-again-300288272.html; Soulaima Gourani, "Why Most Women Give Up on Their Dreams," *Forbes*, July 29, 2019, https://www.forbes.com /sites/soulaimagourani/2019/07/29/why-most-women-give-up-on-their-dreams /?sh=51b893c12082.

17. Stephanie Neal, Jazmine Boatman, and Linda Miller, "Mentoring Women in the Workplace: A Global Study," *DDI (Development Dimensions International)*, https://www.ddiworld.com/research/mentoring-women-in-the-workplace.

18. Ashley Bittner and Brigette Lau, "Women-Led Startups Received Just 2.3% of VC Funding in 2020," *Harvard Business Review*, February 25, 2021, https:// hbr.org/2021/02/women-led-startups-received-just-2-3-of-vc-funding-in-2020; Sophia Kunthara, "Black Women Still Receive Just a Tiny Fraction of VC Funding Despite 5-Year High," *Crunchbase News*, July 16, 2021, https://news.crunchbase .com/diversity/something-ventured-black-women-founders/; Alexandra York and others, "Meet the 71 Black Women Who Raised $1 Million or more in VC Funding Since 2021," *Business Insider,* updated April 21, 2023, https://www.businessinsider .com/black-female-founders-raised-millions-in-vc-this-year-2021-9.

19.Jack Zenger and Joseph Folkman, "Research: Women Score Higher Than Men in Most Leadership Skills," *Harvard Business Review*, June 25, 2019, https:// hbr.org/2019/06/research-women-score-higher-than-men-in-most-leadership-skills; Bob Sherwin, "Why Women Are More Effective Leaders Than Men," *Business Insider*, January 24, 2014, https://www.businessinsider.com/study-women-are -better-leaders-2014-1.

20. Elaine Pofeldt, "The Confidence Gap and Women Entrepreneurs," *Forbes*, May 28, 2013, https://www.forbes.com/sites/elainepofeldt/2013/05/28/the-confidence -gap-and-women-entrepreneurs/?sh=5f6a4bfe42c55.

21. Leanna Garfield and Zoë Ettinger, "14 of the Biggest Marches and Protests in American History," *Business Insider,* updated June 1, 2020, https://www.businessinsider.com/largest-marches-us-history-2017-1.

22. Diana Bruk, "Here's the Full Transcript of Gloria Steinem's Historic Women's March Speech," *Elle,* January 21, 2017, https://www.elle.com/culture/news/a42331/gloria-steinem-womens-march-speech/.

23. Anna Zakrzewski et al, "Managing the Next Decade of Women's Wealth," *Boston Consulting Group,* April 9, 2020, https://www.bcg.com/publications/2020/managing-next-decade-women-wealth; Tamara Gillan, "The Changing Face of Women's Wealth," *Citywire,* October 21, 2022, https://citywire.com/wealth-manager/news/the-changing-face-of-women-s-wealth/a2399508; Fan Cheuk Wan, "Women's Growing Wealth Fuels Impact Investing," *HSBC,* March 1, 2023, https://www.hsbc.com/news-and-views/views/hsbc-views/womens-growing-wealth-fuels-impact-investing.

24. Pooneh Bahai, Olivia Howard, and others, "Women as the Next Wave of Growth in US Wealth Management," *McKinsey & Company,* July 29, 2020, https://www.mckinsey.com/industries/financial-services/our-insights/women-as-the-next-wave-of-growth-in-us-wealth-management; "How Is the US Economy Doing?," *USA Facts,* https://usafacts.org/state-of-the-union/economy/.

25. "Facts about Small Business: Women Ownership Statistics," *US Small Business Administration Office of Advocacy,* March 23, 2023, https://advocacy.sba.gov/2023/03/21/facts-about-small-business-women-ownership-statistics/; updated January 23, 2023, https://www.fundera.com/resources/women-owned-business-statistics; "Behind the Numbers: The State of Women-Owned Businesses in 2018," *WBENC (Women's Business Enterprise National Council),* https://www.wbenc.org/news/behind-the-numbers-the-state-of-women-owned-businesses-in-2018/.

26. "FreshBooks 2021 Annual Self-Employment Report," *FreshBooks,* https://www.freshbooks.com/press/data-research/usemploymentreport.

27. "Havas' Meaningful Brands Outperform Stock Market By 206%," *ResearchLive,* February 3, 2017, https://www.research-live.com/article/news/havas-meaningful-brands-outperform-stock-market-by-206-/id/5018022; Lindsey Perron, "The Importance of Having a Meaningful Brand in the Modern Age," *Viral Solutions,* May 1, 2019, https://viralsolutions.net/the-importance-of-having-a-meaningful-brand/.

28. Rebekkah Smith, "20 Women-Owned Business Statistics You Must Know," *NorthOne,* https://www.northone.com/blog/small-business/women-owned-business-statistics.

29. Smith, "20 Women-Owned Business Statistics You Must Know"; "Consumer Quotient Report: What If You Really Knew Me?," *Hubspot,* https://cdn2.hubspot.net/hubfs/373439/C_Space_Reports/CQ-US-Report-2016.pdf.

30. Kathleen Kusek, "The Death of Brand Loyalty: Cultural Shifts Mean It's Gone Forever," *Forbes,* July 25, 2016, https://www.forbes.com/sites/kathleenkusek

/2016/07/25/the-death-of-brand-loyalty-cultural-shifts-mean-its-gone-forever/?-sh=765369464dde.

31. Alyson Shontell, "Hundreds of Startups Go Public Every Year. Only 20 Are Founded and Led by Women," *Business Insider,* updated January 5, 2021, https://www.businessinsider.com/female-entrepreneurs-face-obstacles-taking-companies-public-2020–12.

32. Lynsey Addario, interview by Kathleen Griffith, https://www.youtube.com/watch?v=FuyMg7J6Juk.

3. Vision

1. Eric Ries, "The 5 Whys," *Harvard Business Review,* February 7, 2012, https://hbr.org/2012/02/the-5-whys.html.

2. Vinoth K. Ranganathan, Vlodek Siemionow, and others, "From Mental Power to Muscle Power—Gaining Strength by Using the Mind," *Neuropsychologia,* 2004, 42(7): 944–56, https://doi.org/10.1016/j.neuropsychologia.2003.11.018; A.J. Adams, "Seeing Is Believing: The Power of Visualization," *Psychology Today,* December 3, 2009, https://www.psychologytoday.com/intl/blog/flourish/200912/seeing-is-believing-the-power-visualization.

3. Mimi Duvall, interview by Kathleen Griffith.

5. Framing

1. Phillippa Lally, Cornelia H.M. van Jaarsveld, and others, "How Are Habits Formed: Modelling Habit Formation in the Real World," *European Journal of Social Psychology,* Volume 40, Issue 6 (July 16, 2009): 998–1009, https://doi.org/10.1002/ejsp.674; James Clear, "How Long Does It Actually Take to Form a New Habit? (Backed by Science)," *jamesclear.com,* https://jamesclear.com/new-habit.

2. Maggie Seaver, "Habit Stacking Is Easiest Way to Make New Habits Last—Here's How It Works," *Real Simple,* updated on March 31, 2023, https://www.realsimple.com/work-life/life-strategies/inspiration-motivation/habit-stacking.

3. Dr. Amishi Jha, interview by Kathleen Griffith, https://www.youtube.com/watch?v=89Y66LLZMX4.

4. Jha interview.

5. Kait Smith Lanthier, "Care.com's Sheila Lirio Marcelo's Advice for Entrepreneurial Women," *Babson Thought & Action,* October 3, 2016, https://entrepreneurship.babson.edu/care-coms-sheila-marcelos-advice-for-entrepreneurial-women/.

6. Martha Beck, "Yes? No? Maybe? How to Make Decisions," *marthabeck.com,* https://marthabeck.com/2013/09/how-to-make-decisions/.

6. Crew

1. Nedra Tawwab, "A Little Secret from a Therapist," *Instagram: nedrataw-wab*, https://www.instagram.com/p/CinUhAkOkd1/; *nedratawwab.com*, https://www.nedratawwab.com/.

2. Noah St. John, "Why Your Mind Is Like an Iceberg," *HuffPost*, updated December 6, 2017, https://www.huffpost.com/entry/why-your-mind-is-like-an_b_6285584; "Our Unconscious Brain Makes the Best Decisions Possible," *ScienceDaily*, December 29, 2008, https://www.sciencedaily.com/releases/2008/12/081224215542.htm.

7. Construction$$

1. Bill Carmody, "3 Reasons Celebrating Your Many Accomplishments Is Critical to Your Success," *Inc.*, August 12, 2015, https://www.inc.com/bill-carmody/3-reasons-celebrating-your-many-accomplishments-is-critical-to-your-success.html; Liz Guthridge, "Recently Succeed at Something? Celebrating Is Good for Your Brain," *Forbes,* June 24, 2019, https://www.forbes.com/sites/forbescoachescouncil/2019/06/24/recently-succeed-at-something-celebrating-is-good-for-your-brain/?sh=2e8a724e3d91.

2. Victoria Williams, "Small Business Facts: Women Owned Employer Businesses," *Small Business Administration Office of Advocacy,* August 2021, https://advocacy.sba.gov/wp-content/uploads/2021/08/Small-Business-Facts-Women-Owned-Businesses.pdf; Julija A., "41 Small Business Statistics: Everything You Need to Know," *SmallBizGenius*, June 17, 2023, https://www.smallbizgenius.net/by-the-numbers/small-business-statistics/#gref; Deyan Georgiev, "Small Business Statistics: Guide to Success in 2023," *Review42*, updated May 20, 2023 https://review42.com/resources/small-business-statistics/.

3. "Small Business Statistics," *Chamber of Commerce*, https://www.chamberofcommerce.org/small-business-statistics/; Devon Delfino, "The Percentage of Businesses That Fail—and How to Boost Your Chances of Success," *LendingTree*, updated May 8, 2023, https://www.lendingtree.com/business/small/failure-rate/.

4. Barbara Huson, interview by Kathleen Griffith.

5. Raija Haughn, "The History of Women and Loans," *Bankrate.com*, September 19, 2023, https://www.bankrate.com/loans/personal-loans/history-of-women-and-loans/.

6. "Life Lessons Madhu Chopra Taught Priyanka Chopra to Become the Successful Woman She Is Today," *Times of India*, updated April 6, 2023, https://timesofindia.indiatimes.com/life-style/parenting/moments/life-lessons-madhu

-chopra-taught-priyanka-chopra-to-become-the-successful-woman-she-is-today
/photostory/99293103.cms?picid=99293120.

10. Landscape

1. Chloe Sorvino, "How a Former Marketing Executive Built a $1.1 Billion Brand Around Frozen Fruits And Vegetables," *Forbes*, June 15, 2022, https://www.forbes.com/sites/chloesorvino/2022/06/15/how-a-former-marketing-executive-built-a-11-billion-brand-around-frozen-fruits-and-vegetables/?sh=405613ace6dd; Roseanne Attia, "How Daily Harvest Did Absolutely Everything Right," *Marketing in the Age of Digital*, February 28, 2021, https://medium.com/marketing-in-the-age-of-digital/how-daily-harvest-did-absolutely-everything-right-689ed6f98401.

2. "Profile: Melanie Perkins, Co-Founder & CEO, Canva," *Forbes*, https://www.forbes.com/profile/melanie-perkins/?sh=7e3a691c1265.

3. Catherine and Geoff Cook and Liz Welch, "How We Founded myYearbook," *Inc.*, May 1, 2012, https://www.inc.com/magazine/201205/liz-welch/catherine-cook-and-geoff-cook-myyearbook.html; "6 Top Women Entrepreneurs Who Succeeded in Online Business," *Ladies Make Money Online*, May 29, 2018, https://www.ladiesmakemoney.com/women-entrepreneurs/.

4. "Evolution of the Dove 'Real Beauty' Campaign," *WithAll*, July 11, 2016, https://withall.org/evolution-of-the-dove-real-beauty-campaign/; Angela Celebre and Ashley Waggoner Denton, "The Good, the Bad, and the Ugly of the Dove Campaign for Real Beauty," *The Inquisitive Mind (in-mind.org)*, Issue 2, 2014, https://www.in-mind.org/article/the-good-the-bad-and-the-ugly-of-the-dove-campaign-for-real-beauty; "Dove Self-Esteem Project: Our Mission in Action," *dove.com*, https://www.dove.com/us/en/dove-self-esteem-project/our-mission.html.

11. Staging

1. Kevin J. Delaney, "Arlan Hamilton Went from Homeless to Running $20 Million in VC Funds. Here's How She Did It," *Time*, March 6, 2022, https://time.com/6155039/arlan-hamilton-crowdfunded-vc-firm/; "Inspiring Quotes from Arlan Hamilton: Diversity in Tech," *The Huntswoman*, November 18, 2019, https://thehuntswoman.com/inspiring-quotes-from-arlan-hamilton-diversity-in-tech/.

2. barefootcontessa.com, https://barefootcontessa.com/cookbooks.

12. Showcase

1. Bronnie Ware, *The Top Five Regrets of the Dying: A Life Transformed by the Dearly Departing* (Carlsbad, CA: Hay House, 2012).

2. Noah Charney, "Maya Angelou: How I Write," *Daily Beast*, updated February 9, 2023, https://www.thedailybeast.com/maya-angelou-how-i-write.

3. "Oprah Winfrey Leadership Academy for Girls," *Oprah Winfrey Charitable Foundation*, https://www.oprahfoundation.org/portfolio-item/oprah-leadership-academy.

4. "200 Million Reasons to Celebrate: Dolly Parton's Imagination Library," *Imagination Library*, https://imaginationlibrary.com/.

ACKNOWLEDGMENTS

While I am the lucky front woman here who gets to rock it onstage, so many people have poured themselves behind the scenes into Build Like A Woman (the book) and BUILD's broader mission. For years. Frankly, without a whole lot of upside. I am truly grateful to . . .

St. Martin's Press, one of the most well-respected publishing imprints around, and some of the people who make it so—Anne-Marie Tallberg, Jessica Zimmerman, Michelle Cashman—and especially:

Sallie Lotz: editor extraordinaire. You made me a published author for the first time and I will never forget that gift of a lifetime. Your editorial notes were surgical and restrained, carefully putting your fingerprint precisely where it mattered most. More detail, more clarity, more context . . . ultimately, more of myself on the page.

Laura Clark: respected leader. You backed this book, thanks to your own very real business acumen.

CAA and my agents across publishing, TV, and speaking who said I represent the future of business talent. I hope we're still doing this together years from now:

Abby Walters: literary magician. So much poise and polished presence. I wouldn't want to run this race with anyone else. Appreciate you holding my hand every step of the way.

Carly Fromm: savvy shark. The first one at the agency to bet on me talent-wise. You fought for me on deals, despite cutting them often with much larger organizations, and have always kept the faith.

Jamie Stockton: legal eagle. The sign of a smart person is someone who can take something complex and reduce it to its simplest parts. You did that.

My BUILD team who helped spur this work on—Eli Stewart (my trusted right hand), Christina Adranly, Kara Ferreira, Natalia Gonzalez, Kara Simonetti—I'm forever grateful:

Katie Cunningham: kindred spirit. Gifted at high-minded strategy and versed in practical execution. You helped shape the brand into the best possible version of what it could be and never once raised an eyebrow at the audaciousness of my plans. Working with you has felt pretty close to manifest destiny.

Claire Bamundo: PR tornado. Fast-talking idea generator. You've been around since this was just a kernel of an idea. It's an honor to have a publishing pro like you as my fierce advocate. The fact I also consider you a friend is icing on the cake.

Kari Jones: lightning strike. Connecting like-minded people from that beautiful mind of yours. Some of my most fun and fond memories are of us collaborating.

John Newall: investigative instigator. We all have core beliefs and you have a way of uncovering that deepest bedrock. Those jam sessions, where you questioned, poked, prodded, summoned and captured, helped with the initial incarnation.

Marissa Le: fierce designer. Thank you for designing the book proposal and the "prepave" for this work.

My core group, friends, and family who've rooted me on throughout the years. Y'ALL!!! Folks like Heidi Hackemer (helping with the original brand strategy), Laura Kelly and Warren Berger (sharing book advice), Claudia Chan (always a sounding board), Mary Miller (the ultimate non-cheerleader, cheerleader), my girlfriends and brother, the smartest person in any room:

Elinor Griffith: THE mother. I am who I am and where I am because of you. This book is what it is because of you. You worked it and then took it back down to the studs to rework it with me. This process brought us closer than ever. You represent all that is good and right and high-minded . . . One day I hope to be a fraction of the woman you are.

Lauren Stever: support blanket. My trusted sister, what can I say . . . you were the first person I let see early chapters and the only person I let weigh in on chapter titles. You hold space for me in a way no one else ever has.

Peter Griffith: lighthearted contrarian. Always keeping it real—questioning assumptions, facts, paths forward, intentions. My favorite person to laugh with at the end of a long writing vortex of a day. Thanks for walking Dash while I was writing.

Marta and John La Rock: shelter. You let me sequester in your home to finish this book without distraction, all while helping with strategic positioning. Friends who are family.

My coaches and teachers, subject-matter experts—folks like Dr. Laura Rose and Barbara Huston—you sharpened me, strengthened me:

Mimi Duvall: empowerment. Probably more than anyone else you made me see my own power. The power to create. The power to persevere. The power to go big. So much of this life I have is because of you.

The Builders who were interviewed while this was still in a nascent stage:

Eva Longoria, Jessica Alba, Tamara Mellon, Rebecca Minkoff, Tina Brown, June Diane Raphael, Grace Helbig, Jennie Baik, Bobbi Brown, Arianna Huffington, Jennifer Fisher, Misha Nonoo, Karla Welch, Jacklyn Johnson, Sophie Hawley-Weld, Shelley Zalis, Shay Mitchell, Amy Emmerich, Brit Moran, Dr. Amishi Jha, Lynsey Addario, Sukhinder Singh Cassidy, Stacey Bendet, and more . . . thank you. And all the women who I admire for their advocacy work and have watched as mentors from afar.

Early readers who I held my breath sending this manuscript to:

Tembi Locke, Arthur C. Brooks, Barbara Corcoran, Mena Harris, I will forever be indebted to you for aligning and endorsing before anyone else. You let me exhale.

The big brand and upstart clients who took a chance on me, thank you. Shout out also to media partners and journalists who have covered my story.

All of the aunties (Liz, Lucero), grandmas (Grayce, June), and great-grandmas going way back, your sacrifices so I might live my wildest dreams was not in vain.

In the spirit of this book, I also want to thank my damn self. With shaky knees I used every ounce of extra life force outside of consulting to pour hundreds of thousands in personal savings to fund Build Like A Woman. It takes a lot of guts to bet on yourself.

You readers, who were in my mind's eye as I was working through the manuscript; you kept me strong and focused on extraordinarily tough days.

And, finally, to those not represented here (you know who you are), thank you.

With love,

Kathleen